REPORT

Asbestos Bankruptcy Trusts

An Overview of Trust Structure and Activity
with Detailed Reports on the Largest Trusts

Lloyd Dixon • Geoffrey McGovern • Amy Coombe

INSTITUTE FOR CIVIL JUSTICE

The research described in this report was conducted by the RAND Institute for Civil Justice, a unit of the RAND Corporation. This research was supported by a coalition of asbestos defendants and insurers and by the RAND Institute for Civil Justice.

Library of Congress Cataloging-in-Publication Data

Dixon, Lloyd S.
  Asbestos bankruptcy trusts : an overview of trust structure and activity with detailed reports on the largest trusts / Lloyd Dixon, Geoffrey McGovern, Amy Coombe.
    p. cm.
  Includes bibliographical references.
  ISBN 978-0-8330-5037-3 (pbk. : alk. paper)
  1. Bankruptcy trustees—United States. 2. Compensation (Law)—United States. 3. Personal injuries—United States. 4. Trusts and trustees—United States. 5. Asbestos—Law and legislation—United States. I. McGovern, Geoffrey. II. Coombe, Amy. III. Title.

  KF1530.R3D59 2010
  346.7307'8—dc22

                                                                                    2010029003

The RAND Corporation is a nonprofit research organization providing objective analysis and effective solutions that address the challenges facing the public and private sectors around the world. RAND's publications do not necessarily reflect the opinions of its research clients and sponsors.

RAND® is a registered trademark.

© Copyright 2010 RAND Corporation

Permission is given to duplicate this document for personal use only, as long as it is unaltered and complete. Copies may not be duplicated for commercial purposes. Unauthorized posting of RAND documents to a non-RAND website is prohibited. RAND documents are protected under copyright law. For information on reprint and linking permissions, please visit the RAND permissions page (http://www.rand.org/publications/permissions.html).

Published 2010 by the RAND Corporation
1776 Main Street, P.O. Box 2138, Santa Monica, CA 90407-2138
1200 South Hayes Street, Arlington, VA 22202-5050
4570 Fifth Avenue, Suite 600, Pittsburgh, PA 15213-2665
RAND URL: http://www.rand.org/
To order RAND documents or to obtain additional information, contact
Distribution Services: Telephone: (310) 451-7002;
Fax: (310) 451-6915; Email: order@rand.org

Preface

Over time, many companies with significant asbestos-related liabilities have filed for bankruptcy, and payments by trusts set up by bankruptcy courts have played an increasingly important role in the compensation of asbestos-related injuries. While the role of trusts in providing compensation to asbestos claimants has grown, information about the operating procedures and activities of these trusts is not readily available in a convenient form.

This report provides an overview of asbestos personal-injury (PI) trusts. It describes how they are created, how they are organized and governed, and how they operate. It also compiles publicly available information on the assets, outlays, claim-approval criteria, and governing boards of the leading trusts.

This report should be of interest to federal and state policymakers, lawyers, judges, and litigants concerned about the compensation of people injured by exposure to asbestos, the performance of the asbestos compensation system, and the economic impact of asbestos litigation on both defendants and the legal community. It is part of a larger research project on asbestos bankruptcy trusts. A second report will examine how trust compensation or the potential for such compensation is addressed by state liability laws and taken into consideration during court proceedings and settlement negotiations.

The research was supported by a coalition of asbestos defendants and insurers and by the RAND Institute for Civil Justice. The views in the report are those of the authors and do not necessarily reflect those of the research sponsors.

The RAND Institute for Civil Justice

The mission of the RAND Institute for Civil Justice (ICJ) is to improve private and public decisionmaking on civil legal issues by supplying policymakers and the public with the results of objective, empirically based, analytic research. ICJ facilitates change in the civil justice system by analyzing trends and outcomes, identifying and evaluating policy options, and bringing together representatives of different interests to debate alternative solutions to policy problems. ICJ builds on a long tradition of RAND research characterized by an interdisciplinary, empirical approach to public policy issues and rigorous standards of quality, objectivity, and independence.

ICJ research is supported by pooled grants from corporations, trade and professional associations, and individuals; by government grants and contracts; and by private foundations. ICJ disseminates its work widely to the legal, business, and research communities and to the general public. In accordance with RAND policy, all ICJ research products are subject to peer review before publication. ICJ publications do not necessarily reflect the opinions or policies of the research sponsors or of the ICJ Board of Overseers.

Information about ICJ is available online (http://www.rand.org/icj/). Inquiries about research projects should be sent to the following address:

James Dertouzos, Director
RAND Institute for Civil Justice
1776 Main Street
P.O. Box 2138
Santa Monica, CA 90407-2138
310-393-0411 x7476
Fax: 310-451-6979
James_Dertouzos@rand.org

Questions and comments about this report should be sent to Lloyd Dixon (Lloyd_Dixon@rand.org).

Contents

Figures

Tables

Summary

Litigation over personal injuries due to asbestos exposure has continued for more than 40 years in the United States with hundreds of thousands of claims filed and billions of dollars in compensation paid. Many companies with significant liability for asbestos-related injuries have filed for bankruptcy, resulting in the creation of asbestos bankruptcy trusts, which pay claims on behalf of bankrupt defendants. These trusts are playing an increasingly important role in the compensation of asbestos-related injuries.

While the role of trusts in providing compensation to asbestos claimants has grown, information about the operating procedures and activities of these trusts is not readily available in a convenient form. Little research has been done on transaction costs, time to claim disposition, claimant satisfaction, and other metrics of trust performance. In addition, there is little analysis of how the trusts have affected the overall compensation that asbestos claimants receive and the asbestos liabilities of solvent defendants and their insurers.

This report provides an overview of asbestos PI trusts. It describes how they are created, how they are organized and governed, and how they operate. It also compiles publicly available information on the assets, outlays, claim-approval criteria, and governing boards of the leading trusts. This report does not attempt to evaluate trusts' performance or assess how they have affected the overall compensation of asbestos claimants. Rather, it is meant to provide a readily accessible source of information on asbestos trusts that will help interested parties better understand how trusts operate and their activities to date. This report is part of a larger research project on asbestos bankruptcy trusts. A second report will examine how trust compensation or the potential for such compensation is taken into consideration in court proceedings and settlement negotiations.

Data and Methods

Data on the trusts were abstracted from publicly available sources including bankruptcy documents, trust websites, trust annual reports, and U.S. Securities and Exchange Commission (SEC) filings. To concentrate our efforts on the largest trusts, we selected a subset of the 54 trusts that had been set up through 2009. Twenty-six active trusts were chosen that met specified cutoffs based on the magnitude of assets available to the trust when it was established and the amount of claim payments through 2008. The 26 active trusts that met the criteria accounted for more than 99 percent of the claim payments that we could identify for all trusts through 2008.

Detailed reports on the 26 selected trusts were prepared and then submitted to the relevant trusts for review. Twenty-three of the trusts were able to review the data, and the data were revised accordingly. The reports for the 26 active trusts, as well as for the three largest proposed trusts, are provided in Appendix B to this report. The overview of trust activity that follows is based on the 26 selected active trusts. Trusts do not publicly release individual claim information; thus, neither the variation of payments by a given trust across individuals nor payments by multiple trusts to the same claimant can be examined.

Findings

Number of Bankruptcies and Trusts

Figure S.1 shows the cumulative number of bankruptcies filed that involved at least some asbestos liability and the number of asbestos bankruptcy trusts that have been established. Fifty-four trusts have been established through June 2010, with a considerable acceleration in the number of trusts established in the second half of the 2000s. Nine more trusts are in the pipeline, with undoubtedly more to come.

Aggregate Claim Activity

Figure S.2 displays the cumulative number of claims paid and the claim payments for the 26 selected active trusts. Data for the years prior to 2006 are aggregated because we were not able to break down pre-2006 figures by year for some major trusts. Data on pre-2006 claim payments for two trusts are incomplete because complete records could not be located for these

Figure S.1
Cumulative Number of Asbestos-Related Bankruptcies Filed and Trusts Established as of June 2010

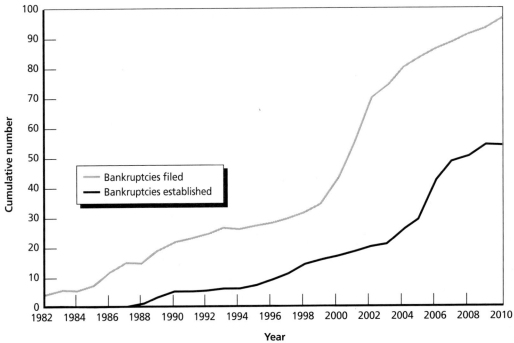

Figure S.2
Cumulative Number of Claims Paid and Value of Claim Payments at the Selected Trusts

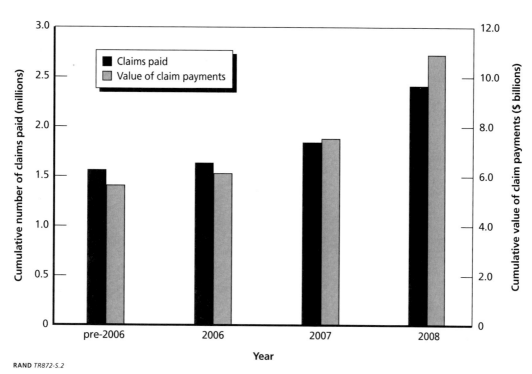

older trusts. Also, it appears that data on the number of paid claims are incomplete for three of the 26 trusts. Thus, the data in Figure S.2 provide lower bounds on the number of claims paid and the value of claim payments. Plaintiffs' attorneys' fees must be removed from trust payments in order to determine the amount ultimately received by claimants.

Reflecting the influx of new trusts in 2006 and 2007, both the number of claims paid and annual value of claim payments surged in 2007 and 2008. Approximately 575,000 claims were paid, for a total value of $3.3 billion in 2008. Because multiple trusts can make payments to the same individual, the number of claims paid exceeds the number of individuals receiving compensation from the trusts, but by how much is unknown. To put these numbers in perspective, a 2005 RAND report estimated that $7.1 billion was paid in compensation by asbestos defendants (not including asbestos trusts) in 2002 (Carroll, Hensler, et al., 2005, p. 92). Comprehensive data on which to base more-current estimates of tort compensation are not available.

Trust compensation payments have been considerable to date, and the assets under trust control indicate that significant payments will continue. As of year-end 2008, the assets of the selected active trusts totaled $18.2 billion, and this total does not include the assets of four recently formed trusts that had not filed financial statements as of 2009. The total also does not include the estimated assets of currently proposed trusts. Estimates of the initial assets at eight of the nine proposed trusts for which information is available total $14.5 billion.

Breakdown of Payments by Injury Type

The compensation paid to claimants with more-severe diseases relative to those with less severe diseases has been an ongoing issue in asbestos compensation. Ten of the 26 active trusts provide separate figures on malignant and nonmalignant claims. *Malignant claims*, by and large, refers to claims involving mesothelioma, lung cancer, and other cancers. *Nonmalignant claims* refers to claims involving severe asbestosis, asbestosis and pleural disease, or other asbestos-related diseases.

Taking 2007 and 2008 together, 86 percent of the total number of claims that these trusts paid were for nonmalignant injuries. Nonmalignant claims accounted for 37 percent of 2007 and 2008 expenditures at these ten trusts, reflecting an average payment per claim that was roughly one-tenth that for malignant claims.

While legislative and judicial reforms have made it increasingly difficult to obtain compensation for nonmalignant injuries in the tort system, the large number of nonmalignant claims paid by trusts indicates that the trust system remains a source of compensation for such injuries. How the total compensation a claimant receives from the trusts for nonmalignant injuries has changed over time, however, is uncertain. On the one hand, some trusts have cut payments for the least serious nonmalignant claims. On the other hand, an increase in the number of trusts means that a claimant may be able to obtain compensation for nonmalignant claims from more trusts.

Trust Transaction Costs

Trusts strive to deliver compensation with minimal legal and other transaction costs, at least compared with the transaction costs associated with the tort system. Trust financial statements allow estimates of gross claimant compensation as a percentage of trust expenditures. The claimant compensation is gross in the sense that it includes any fees the claimant pays to his or her attorney for services related to the recovery.[1]

As trust claim payments rose rapidly between 2006 and 2008, the gross claimant-compensation percentage rose from between 71 and 75 percent in 2006 to approximately 95 percent in 2008. These levels compare favorably to estimates of gross compensation as a percentage of defendant expenditures in the tort system. Carroll, Hensler, et al. (2005, p. xxvi) estimated that gross claimant compensation through 2002 amounted to 69 percent of total spending by defendants and insurers. It should be noted, however, that the gross compensation percentages for the trusts do not include the legal and other transaction costs incurred in negotiating the trust terms during the bankruptcy proceedings.

Claim Valuation Schedules

When a trust receives an asbestos PI claim, it must review the submitted claim documents and assign a value to the claimant's injuries. Trusts typically offer claimants two primary options for claim review: expedited review or individual review.

Under expedited review, claims that meet the medical and exposure criteria for the alleged disease (referred to as the disease level) will be assigned a scheduled value for the disease. According to a party that has worked closely with trusts, the scheduled value is typically set slightly above the 50th percentile of the historical settlements that the debtor paid for the particular disease before bankruptcy. We, however, have not been able to evaluate the extent to which this is actually the case.

---

[1] Informed parties indicated that plaintiffs' attorneys' fees typically run about 25 percent of the award.

As an alternative to expedited review, individual review provides a claimant the opportunity to receive individual consideration of his or her medical condition and of the claim's value. Individual-review claims are meant to be valued at the historical liquidated value of similarly situated claims in the tort system. We have not been able to evaluate the extent to which this is the case either. Most trusts also publish so-called average values of different disease levels. For most trusts, the average value is the trust's target for the average value assigned to claims, including claims that go through either expedited or individual review.

The top rows of Table S.1 show the scheduled and average values for mesothelioma claims for the trust-claim-class combinations at the selected trusts reporting this information.[2] The scheduled value for mesothelioma claims varies from $7,000 to $1.2 million across the 30 trust-claim-class combinations, with a median of $126,000. The median of the average value for mesothelioma claims is $180,000—again, with a large spread. The wide spread in both the scheduled and average values reflects, in part, the differences across debtors in the settlement values for mesothelioma claims prebankruptcy.

Most trusts do not have sufficient funds to pay every claim in full and, thus, set a payment percentage that is used to determine the actual payment a claimant will be offered. As shown in the Table S.1, the median of the payment percentage is 25 percent across the trust-claim-class combinations reporting, with the range running from 1.1 percent to 100 percent. Thus, the assets available to some trusts allow them to pay only a very small proportion of the value assigned to the claim while other trusts are fully funded and can pay the entire amount.

The bottom rows in Table S.1 show the scheduled and average values once the payment percentage has been applied. Average values for mesothelioma claims net of the payment percentage range from $13,000 to $238,000 across the trust-claim-class combinations.

Trusts recognize various disease levels, and scheduled and average values are usually set for each. While mesothelioma is always considered a separate disease level, the number of other

Table S.1
Mesothelioma Claim Values

Item	Minimum	Percentile			Maximum
		20th	50th	80th	
Prior to applying payment percentage					
Scheduled value ($ thousands) (30 trust-claim-class combinations)	7	59	126	203	1,200
Average value ($ thousands) (23 trust-claim-class combinations)	45	99	180	262	524
Payment percentage (29 trust-claim-class combinations)	1.1	9.4	25.0	46.3	100.0
After applying payment percentage					
Scheduled value ($ thousands) (28 trust-claim-class combinations)	1	13	27	68	240
Average value ($ thousands) (21 trust-claim-class combinations)	13	23	41	101	238

---

[2] A number of trusts set different scheduled values for the separate classes of claims they accept. We consider each of these trust-claim-class combinations separately.

disease levels varies by trust. Comparison of scheduled and average values after application of the payment percentage for trusts with comparable disease levels shows that scheduled and average values for other cancers and severe asbestosis are considerably below those for mesothelioma but substantially higher than those for asbestosis/pleural disease and other asbestos disease.

Composition of Trust Governing Bodies

Trusts are governed by trustees, who operate the trust for the benefit of claimants. Because trusts often have hundreds of thousands of beneficiaries who cannot directly control the trustees, committees are set up to represent the interests of current and future claimants. Trustees are required to obtain the consent of the trust advisory committee (TAC) (representing current claimants) and the future claimants' representative (FCR) (representing future claimants) before major actions by the trust can be taken (such as revising trust distribution procedures, or TDPs).

To better understand who is running the trusts, we determined the professional affiliations of key trust personnel. At the 26 selected trusts, we identified a total of 255 different positions for trustees, TAC members, FCRs, trust counsel, TAC counsel, and FCR counsel. There were 122 different individuals filling these 255 positions, representing 83 different organizations. While the lists assembled for trustees, TAC members, and FCRs are fairly complete, the lists for trust counsel, TAC counsel, and FCR counsel are less complete because it is more difficult to obtain the information on who is serving in these capacities.

Table S.2 shows the organizations represented at more than five different trusts. Kazan, McClain, Abrams, Lyons, Greenwood and Harley is represented at more than half of the 26 trusts, and the other firms are represented at sizable percentages. These organizations tend to be represented at the larger trusts, which can be inferred by comparing the second and leftmost columns of Table S.2.[3] Seven of the nine firms listed are plaintiffs' attorney firms and are represented on the TACs. Campbell and Levine is trust counsel at multiple trusts, and Caplin and Drysdale is TAC counsel at multiple trusts. The involvement of all of these firms at a sizable share of the selected trusts reflects the leading role that these firms play in asbestos litigation or in the bankruptcy process and the creation of asbestos trusts.

Limitations of Publicly Available Trust Data

The publicly available information on asbestos bankruptcy trusts is a useful resource and provides an informative overview of trust practices and activity. However, it is limited in many important ways. Data on important variables, such as the number of claims filed, are incomplete, and information for the early years of the older trusts is not readily available. Data by disease level are uneven, with less than half of the selected 26 trusts breaking out information for malignant and nonmalignant claims. Only a few trusts report data by disease level beyond the malignant/nonmalignant breakdown. In addition, disease-level categories vary across trusts, adding to the challenges of comparing claim valuations and payments by disease level across trusts. Trusts do not follow a common set of accounting principles when preparing finan-

---

[3]   Specifically, the combined assets of the trusts at which a firm is represented as a percentage of total year-end 2008 assets of the selected trusts are larger than the percentage of trusts at which the organization is represented.

Table S.2
Organizations Most Frequently Represented at the 26 Selected Trusts

Organization	Number of Trusts at Which Firm Was Represented		2008 Assets of Trusts at Which Firm Was Represented	
	Number	Percentage of Selected Trusts	Assets ($ billions)	Percentage of Assets of Selected Trusts
Kazan, McClain, Abrams, Lyons, Greenwood and Harley	15	58	11.6	64
Baron and Budd	11	42	11.5	63
Cooney and Conway	11	42	13.3	73
Weitz and Luxenberg	11	42	13.4	74
Motley Rice	8	31	9.4	52
Bergman Draper and Frockt	6	23	5.5	30
Campbell and Levine	6	23	8.0	44
Caplin and Drysdale	6	23	10.4	57
Goldberg Persky White	6	23	10.3	57

cial statements, which makes it difficult to compare financial performance across trusts and develop measures of gross claimant compensation as a percentage of trust expenditures.

From the perspective of trying to understand the role of the trusts in the compensation for asbestos-related injuries, perhaps the most significant limitation of the publicly available data is the inability to link payments across trusts to the same individual. It is not possible to use trust-level data to determine the number of trusts providing payments to the same individual or the amount the trusts together pay to an individual claimant. This lack of information makes it difficult or perhaps impossible to evaluate the trusts' effect on the total compensation provided to individual claimants, as well as on the compensation paid by solvent defendants.

Information on individual settlements is very difficult to obtain from solvent defendants and from plaintiffs' attorneys as well. In the past, researchers have had success obtaining individual settlement data from a number of solvent defendants on a confidential basis (see, for example, Carroll, Hensler, et al., 2005). Researchers have likewise been able to obtain individual data from the Manville Personal Injury Settlement Trust in the past, although, in recent years, the Manville Trust has declined to make these data available for research purposes. Researchers have not been successful in obtaining individual asbestos compensation data from plaintiffs' attorneys.

The ability to understand the trusts' effect on overall claimant compensation and the compensation paid by solvent defendants will depend, to a large extent, on whether solvent defendants, trusts, and plaintiffs' attorneys are willing to release individual compensation information on a confidential basis for research purposes.

Acknowledgments

Many people made important contributions to this report. We would first like to thank Marc Scarcella at Bates White and Peter R. Kelso at Litigation Resolution Group for helping us access and interpret the publicly available data on the trusts that had already been collected by Bates White. We would also like to thank the 23 trusts that reviewed the information we assembled on their trusts for accuracy and completeness. The substantial time that many of them spent reviewing the data is much appreciated.

Insightful peer reviews were provided by James M. Anderson and Frank Camm at RAND. Helpful comments on the draft were provided by Charles E. Bates of Bates White; Melissa H. Brown of Georgia-Pacific; Stephen J. Carroll, recently retired from RAND; Deborah Greenspan of Dickstein Shapiro; Elihu Inselbuch of Caplin and Drysdale; Harold Kim of the U.S. Chamber of Commerce Institute for Legal Reform; John Kinney of the Hartford Financial Services Group; William M. Lynch of Liberty Mutual Group; Joseph J. O'Hara of Owens-Illinois; Thomas O'Kane of Munich Reinsurance America; and Paul D. Rheingold of Rheingold, Valet, Rheingold, Shkolnik and McCartney.

At RAND, we thank ICJ quality-assurance director Susan M. Gates for moving this document through the RAND quality-assurance process and for providing useful comments on the draft; James Dertouzos, ICJ director, for helpful advice during the course of the project; Steve Carroll for his help in scoping the project and for advice throughout the project; Lisa Bernard for skillful editing; Stephanie Lonsinger for manuscript-preparation assistance; and Fred Kipperman, ICJ associate director, and Jamie Morikawa, development director, for helping scope and secure funding for the project, as well as liaising with project sponsors.

Glossary

524(g) trust. See *asbestos personal-injury trust.*

asbestos personal-injury claim. Any claim or demand, whether against a debtor asbestos company or an asbestos personal-injury trust, that arises from harm or alleged harm due to direct or indirect exposure to asbestos or asbestos-containing products.

asbestos personal-injury trust. A trust established pursuant to Section 524(g) of the U.S. bankruptcy code to pay asbestos-related liabilities. The trust is established as part of a debtor's reorganization plan under Chapter 11 of the bankruptcy code.

asbestosis. A noncancerous lung disease caused by asbestos fibers.

average value. A monetary value that trusts use as a guide for payment amounts under a specific disease category. Over time, the combined payments offered under both expedited and individual review are expected to trend toward the average value for each disease category.

bankruptcy date. The date the debtor filed a petition for reorganization with the bankruptcy court under Chapter 11 of the bankruptcy code.

channeling injunction. An element of Section 524(g) of the bankruptcy code that shifts all asbestos-related liabilities to the newly formed asbestos personal-injury trust and bars suits against the reorganized debtor.

claim administrator. A company that asbestos trusts employ to manage claim processing in accordance with the standards of the trust distribution procedures. Some claim administrators process claims from several trusts.

claim payment ratio. A ratio that sets a limit on the percentage of the maximum annual payment that can be paid to claimants with malignancies and severe asbestosis and to claimants with less severe injuries.

claim ratio. See *claim payment ratio.*

claimant. The holder of an asbestos claim who either presently seeks or may in the future seek payment from the trust.

company exposure. A component of the exposure criteria for expedited review, company exposure requirements set the minimum time requirement for exposure to the debtor's job sites or asbestos-containing products.

confirmation date. The date the bankruptcy court confirmed the debtor's plan for reorganization in accordance with the provisions of Chapter 11 of the bankruptcy code.

debtor. The former asbestos-producing company that has sought bankruptcy reorganization and funded, in whole or in part, the asbestos personal-injury trust.

diffusing capacity of the lung for carbon monoxide (test). A pulmonary test to measure the amount of carbon monoxide absorbed by the lungs.

exigent-hardship claim. A claim classification defined by each trust that improves a settled claim's position in the payment queue. Many trusts limit exigent cases to the malignant diseases and severe asbestosis. Furthermore, trusts condition such claims on a claimant's immediate financial need that resulted from the claimant's asbestos-related disease.

expedited review. A claim-processing category available to claimants alleging certain diseases. Expedited review consists of submitting documentation on both medical and exposure criteria and is available only for disease classifications as described in the trust distribution procedures. Successful expedited review results in a fixed and certain payment in accordance with the procedures and scheduled values described in the trust distribution procedures.

extraordinary claim. Claim for which a claimant's asbestos-related exposure was predominantly the result of one specific debtor's products or manufacturing facility.

first-in, first-out principle. Claims are placed in the processing queue and the payment queue in the order in which they are received.

forced expiratory volume in one second/forced vital capacity ratio. A pulmonary test measuring the volume of air expired in the first second, expressed as a percentage of forced vital capacity.

future claimants' representative. A court-appointed representative who represents the interests of future claimants in matters of trust administration. Any changes made to the trust distribution procedures, including the payment percentage and the claim payment ratio, must receive approval from the future claimants' representative.

indirect trust claim. Claim filed against the trust by parties other than the asbestos claim-holder (e.g., by a claim asserting a theory of contribution).

individual review. A claim-processing category that requires individualized review of a claimant's records to determine the extent of disease, its likely connection to asbestos exposure, and its corresponding payment amount. Some categories of disease may be compensated only through individual review (i.e., lung cancer without underlying asbestosis).

International Labour Organization reading. An interpretation of pulmonary x-rays using the International Labour Organization's International Classification of Radiographs of Pneumoconioses.

interstitial fibrosis. A scarring of the lung tissue.

latency period. The length of time between the date a claimant was first exposed to asbestos or asbestos-containing products and the date of medical diagnosis of asbestos-related disease or asbestos-related death.

liquidated claim. An asbestos claim, either in the tort system or processed through the trust, in which the monetary value of the claim has been fixed, though not necessarily paid to the claimant.

maximum annual payment. The annually determined upper limit to the amount of money the trust can pay to claimants in the aggregate for that year.

mesothelioma. A cancer of the mesothelium, a protective membrane that covers the internal organs. Mesothelioma is the most severe disease category recognized by asbestos trusts.

occupational exposure. Years on the job during which the claimant was exposed to asbestos.

payment percentage. A percentage applied to the value that a trust assigns to a claim to determine the amount that will be actually paid to the claimant. Payment percentages are initially set during the trust formation but may be changed with the consent of the trust advisory committee and the future claimants' representative. Payment percentages are used as a means to preserve trust assets to pay future unknown claims.

payment queue. The order in which an asbestos personal-injury trust pays liquidated claims. The payment queue is governed by the first-in, first-out principle but subject to the maximum annual payment and the claim payment ratio.

pleura. A membrane that surrounds the lungs.

pleural calcification. A calcium buildup on the pleura.

pleural disease. Common name for a number of ailments of the pleura.

pleural plaques. A localized scarring of the pleura.

pleural thickening. Diffuse scarring of the pleura.

pre- or post-petition claim. A claim filed against a debtor company either before (prepetition) or after (post-petition) the debtor's filing for bankruptcy protection.

prepackaged bankruptcy. A bankruptcy reorganization plan that is negotiated *before* filing for bankruptcy protection.

processing queue. The order in which asbestos personal-injury claims, whether filed against the debtor or against the trust, are processed, reviewed, and assigned a liquidated settlement value.

scheduled value. The monetary value assigned to a claim through expedited review.

significant occupational exposure. An exposure criterion required for specific diseases. The standard definition provided in the trust distribution procedures is

> employment for a cumulative period of at least five (5) years with a minimum of two (2) years prior to December 31, 1982, in an industry and an occupation in which the claimant (a) handled raw asbestos fibers on a regular basis; (b) fabricated asbestos-containing products so that the claimant in the fabrication process was exposed on a regular basis to raw asbestos fibers; (c) altered, repaired or otherwise worked with an asbestos-containing product such that the claimant was exposed on a regular basis to asbestos fibers; or (d) was employed in an industry and occupation such that the claimant worked on a regular basis in close proximity to workers engaged in the activities described in (a), (b), and/or (c). (Kaiser Aluminum and Chemical Corporation, 2007)

trust advisory committee. A court-appointed trust administrative committee that represents the interests of current claim-holders in matters of trust administration. Any changes made to the trust distribution procedures, including the payment percentage and the claim payment ratio, must receive approval from the trust advisory committee.

trust distribution procedure. The document that describes the process by which claims will be collected, reviewed, and paid.

Abbreviations

ADR	alternative dispute resolution
CT	computed tomography
FCR	future claimants' representative
FEV1	forced expiratory volume in one second
FIFO	first-in, first-out
FVC	forced vital capacity
GAAP	generally accepted accounting principle
ILO	International Labour Organization
MAP	maximum annual payment
PI	personal injury
SEC	U.S. Securities and Exchange Commission
TA	trust agreement
TAC	trust advisory committee
TDP	trust distribution procedure
THAN	T. H. Agriculture and Nutrition
TLC	total lung capacity

CHAPTER ONE

Introduction

Over the past ten years, payments by asbestos personal-injury (PI) trusts have played an increasingly important role in the compensation of asbestos-related injuries. These trusts pay claims on behalf of companies that have filed for bankruptcy at least in part to resolve their asbestos liabilities. The trusts are created during the bankruptcy process and, once formed, become the only source of compensation from the bankrupt defendants for asbestos-related injuries. The formation of an asbestos PI trust bars parties alleging asbestos-related injuries from suing the bankrupt defendants in the tort system.

While the numbers of asbestos-related bankruptcies and resulting trusts have grown, information about the operating procedures and activities of these trusts is not readily available in a convenient form. Little research has been done on transaction costs, time to claim disposition, claimant satisfaction, and other metrics of trust performance. In addition, there is little analysis of how the trusts have affected the overall compensation that asbestos claimants receive and the trusts' effect on the asbestos liabilities of solvent defendants and their insurers.

This report provides an overview of asbestos PI trusts. It describes how they are created, how they are organized and governed, and how they operate. It also compiles publicly available information on the assets, outlays, claim-approval criteria, and governing boards of the leading trusts. This report does not attempt to evaluate trusts' performance or assess how they have affected the overall compensation of asbestos claimants. Rather, it is meant to provide a readily accessible source of information on asbestos trusts that will help interested parties better understand how trusts operate and their activities to date. This report is part of a larger research project on asbestos bankruptcy trusts. A second report will examine how trust compensation or the potential for such compensation is addressed by state liability laws and taken into consideration during court proceedings and settlement negotiations. In the remainder of this introductory chapter, we provide a brief overview of asbestos litigation and the rise of the trusts and an outline of the remainder of the report.

Asbestos Litigation and the Rise of the Trusts

Asbestos is a naturally occurring fiber that was widely used in the United States in industrial products throughout much of the 20th century. Despite its usefulness as a basic material, asbestos is toxic and has been linked to several diseases, such as mesothelioma, lung cancer, and asbestosis. The combination of asbestos' toxicity and its widespread use in industrial products caused one of the major litigation episodes in U.S. history. In the 1960s, U.S. courts began to hear asbestos-related PI claims,[1] and the Fifth Circuit upheld the first successful suit in 1973.[2] The litigation subsequently exploded. A 2005 RAND report (Carroll, Hensler, et al., 2005) estimated that, through 2002, approximately 730,000 people had filed asbestos claims against at least 8,400 corporate defendants. These defendants included miners and manufacturers of asbestos or asbestos-containing products, purchasers of asbestos products, insurers, and businesses that used asbestos or asbestos-containing products in the course of their industry. Awards, legal fees, and other claim-related costs rose into the billions of dollars. Indeed, asbestos litigation became "the longest-running mass tort litigation in the United States" (Carroll, Hensler, et al., 2005, p. xvii).

Several factors contributed to the courts' difficulty in resolving the litigation: the widespread use of asbestos, which exposed as many as 27.5 million Americans to asbestos in the course of their employment (American Academy of Actuaries, 2007, p. 1); a long latency period for asbestos diseases; a segment of the plaintiffs' bar that sought to capitalize on the asbestos-litigation boom by seeking settlements for plaintiffs with no known diseases (Hensler et al., 1985; McGovern, 2002); and the failure of global settlements through class-action lawsuits.

Various reform efforts were introduced to try to better manage the resolution of the massive number of asbestos claims and to provide compensation for asbestos claimants. For example, beginning in 1977, proposals before Congress called for a federal trust fund that would oversee asbestos claimants' compensation.[3] These efforts encountered fierce political resistance and were ultimately unsuccessful despite endorsement from the Supreme Court.[4] Many state-level reforms were implemented. These include statutory medical criteria requirements that identify which asbestos-related injuries are actionable in a state tort suit, revisions to joint- and several-liability rules regarding the apportionment of monetary damages across multiple defendants, and inactive and expedited dockets.[5]

Despite the judicial remedies, legislative wrangling, and more than 40 years of lawsuits, asbestos claims continue to this day—albeit in an altered form. Whereas the asbestos compensation of the past predominantly involved submitting claims directly to defendants or filing tort claims in court, the current asbestos landscape is set jointly in the tort system and in an extrajudicial trust system.

The trust system was created as the by-product of asbestos bankruptcies. Major asbestos defendants faced crushing and often-unpredictable liabilities for the harms caused by asbestos. Bankruptcy was one option for coping with these liabilities because it grants a bankrupt defen-

---

[1] See, e.g., *Tomplait v. Combustion Eng'g, Inc.*, No. C.A. 5402 (E.D. Tex. 1967); *Borel v. Fibreboard*, 493 F.2d 1076 (5th Cir. 1973) at 1104 (indicating that the initial suit was filed in 1969). The first suits filed against Johns-Manville, however, came as early as the 1930s but were ultimately settled (Macchiarola, 1996, p. 592).

[2] *Borel v. Fibreboard*, 493 F.2d 1076 (5th Cir. 1973).

[3] H.R. 8689 (1977).

[4] *Amchem Prods. v. Windsor* (521 U.S. 591, 1997) (Ginsburg, at 628–629: "the argument is sensibly made that a nationwide administrative claims processing regime would provide the most secure, fair, and efficient means of compensating victims of asbestos exposure"). See also *Ortiz v. Fibreboard Corp.* (527 U.S. 815, 1999).

[5] An inactive docket, sometimes called a pleural registry, is an administrative procedure by which the claims of plaintiffs who were exposed to asbestos but who do not yet show signs of injury are held until symptoms of disease appear. The procedure helps prevent court dockets from becoming clogged with unimpaired asbestos claims while preserving the plaintiffs' right to sue without fear of running into a statute of limitations. An expedited docket, on the other hand, fast-tracks the judicial process for asbestos victims who have the most-severe claims. For more, see Carroll, Hensler, et al. (2005, pp. 26–28).

dant (also known as the debtor) an injunction against civil lawsuits. For asbestos bankruptcies, that means that parties alleging injury due to asbestos exposure are barred from suing the companies that were the major producers of asbestos and asbestos-containing products.

Bankruptcy protection thus changed the tenor and tone of asbestos litigation by barring suits against bankrupt defendants. In 1982, the Johns-Manville Corporation filed one of the first asbestos-related bankruptcy petitions, and, in 1987, the Manville Personal Injury Settlement Trust was the first asbestos bankruptcy trust established.[6] Since then, there has been a dramatic surge in the number of asbestos manufacturers seeking bankruptcy protection. In fact, "nearly all of the major manufacturers" have declared bankruptcy (American Academy of Actuaries, 2007, p. 5). Because the major asbestos manufacturers are protected from lawsuits, plaintiffs are left with "peripheral" companies: those that played less prominent roles in asbestos production and use (e.g., companies that may have asbestos "encapsulated in their products or [companies] having asbestos on their premises") (American Academy of Actuaries, 2007, p. 7; see also Bates, Mullin, and Marquardt, 2009).

Asbestos bankruptcy trusts are established under Section 524(g) of Chapter 11 of the bankruptcy code[7] and exist for the sole purpose of compensating asbestos claimants who are either currently ill or may develop diseases in the future. The goal is to treat current claims and future demands in substantially the same manner by managing a trust fund paid for by the bankrupt asbestos defendant.

In general, the trust system works in the following way. A company facing asbestos liabilities petitions the bankruptcy court for bankruptcy protection and reorganization. All lawsuits against the company are immediately halted. After negotiations with the company's creditors—including asbestos plaintiffs' lawyers—the company submits a plan of reorganization to the court. Among other details, the plan establishes and funds an independent asbestos PI trust. The trust will use the debtor's assets to collect, process, and pay all of the valid asbestos PI claims. Individuals suffering asbestos-related injuries may file claims with any and all trusts. If the claimant meets exposure requirements relating to a trust's debtors' products, as well as medical criteria, the trust will pay compensation to the claimant. In return for funding the trusts, the reorganized company is shielded against all current and future asbestos-related liability. Asbestos PI trusts are now "answering for the liability of many of the most culpable companies" (Shelley, Cohn, and Arnold, 2008, p. 258).

Organization of This Report

In Chapter Two, we describe the trust mechanism: its historical formation, codification in bankruptcy law, and purpose in response to the asbestos-litigation boom. Chapter Three discusses the internal working structures of the trusts by identifying key players, governing processes, and common elements of trust administration, such as the trust distribution procedures (TDPs), which are used to guide claim processing.

In Chapter Four, we provide a descriptive overview of bankruptcy trusts, including trends in the number of trusts, claim payments, and assets. We also report the target average payment

---

[6]   *In re Johns-Manville Corp.* (68 B.R. 618, Bankr. S.D.N.Y. 1986; decision affirmed in part, reversed in part, 78 B.R. 407, S.D.N.Y. 1987; order affirmed, 843 F.2d 636, 2d Cir. 1988).

[7]   11 U.S.C. § 524(g).

per claim by disease category, the breakdown of payments between malignant and nonmalignant claims, and initial estimates of trust transaction costs. Concluding observations in Chapter Five are followed by appendixes presenting detailed information on the trusts. Appendix A lists companies that have filed for bankruptcy with at least some asbestos liability and the trusts that have been consequently established. Appendix B presents detailed information on each of the 26 largest active trusts and the three largest proposed trusts.

CHAPTER TWO

History of and Statutory Framework for Asbestos Bankruptcy Trusts

This chapter provides an overview of the development of asbestos PI trusts. The discussion begins with a brief case history of the first trust, the Manville Trust, and follows up with the codification of the trust mechanism in bankruptcy law.

The Johns-Manville Corporation Bankruptcy and the First Asbestos Personal-Injury Trust

In the wake of an "avalanche" of litigation,[1] the major asbestos manufacturers quickly discovered that their liabilities were escalating, unpredictable, and, therefore, unmanageable.[2] Many of these businesses sought reorganization of their debts through bankruptcy. Chapter 11 of the bankruptcy code allows indebted companies to continue operations while paying debtors over an extended period of time (as opposed to a liquidation of all business assets and the shuttering of the company under Chapter 7 rules). The choice to undergo bankruptcy reorganization is "a difficult one for corporations" (Carroll, Hensler, et al., 2005, p. 109). Yet, bankruptcy is "the only generally recognized legal vehicle that is currently available for imposing finality on a defendant's asbestos liability" (McGovern, 2002, p. 1756). Given the challenges posed by asbestos liability and the difficulty of protecting future claimants in particular, reorganization is an attractive option, at least for some parties (see Mabey and Zisser, 1995).

One of the first companies to petition for reorganization was the Johns-Manville Corporation—at the time, the largest producer of asbestos-containing products and a leading defendant in asbestos lawsuits (Carroll, Hensler, et al., 2005, p. 110). Johns-Manville petitioned for Chapter 11 reorganization in 1982. Six years later, it emerged from bankruptcy, having shifted its asbestos liabilities to a new entity known as the Manville Personal Injury Settlement Trust.[3] This use of bankruptcy protection to shed asbestos liability was, as one author put it, "a radical new use of bankruptcy law" (Macchiarola, 1996, p. 583).

The creation of the trust was a novel approach to managing the company's asbestos liabilities. The arrangement was straightforward. The new Johns-Manville's financial assets, including a majority stake in the company's common-stock and product-liability insurance payouts on insurance policies it had purchased, were transferred to the trust. The combined value was

---

[1] *In re Combustion Eng'g., Inc.* (391 F.3d 190, 200, 3d Cir., 2004).

[2] The toxicity of asbestos and the long latency period for asbestos-related diseases combined to create an unmanageable future liability risk. For more, see Carroll, Hensler, et al. (2005).

[3] *In re Johns-Manville Corp.* (1988).

estimated at $2.5 billion when the trust was established (see Chapter Four). In return, the trust was responsible for processing and paying Johns-Manville's asbestos PI claims. The newly reorganized successor known as Manville Corporation was shielded from all future asbestos liability. This liability shield, known as a *channeling injunction*, barred all future asbestos claimants from suing Manville. All demands had to be filed with the trust, which would manage the funds for the sole benefit of the claimants.

Initially, the Manville Trust was set up to pay claimants 100 percent of the settlement value of their claims (i.e., what the claims would have received, on average, in the tort system). These claims would be paid according to a first-in, first-out (FIFO) rule, paying each claimant based on the date his or her claim was filed. During the bankruptcy negotiations, the trust was expected to settle 83,000–100,000 claims (Issacharoff, 2002, p. 1932; see also Manville Personal Injury Settlement Trust, 1996), and, at one point, the trust expected claim values to average about $25,000 (Macchiarola, 1996, p. 603).

The estimates were too optimistic, and a wave of litigation impleading the trust demonstrated the inadequacy of the first attempt (see Peterson, 1990). These new claims were, in part, the product of mass screenings conducted by plaintiffs' law firms (Hensler et al., 1985). On the other front, fearing that the money currently held in the trust would run out, current claimants awaiting payment sued the trust.[4] Current claimants rushed to recover what they could, motivated by fears that an unfavorable position in the FIFO queue and the onslaught of new claims jeopardized the chance of recovery.[5]

By 1992, "more than 190,000 claimants were seeking compensation from the trust" (Manville Personal Injury Settlement Trust, 1996).[6] Swamped by claimants, the trust was insolvent just a few years after it was created.

A 1995 settlement revised the claim-processing procedures contained in the original plan of reorganization, as well as restructured the financial arrangement with Manville. The settlement corrected some critical oversights in the previous arrangement. First, it established a new compensation plan that gave priority to the most-seriously ill. Second, it established processes for resolving disputes between claimants and the trust. These guidelines sought to prevent the flood of litigation by disgruntled claimants, which had quickly exhausted trust assets and triggered the need for new procedures. Third, the new settlement created an administrative role for a future claimants' representative (FCR), whose duty it was to protect the interests of claimants who had not yet filed with the trust.[7]

These new elements were not merely patches on a dysfunctional trust. They would have lasting significance for all future asbestos PI trusts and broad ramifications for public policy regarding the compensation of asbestos claimants. The revisions reaffirmed the policy goal that the sickest claimants should receive the highest compensation (both individually and in the aggregate). This reaffirmation stood in sharp relief to a litigation history in which claims for nonmalignant diseases dwarfed the number of claims for malignant cancers (see Carroll,

---

[4]   A provision in the trust plan allowed the trust to put claims for which litigation was pending in the front of the claim-processing queue.

[5]   *In re Joint E. & S. Dist. Asbestos Litig.* (129 B.R. 710, 758, Bankr. E. & S.D.N.Y., 1991).

[6]   Illustrating how optimistic the original estimates were, as of September 30, 2009, the trust had received 817,264 claims and had already paid $3.9 billion (Manville Personal Injury Trust Settlement, 1996).

[7]   *In re Joint E. & S. Dists. Asbestos Litig. v. Falise* (878 F. Supp. 473, E. & S.D.N.Y., 1995).

Hensler, et al., 2005, p. 75). It also foreshadowed the establishment of disease levels, corresponding payment schedules, and claim payment ratios.[8] Each of these is discussed in more detail in Chapter Three.

Furthermore, the appointment of an FCR signaled that the court recognized an inherent tension between different classes of claimants. In the court's own words, "The goal of the Plan and the purpose of the [channeling] Injunction is to preserve the rights and remedies of those parties who by accident of their disease cannot even speak in their own interest."[9] Those future claimants who were not yet aware of their diseases could not be shut out of potential recovery by claimants whose diseases were already manifest. Failure to protect the future claimants' rights to recover from the trust would have closed off all avenues to recovery (since the channeling injunction closes the door to the tort system).

The Codification of Asbestos Personal-Injury Trusts in Bankruptcy Law

Although the first iteration of the Manville trust had its operational difficulties, Congress granted its imprimatur to the "creative solution"[10] when it amended Section 524 of the bankruptcy code in 1994.[11] The new rules essentially borrow the Manville solution, including the post hoc revisions. The 1994 amendments allow companies that face crushing asbestos liabilities to fund a trust that pays all of the debtor's asbestos claims in exchange for a channeling injunction forever shielding the debtor from asbestos tort actions.[12]

Not all asbestos-related bankruptcies result in the creation of a trust,[13] but, for those companies that want to establish a trust in exchange for the valuable channeling injunction, statutory criteria have been established that govern the confirmation of an asbestos trust. Seven conditions, in addition to the standard bankruptcy requirements under Section 1129 of the bankruptcy code, must be met prior to a bankruptcy court approving a 524(g) trust and the issuance of the valuable channeling injunction as part of Chapter 11 reorganization:

---

[8] Disease levels are classifications of different types of illnesses (e.g., mesothelioma, asbestosis, lung cancer). Each disease level is assigned a monetary value, called the *scheduled value*, which a trust will offer if the claimant elects for an expedited (nonindividualized) claim review process. Scheduled values generally correspond to the severity of the disease, with mesothelioma, the most-severe condition, assigned the highest scheduled value. Claim payment ratios are guidelines the trusts use when allocating annual payments. For example, a 60-40 claim payment ratio might indicate that mesothelioma and lung-cancer claimants will get at least 60 percent, by value, of the payments for the year. The claim payment ratio is used to ensure that the most-severely ill claimants receive the majority of the annual compensation.

[9] *In re Johns-Manville Corp.* (68 B.R. 618, 627, 1986).

[10] H.R. Rep. 103-835 at 40 (1994).

[11] The provision was part of the Bankruptcy Reform Act of 1994 (Pub. L. 103-393, § 111), and the key provisions are contained in 11 U.S.C. 524(g)(1) et seq.

[12] Section 524(g) also allows bankruptcy judges to issue injunctions for third-party "nondebtors" that contribute funds or assets to the trust. Issues surrounding the nondebtor release clause are timely but beyond the scope of the present study. See, e.g., Silverstein (2009).

[13] It is possible, for example, that a company will go into liquidation under Chapter 7 rather than seek reorganization under Chapter 11. In such a case, the company effectively shuts down. The 524(g) mechanism, on the other hand, allows the company to continue creating its nonasbestos products. For a discussion of whether 524(g) requires the debtor to engage in "substantial" business activities post-confirmation, see Esserman and Parsons (2006).

1. There is a trust for present and future asbestos claims.
2. The trust is funded by securities or debt from the debtor.
3. The trust owns a majority of the voting stock of the debtor, of the parent company of the debtor, or of a subsidiary of the debtor.
4. The trust will pay present and future asbestos claims against the debtor.
5. The present and future claims are valued and paid in substantially the same manner.
6. The plan is approved by a 75-percent vote of current claimants in number and by two-thirds of the voting claims in terms of claim value.
7. An FCR is appointed (McGovern, 2002, p. 1754).

The first three conditions concern trust creation and funding. Importantly, Section 524(g) does not allow a debtor to inject money into a trust and walk away. Instead, the trust is entitled to a majority of the voting stock of the reorganized company. The result is a confluence of interest between debtor and trust: "Because the trust is funded in part with the stock of the reorganizing debtor, the trust/injunction combination aligns the future claimants' desire for payment with the company's desire to survive as an ongoing entity" (Effross, 1994). This does not interfere with the independence of the trust. The debtor has no controlling interest in the trust's activities.

The assets transferred to the trust may consist wholly of the debtor's, the debtor's parent company's, or the debtor's subsidiary's common stock or may be a portfolio of assets, such as stock, cash, and insurance policies (or the rights to settlements therefrom). The funding may come as one large lump sum or, more commonly, be disbursed over a number of years according to a prenegotiated schedule. The trust reports included in Appendix B contain information about the funding sources of the leading trusts.

The fourth through seventh conditions primarily concern the claimants, their interests, and the mechanisms by which those interests are expressed. The fourth condition is the effect of the channeling injunction: The trust becomes the sole venue for claiming against the debtor. This channeling injunction applies to both current and future claimants.

Per the fifth requirement, those claimants must be treated in a substantially similar manner. To satisfy this requirement, trusts use a matrix of diseases and corresponding monetary values assigned to those diseases to help ensure that similarly situated claimants receive equitable treatment. In most cases, a claimant who meets established medical criteria would be paid an amount equal to all similarly situated claimants.[14]

Condition 6 states that 75 percent of current claimants in number and two-thirds of the claimants by value of the claims must approve the bankruptcy reorganization plan prior to creation of a 524(g) trust. Current claimants for this purpose are plaintiffs who filed asbestos PI claims against the debtor. In practice, this precondition is accomplished by garnering support from lawyers who represent a sufficient number of claimants to reach these threshold values.[15] Note, however, that these voting thresholds count only current claimants. Neither

---

[14] According to 11 U.S.C. 524(g)(2)(b)(ii)(V), the trust must process claims "through mechanisms such as structured, periodic, or supplemental payments, pro rata distributions, matrices, or periodic review of estimates of the numbers and values of present claims and future demands, or other comparable mechanisms."

[15] The process by which trust reorganization plans are approved has been criticized, and reorganization plans that have been negotiated in advance of filing a petition (known as *prepackaged bankruptcies*) have particularly been lambasted as providing too few protections to the creditors. See, e.g., Parloff (2004) and Plevin, Ebert, and Epley (2003).

future claimants, for whom the trusts ostensibly are created, nor the FCR is included in the voting class (see generally Brown, 2008). Future claimants, by statute, are considered to hold future demands against the trust. Demands, as opposed to claims, do not trigger a right to vote whether to confirm a plan of reorganization (Mabey and Zisser, 1995, p. 502).

Strategies for Gaining Support for a Bankruptcy Plan

Debtor companies in bankruptcy, whether or not they face asbestos-related liabilities, have used two different approaches for garnering the necessary creditors' approval for a plan of reorganization and ultimate certification by the bankruptcy court. Under the most-common approach, sometimes called a *freefall bankruptcy*, a debtor files for bankruptcy protection and engages in a lengthy process of negotiations with creditors. After a petition for bankruptcy protection is filed with the court, all parties with a claim against the debtor, including the (often large number of) asbestos claimants, are entitled to participate in negotiations and to vote on the plan of reorganization.[16] In a freefall bankruptcy, the filing of the bankruptcy is the formal trigger of negotiations between debtor and creditor. For asbestos bankruptcies in this process, an FCR must be appointed by the court to ensure that attention is paid to equity between current and future claimants.

The second method, known as a *prepackaged* or *prepack bankruptcy*, takes a "streamlined" approach by negotiating a plan of reorganization *before* filing for bankruptcy protection (Barliant, Karcazes, and Sherry, 2004). Under the prepackaged approach, the debtor does the negotiating legwork before filing with the bankruptcy court, delivering to the judge a plan of reorganization that satisfies the voting requirements of Section 524(g) as well as other Chapter 11 requirements. This approach allows the debtor considerably more flexibility in plan negotiations because they take place behind closed doors on an individual basis. These negotiations may still last for years, however, and creditors can still object once a plan is filed. Importantly, a prepack asbestos bankruptcy does not trigger the need for a court-appointed FCR until the formal petition is filed with the court.

Some researchers have claimed that prepack bankruptcies have allowed debtors to attempt to manipulate the pool of voting claimants by settling some claims through prepetition trusts[17] and by making settlement of these claims contingent upon an affirmative vote for reorganization (Barliant, Karcazes, and Sherry, 2004, p. 458). Other researchers have dismissed concern over debtors acting "in cahoots with" dominant asbestos lawyers with vast portfolios of asbestos claims against the interests of other creditors or of the debtors' co-defendants in asbestos cases (see, e.g., Snyder and Siemer, 2005, p. 803; Green et al., 2007–2008).

The first such prepackaged bankruptcy was approved in the bankruptcy trial of the Fuller Austin Insulation Company. In that case, the time from filing to confirmation was a mere 70 days,[18] far shorter than the nearly four-year average for all bankruptcies with asbestos-

---

[16] The debtor's product-liability insurers typically are not successful in convincing the bankruptcy judge to grant them standing in the case. Parties that were co-defendants with the debtor on asbestos claims before it filed for bankruptcy are in a similar situation.

[17] A prepetition trust is a fund established to pay settlements that were liquidated prior to the debtor's bankruptcy filing.

[18] Voluntary Chapter 11 petition, *In re Fuller-Austin Insulation* (1998 U.S. Dist. LEXIS 23567, at 1, Bankr. D. Del, November 10, 1998).

related liabilities (see Chapter Four). Other prepack asbestos bankruptcies include Combustion Engineering, T. H. Agriculture and Nutrition (THAN), and J. T. Thorpe and Son Inc.

Prepackaged bankruptcies are common in corporate bankruptcy cases (Ehrenfeld, 2003, p. 634). Yet, the special considerations of asbestos bankruptcies (including the special concern for future claimants) have raised questions about whether prepackaged asbestos bankruptcies serve all claimants' interests equitably. A former bankruptcy court judge and his co-authors have derided the prepackaged approach because "procedural and substantive requirements of the Bankruptcy Code [have] been sacrificed in the haste" (Barliant, Karcazes, and Sherry, 2004, p. 446).

For example, the Third Circuit vacated a confirmation order, tossing out Combustion Engineering's reorganization plan.[19] In that case, the bankruptcy negotiations resulted in special payments to numerous prepetition asbestos claimants such that they were paid a settlement that covered the majority of the claim but retained a "stub claim" that entitled them to vote on the plan of reorganization. This "artificial impairment" for voting purposes did not provide adequate assurance that the plan was equitably treating current post-petition and future claimants. The potential manipulation of voting rules, rather than the protection of all claimants' rights to an equitable recovery, led the Third Circuit to vacate the confirmation and remand the case for further consideration.

Once a bankruptcy plan satisfies the requirements of Section 1129 and Section 524(g) and is certified by the bankruptcy court and approved by the district court, a permanent litigation ban known as a *channeling injunction* is put in place, barring all civil suits against the debtor. A new asbestos bankruptcy trust will then soon be established, and the newly reorganized company will emerge from bankruptcy and resume business operations.

---

[19] *In re Combustion Engineering* (391 F.3d 190, 248–249, 2004).

CHAPTER THREE

Trust Governance, Administration, and Procedures for Compensating Claimants

Pursuant to Section 524(g) of the bankruptcy code, asbestos PI trusts must establish an organizational structure and operating procedures that meet statutorily defined standards. To this end, trust administrative functions, the amount of compensation claimants may receive, and the processes that determine compensation are established for each trust prior to confirmation of the bankruptcy reorganization plan.[1] These determinations are contained in two core documents: the asbestos trust agreement (TA) and the TDP. The TA formally establishes the trust and details the authorities of its administrative officers, and the TDP describes the process by which claims will be collected, reviewed, and paid.

Although each asbestos bankruptcy is different, and although asbestos trusts have evolved over the years (McGovern, 2006), there is a great deal of similarity across asbestos trusts in terms of organization, structure, and purpose (as reported in the TA and the TDP). For example, all trusts exist for the sole purpose of assuming a debtor's asbestos-related liabilities and, by law, must use the assets held in trust to treat current and future PI claimants equitably. In addition, the newer trusts have nearly identical criteria and governing structures. This similarity may be the product of repeat players in the asbestos bankruptcies: a small group of asbestos plaintiffs' attorneys representing a large number of claims, defense firms with expertise representing asbestos debtors, and insurance counsel representing companies that insured several asbestos defendants.

This section reviews the general provisions of the TAs and uses the elements of the TDPs to describe how claims are filed, evaluated, and paid. It should not be assumed that this process is the same for all trusts; rather, this chapter describes common practices and notes important exceptions. Here, we present information about the internal functions. The discussion of TAs outlines the purpose of the trust institution, introduces the key stakeholders and administrators, defines their relationships with one another, and specifies what information about the trust will be provided to the bankruptcy court and the public. The walk-through of TDPs is intended to reveal the nuts and bolts about claim processing and payment.

Asbestos Trust Agreements and Key Actors in Trust Administration

TAs constitute the founding document of the asbestos PI trust. The contents, though now fairly standardized, are negotiated prior to confirmation of the bankruptcy reorganization plan and certified by the bankruptcy court. At minimum, a TA will contain an agreement of trust

---

[1] These elements are not static, however. They can be amended post-confirmation through procedures listed in the TA.

(which will state the trust's purpose, acknowledge the transfer and acceptance of assets, and assume the debtor's liabilities), and a description of the key actors in the trust's administration. These elements are described in this section.

Agreement of Trust

The agreement-of-trust provisions formally establish and name the trust. For all asbestos PI trusts, the purpose of the trust is to assume liability under the plan of reorganization, to pay valid claimholders pursuant to the TDP (described later in this chapter), and to otherwise meet the legal conditions of a 524(g) trust (described in Chapter Two). The debtor company is then obligated to transfer the agreed-upon assets to the trust. Once the assets are transferred, the trust is authorized to accept the assets in exchange for acceptance of all asbestos liability and all legal defenses that would be available to the debtor. In other words, the trust contractually accepts the funds and willingly stands in place of the debtor for legal liability, insurance (as a beneficiary of the debtor's insurance policies), and indemnity purposes.

Key Actors in Trust Administration

Trustees. Following the acceptance of assets and liabilities, the TAs outline the powers of the trustees who manage the daily operations of the trust. The bankruptcy court approves the trustees. Thus far, trusts have had from one to six trustees, although, in theory, there is no limit to the potential number of trustees. When a trust has several trustees, one is designated as the managing trustee. Service as a trustee for one trust does not preclude concurrent service to other trusts.

The trustees function as the executive officers of the trust and are assigned a slate of management responsibilities, including the following:

1. Manage the investments of the trust, including the exercise of all voting rights with respect to the trust's majority stake in the reorganized debtor.
2. Hire and supervise a support staff and outside advisers to assist with legal, financial, accounting, claim processing, and other professional matters.
3. File tax[2] and other returns, including required annual reports to the bankruptcy court.
4. Stand in the debtor's place as plaintiff or respondent, including filing suit for recovery from the debtor's insurance carriers.

Most often, the TAs outline the managerial responsibilities in very general terms. On occasion, the instructions to the trustees are more specific; this level of detail is reserved for guidance in managing the trust's assets. Such guidance ranges from delegated judiciousness[3] to prescriptions regarding the type of asset classes in which the trust may invest and the portfolio allocation that may be employed.[4]

---

[2] For tax purposes, the trusts are considered "qualified settlement funds" as described in Section 1.468B-1 et seq. of the Treasury regulations and the Internal Revenue code.

[3] For the H. K. Porter Company (1998, p. 9), the TA instructs trustees to invest monies "in the manner in which individuals of ordinary prudence, discretion and judgment would act in the management of their own affairs."

[4] For example, the C. E. Thurston and Sons Asbestos Trust includes a proscription on long-term debt securities rated lower than BBB by Standard and Poor's (C. E. Thurston and Sons, undated, p. 10).

Trustees are compensated from the trust assets. Not all TAs specify the level of compensation; some agreements leave the compensation amount to the trust advisory committee (TAC) and FCR to decide. Some agreements specify an hourly rate—$500 per hour is common. Others set annual compensation—for example, $60,000–$75,000 per annum plus hourly compensation for travel and attendance at meetings.[5] Trustee compensation is reported annually to the bankruptcy court, the TAC, and the FCR.

Additional oversight of general trust activity is provided through regular reporting to the bankruptcy court. Required court filings include an annual report with the trust's balance sheet and a summary of the number and type of claims the trust disposed over the previous year. These documents are available for public review and constitute the raw data for the trust reports in Appendix B.

Support staff and trust overhead expenses are also paid from the trust assets. Operating costs vary widely, depending on the size of the trust, the number of claims it processes, the extent of legal engagement with third parties (such as insurers), and the like. An analysis of costs is provided in Chapter Four.

TAC Members and the FCR. The trustees manage the asbestos trust for the sole benefit of the claimant beneficiaries. Although trusts often have hundreds of thousands of beneficiaries, the trustees are not under the influence and control of hundreds of thousands of claimants. Instead, a committee of advocates represents the claimants' interests. This oversight comes via the TAC and the FCR. These advisers, as described later in this chapter, provide advice and must consent to significant changes in trust administration and the implementation of TDPs.

Claimant beneficiaries come in two varieties. Current claimants have submitted applications for compensation based on diseases that are presently manifested. Future claimants have not yet filed with the trust. This latter group includes individuals with current diseases who have not yet submitted a demand to the trust and individuals who do not yet have symptoms of asbestos-related diseases.

The interests of current and future claimants are often divergent: "Although the current and future claimants are allied in seeking the largest amount possible for all asbestos personal injury plaintiffs, they may have differences in how that amount should be divided" (McGovern, 2006, p. 164). Current claimants seek speedy payment at a claim's full value. Future claimants, on the other hand, do not yet exist or are unknown to the trust. From the future claimants' perspective, the highest priority is preservation of the trust's assets until future claimants apply for compensation. In practical terms, future claimants often want to withhold payments from current claimants or apply a discount to a current claim's value to enable the pool of money to last for many years (recall the Manville Trust's initial problems: No provisions were made to reserve a portion of the trust's assets to pay future claims, pushing the trust into insolvency).

To ensure that both current and future claimants' interests are adequately protected, the role of the claimants' representative and the related fiduciary duty was split between the TAC and the FCR. Although the TAC often consists of many representatives while the FCR is a solitary delegate, the TAC and FCR have equal authority. The consent of both the FCR and

---

[5] The J. T. Thorpe Settlement Trust has set annual compensation at $15,000 for a nonmanaging trustee plus an hourly adjustment for travel and time spent in preparation for and attendance at meetings. This compensation level is particularly low and bears special notice. The managing trustee's compensation is not reported in the most-current TA (J. T. Thorpe Settlement Trust).

the TAC is required before undertaking substantial trust activities (such as selection of a new trustee or revising the TDP or TA).

The FCR position (sometimes called the *legal representative*) is statutorily required under Section 524(g) of the bankruptcy code. Section 524(g)(4)(B)(i) states that the channeling injunction may be granted only if, as part of the proceedings, "the court appoints a legal representative for the purpose of protecting the rights of persons that might subsequently assert demands" against the trust.[6] Perhaps because the FCR position is a statutory requirement, the TAs do not always address the FCR's duties.[7] For those that do mention the FCR, the discussion tends to be perfunctory and generally limited to compensation. Commonly, the FCR is remunerated at $600 per hour, or a "reasonable hourly rate set by the PI trustees" that sometimes requires consent of the TAC. The duration of the FCR's term of office varies from trust to trust, as do the procedures for replacing an FCR. Service as FCR for one trust does not preclude concurrent service to other trusts.

The TAC's role arises from the prebankruptcy confirmation negotiations between the plaintiffs' attorneys, the creditor committees, and the debtor. TAC roles are always established in the TA. Often, the TAC includes representatives of the plaintiffs' law firms with the largest number of claimants. Service as a TAC member for one trust does not preclude concurrent service to other trusts.

The TAs commonly set TAC member compensation. Usually, the rate falls in the range of $450–$500 per hour or a "reasonable hourly rate set by the PI trustees." The duration of the TAC members' term of office varies from trust to trust, as do procedures for replacing TAC members.

Both the TAC and FCR have the right to employ, at the trust's expense, independent counsel or advisers (in pursuit, for example, of accurate estimates of likely future claims). More importantly, the TAC and FCR must give consent before any changes are made to the TA or the TDP, including the claim payment ratio, the disease levels, and the payment percentage. If disagreements arise that cannot be resolved through internal dispute-resolution mechanisms, recourse reverts to the bankruptcy court.

Claim-Processing Procedures

The processes that govern claim filing and payment are contained in the trusts' TDPs. TDPs (sometimes called *claim-resolution procedures*) are central to reviewing, liquidating (i.e., establishing a monetary value for a claim), and paying asbestos claims. TDPs establish procedures that aim to ensure that all claimants receive fair, equitable, and substantially similar treatment.

---

[6]   In the course of our research, two perspectives arose regarding the role of the FCR. One perspective, expressed by a TAC representative, seemed to suggest that the FCR was required only during the confirmation process for the plan of reorganization. Indeed, there is no statutory requirement for an FCR once a plan has been confirmed; however, all trusts currently in existence have provisions for a continuing role for the FCR.

A second perspective holds that the FCR's fiduciary duty extends not only to future claims by asbestos victims but also to holders of indirect PI claims. Indirect claims are those held by entities that have paid claims on behalf of the trust. Indirect claimants are seeking contribution from the trust as reimbursement for those payments. The statutory language about "persons [who] might subsequently assert demands" against the trust does not specify whether the FCR represents the interests of these claimholders.

[7]   For example, see the H. K. Porter Company (1998) asbestos TA.

They coordinate claim processing, assign liquidated values for various diseases, set medical criteria for the different diseases, prescribe review procedures that will be followed by the claim-processing facility, and establish an alternative dispute resolution (ADR) process to resolve disputes between the claimant and the trust.

In this section, we outline the general process through which a claim is filed, evaluated, assigned a monetary value, and paid to a claimant. In doing so, we describe the devices and procedures as outlined in the TDPs. The description in this section is intended to be a generalization based on similarities in many trusts' TDPs. The process may differ for specific trusts.

Stage 1: Claim Filing and Selection of Claim Review Method

The first stage of a PI claim against an asbestos trust involves a claimant with an asbestos-related disease identifying the trust or trusts against which to file a claim (see Figure 3.1). A claimant's work history determines the trusts to which a claim may be submitted. In theory, a claimant can recover money from a trust only if the claimant was exposed to asbestos that was produced, manufactured, or used by the trust's debtor company. For example, a claimant who worked with products manufactured by Johns-Manville would file a single claim with the Manville Trust. However, a claimant who used products made by Johns-Manville, Kaiser, U.S. Gypsum, and J. T. Thorpe, would likely file with each of those debtors' trusts. Section 524(g) of the bankruptcy code does not set a numerical limit on the number of trusts against which a claimant may file; nor is there a monetary cap on the amount a claimant may recover in the aggregate from the trusts. Trust claimants can and frequently do file claims with, and collect money from, multiple trusts. Claimants may also recover from solvent defendants through the tort system.

Once the appropriate trusts are identified, the claimant selects the method of review to be used in processing the claim. Almost all trusts have two main methods of review: expedited review and individual review. With some important exceptions, discussed later in this chapter, a claimant may choose either method.

The expedited-review procedure seeks to pay claims quickly at a fixed value. Different diseases (such as mesothelioma and asbestosis) are valued differently, with the more-severe diseases valued more highly. The claimant knows the payment amount, known as the *scheduled value*, in advance; scheduled values are published in the TDPs. To determine whether a claimant qualifies for the quick, fixed payment available through expedited review, the trusts use a preestablished set of criteria for medical evidence and work history; these criteria are also published in the TDPs. Trusts will presume that claims supported by sufficient evidence documenting the medical diagnosis and work history are valid. Hence, a claimant selecting expedited review gathers the requisite evidence and sends all supporting documentation to the claim-processing facility for review.

As an alternative to expedited review, individual review gives claimants with certain diseases the opportunity to receive individual consideration of their specific medical condition and work history in hopes of justifying a higher payment. Individual review is mandatory in cases in which the claimant cannot meet the medical or exposure criteria under the expedited-review process. Furthermore, for certain medical conditions (such as lung cancer in a claimant who is a smoker), individual review is required.

Under individual review, there are no presumptively valid claims, and the time it takes to process an individual case may be considerably longer than under expedited review. Individual-review claims do not have a fixed scheduled value. Each claim is liquidated based on the indi-

Figure 3.1
Schematic of Claim Payment Process

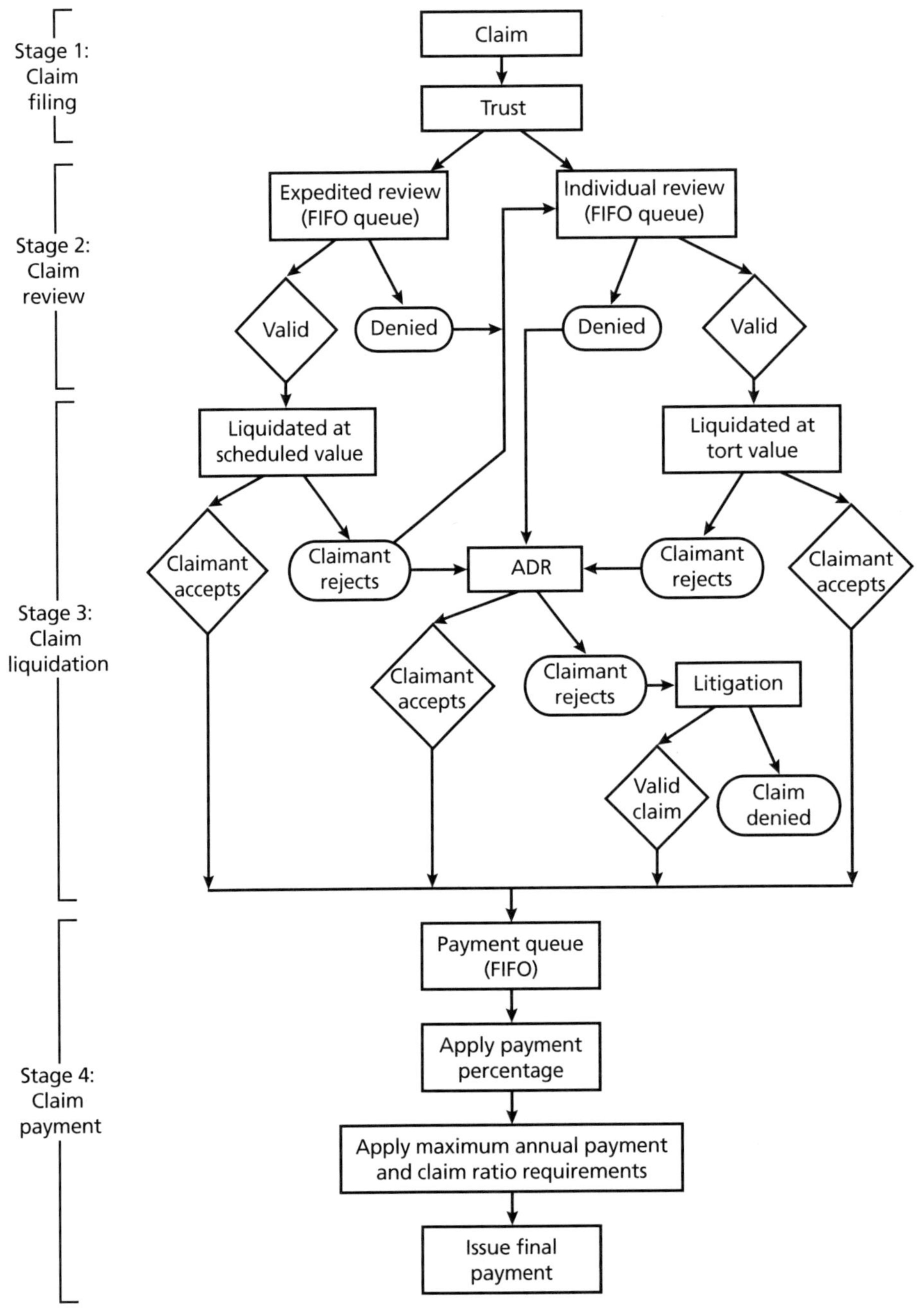

RAND TR872-3.1

vidual circumstances. The liquidated value may or may not be greater than the scheduled value for a similar disease.

Because individual review is designed to take individual circumstances into account, an individual-review claim is likely supported by more-substantial medical evidence and a more-detailed work history than for expedited review. This supporting material is forwarded to the claim-processing facility and awaits review.

Stage 2: Claim Review

Upon receipt of all claim documents, the claim-processing facility begins the review process according to the method selected by the claimant. To begin this process, the facility assigns the claim a place in the FIFO processing queue. There are separate FIFO queues for expedited-review claims and individual-review claims. For claims filed after the trust was established, the date of receipt of the completed claim documents establishes the claimant's place in the FIFO processing queue.

About six months before a claimant enters the actual processing phase, the trust sends notice thereof to the claimant, requesting any updates to the medical history or exposure evidence. Assuming that there is none, or upon receipt of the new evidence, the facility begins to review the submitted materials.

For claims filed under expedited review, the facility determines whether the claimant's medical and exposure evidence satisfies the requirements outlined in the TDP for a presumptively valid claim. Each disease that a trust recognizes has different requirements, and these requirements are summarized for the largest trusts in Appendix B. Both disease level and the requirements merit further discussion.

Asbestos exposure has been linked to a variety of diseases. The bankruptcy code conditions the channeling injunction upon the creation of a trust system of compensation that treats claimants with similar diseases equitably. To do this, the trusts have established disease levels. A disease level is a category of asbestos-related disease. It is coupled with a set of medical and exposure requirements and an associated liquidated value that is offered to claimants who meet those requirements. The disease levels are used to review all expedited-review claims that are filed against the trust.

The trusts generally recognize eight disease levels.[8] There is variation in the number of levels used across trusts, and the following list of eight disease levels represents the most extensive list. In order of the most severe to the least severe condition, the disease levels are

- mesothelioma (level VIII)
- lung cancer, with evidence of bilateral asbestos-related nonmalignant disease[9] (often asbestosis) (level VII, also referred to as lung cancer 1)
- lung cancer, without evidence of bilateral asbestos-related nonmalignant disease (level VI, also referred to as lung cancer 2)[10]
- other cancers, with evidence of bilateral asbestos-related nonmalignant disease (level V)

---

[8] For an exception, see NGC Bodily Injury Trust (2002). NGC uses six core categories covering ten recognized diseases. Only the core categories are assigned monetary values.

[9] The standard definition of "evidence of bilateral asbestos-related nonmalignant disease," as used in the TDPs for levels I, II, III, V, and VII, refers to

> (i) a chest X-ray read by a qualified B reader of 1/0 or higher on the ILO [International Labour Organization] scale or,
> (ii) (x) a chest X-ray read by a qualified B reader or other Qualified Physician, (y) a CT [computed tomography] scan read by a Qualified Physician, or (z) pathology, in each case either showing bilateral interstitial fibrosis, bilateral pleural plaques, bilateral pleural thickening, or bilateral pleural calcification.

See, for example, Armstrong World Industries (2008, p. 10).

[10] Level VI claims are for lung cancer without evidence of asbestos-related disease. Because carcinogens other than asbestos may cause lung cancer, level VI claims are not presumptively valid. As a result, these claims are not eligible for expedited review and are expected to have relatively low liquidated values. This is especially true if the claimant was also a smoker.

- severe asbestosis (level IV)
- asbestosis/pleural disease with significantly restricted pulmonary function (level III, also referred to as asbestos/pleural disease 2)
- asbestosis/pleural disease without significantly restricted pulmonary function (level II, also referred to as asbestosis/pleural disease 1)
- other asbestos disease (level I).

These disease levels may be augmented or reduced with the consent of the TAC and FCR.

For each disease level, there is a set of medical and exposure criteria. The medical criteria consist of a diagnosis and a statement of latency. Below are some of the most common standards:

- For diagnoses of malignant conditions (levels V–VIII), the trusts require diagnosis by physical examination, by a board-certified pathologist's report, or by a pathology report from a hospital accredited by the Joint Commission.
- For nonmalignant diseases (levels I–IV),
  - living claimants must present a diagnosis by physical examination
  - decedents' claims must be supported
    - o by a diagnosis by physical examination when the claimant was alive
    - o by pathological evidence
    - o by evidence of bilateral asbestos-related nonmalignant disease (for levels I–III) and an ILO reading of 2/1 or greater (for level IV)[11] and pulmonary-function testing (for levels III and IV only).
- Pulmonary-function testing is required for levels III and IV. The purpose of these tests is to establish severely restricted lung capacity for claims worthy of a higher liquidated value. Normally, level III claims must be supported by results of a pulmonary-function test demonstrating a total lung capacity (TLC) of less than 80 percent or by a forced vital capacity (FVC) level less than 80 percent and a forced expiratory volume in 1 second (FEV1)/FVC ratio greater than or equal to 65 percent.[12] Normally, level IV claims must be supported by results of a pulmonary-function test demonstrating a TLC of less than 65 percent or by an FVC level less than 65 percent and an FEV1/FVC ratio greater than 65 percent. Level IV claims must also be accompanied by an ILO score of 2/1 or greater.
- Disease levels III–VII require supporting medical documentation that establishes asbestos as a contributing factor in causing the claimed disease.

In addition to the diagnosis, the medical criteria compel a physician's statement that the claimant's medical history satisfies a latency requirement. Typically, the latency requirement establishes that "at least ten years have elapsed between the date of first exposure to asbestos or asbestos-containing products and the diagnosis" (Babcock and Wilcox Company, 2009).[13]

---

[11] An ILO reading is an interpretation of pulmonary x-rays using the ILO International Classification of Radiographs of Pneumoconioses (Carroll, Dixon, et al., 2009, p. 7).

[12] The FEV1/FVC ratio measures the amount of air that can be forcibly exhaled in 1 second as a percentage of FVC.

[13] Latency requirements are used to determine whether asbestos was likely a contributing cause of the illness. People with asbestos-related diseases first display symptoms many years after exposure. The latency requirement aims to increase the

Evidence of an asbestos-related disease is not sufficient to justify a claim against an asbestos PI trust. Trusts also review claims for occupational exposure to asbestos and exposure to the trust's debtor's products, manufacturing facilities, or other conduct for which the debtor is liable. Criteria for exposure to the debtor's products, facilities, or other conduct aim to establish a potential link between the claimant's disease and the trust or trusts against which the claimant has chosen to file a claim.[14]

There are typically separate requirements for occupational exposure and exposure related to debtor activities, and these requirements typically vary by disease level. To satisfy the debtor's exposure criteria, a claimant needs credible evidence that he or she worked with or around asbestos at the debtor's facilities or with or around the debtor's asbestos-containing products during the period of time when asbestos was in use. Credible evidence may be a work history at a site where the trusts know asbestos products were used; an affidavit; employment records, invoices, or other business documents; or other evidence that the trust deems reliable. Certain disease levels carry a higher standard for exposure criteria.[15]

Trusts generally do not coordinate with other trusts to determine whether the occupational or debtor exposure evidence submitted to one trust is consistent with the evidence submitted to other trusts.

Trusts do not require specific evidence about the amount of asbestos dust that a claimant may have inhaled during his or her time working with the debtor or the debtor's products. This puts the trust system in direct contrast to some legal jurisdictions when it comes to causation evidence.[16] It should be noted, however, that the ability or inability to sustain a claim in the tort system is immaterial to whether the claimant is entitled to recovery through the trust processes under expedited review. If the claimant has the documentation to satisfy all of the medical and exposure elements for a disease level under expedited review, the claim is valid for purposes of trust compensation. If the trust determines that a claim under expedited review does not satisfy the medical or exposure requirements, the claim will be assigned to the individual-review FIFO queue.

Individual-review claims are used to determine "whether the claim would be compensable in the tort system even though it does not meet the presumptive Medical/Exposure Criteria for any of the Disease Levels" (Kaiser Aluminum and Chemical Corporation, 2007). In addition, individual review can be used if a claimant believes that his or her individual cir-

---

probability that the injury was at least in part caused by exposure to asbestos.

[14] McGovern (2006) describes how exposure criteria have evolved over the years. Since the Celotex plan was established in 1999, all trusts have required proof of exposure to a specific debtor's products.

[15] For disease levels III, IV, V, and VII, claimants need to supply evidence of significant occupational exposure. *Significant occupational exposure* is defined as employment for a cumulative period of

> at least five (5) years with a minimum of two (2) years prior to December 31, 1982, in an industry and an occupation in which the claimant (a) handled raw asbestos fibers on a regular basis; (b) fabricated asbestos-containing products so that the claimant in the fabrication process was exposed on a regular basis to raw asbestos fibers; (c) altered, repaired or otherwise worked with an asbestos-containing product such that the claimant was exposed on a regular basis to asbestos fibers; or (d) was employed in an industry and occupation such that the claimant worked on a regular basis in close proximity to workers engaged in the activities described in (a), (b), and/or (c). (Kaiser Aluminum and Chemical Corporation, 2007)

[16] See, for example, *Borg-Warner Corp. v. Flores* (232 S.W.3d 765, 2007) (indicating that mere exposure to "some" asbestos fibers was insufficient to prove that an asbestos-containing product was a substantial factor in causing the plaintiff's asbestosis).

cumstances merit a liquidated value in excess of the scheduled value offered under expedited review for his or her disease.

If the processing facility does not believe that the claimant presents a claim that is compensable in the tort system, it will deny the claim. If, however, the facility believes that the claim would be cognizable and valid in the tort system, the claim will be liquidated pursuant to procedures described in the next section.

Stage 3: Claim Liquidation

Once the processing facility has determined that a claim is valid, through either expedited or individual review, the claim must be liquidated, or assigned a monetary value. Liquidating a claim is treated differently under expedited and individual review.

For expedited review, claims are liquidated according to the values assigned to the diseases listed in the TDP. These values are called scheduled values. The scheduled value is a standard monetary amount for a specific disease level.[17] It is a one-size-fits-all amount. Specific aspects of a claimant's work history or medical situation are not used to tailor an award beyond classification by disease level. According to a party that has worked closely with trusts, the scheduled value is typically set slightly above the 50th percentile of the historical settlements that the debtor paid for the specific disease before bankruptcy. However, we have not been able to assess the extent to which this is actually the case. The scheduled value is set at such a level to encourage most claimants to choose expedited rather than individual review. Because individual circumstances can vary greatly, the scheduled value may or may not be significantly less than the amount a claimant would receive under individual review.[18]

Individual-review claims are meant to be valued at the historical liquidated value of similarly situated claims in the tort system. Valuation factors may include, among others, age, disability, number of dependents, noneconomic damages, and the settlement and verdict history of the claimant's law firm. At least one trust purports to derive the settlement value by "statistically analyzing previously settled claims, and identifying claim characteristics that have historically correlated with settlement values" (NGC Bodily Injury Trust, 2002, p. 11). Regardless of individual circumstances, however, liquidated claims may not be greater than the maximum value associated with the corresponding disease level. This maximum value is a monetary upper limit established by the TDP.[19]

One special exception to this liquidation process concerns a type of claim called *extraordinary claims*. A claimant may be classified as having an extraordinary claim for some types of asbestos-related diseases if his or her asbestos-related exposure was predominantly the result of one specific debtor's products or manufacturing facility. Typically, an extraordinary claim meets the presumptive medical and exposure criteria under expedited review but, because of the special employment or exposure circumstances, will be treated for liquidation purposes as an individual-review claim. The clear line of culpability triggers the possibil-

---

[17] Sometimes this is referred to as the *allowed liquidated value* (e.g., NGC Bodily Injury Trust, 2002).

[18] All disease levels except level VI are assigned values; level VI claims must undergo individual review and, therefore, do not have an established scheduled value.

[19] We have not evaluated the extent to which scheduled values or the values set in the individual-review process approximate either the midpoint of the distribution of previous settlements or the value of similarly situated claims in the tort system.

ity of a higher liquidated value than would be allowed under expedited review.[20] For example, consider a 30-year employee who spent his entire career at Johns-Manville. If he meets the criteria for mesothelioma under expedited review, the Manville Trust would likely classify his as an extraordinary claim for liquidation purposes.

Upon completion of a claim's review, the valid claimant will be offered an amount in satisfaction of the claim.[21] Claimants may accept the offer, at which time his or her claim enters the payment queue, discussed in the next section. If a claimant refuses the offer, the claim is submitted for ADR under preestablished procedures for either binding or nonbinding arbitration. If nonbinding arbitration fails, claimants have the right to bring suit against the trust in the tort system. According to parties knowledgeable about trust operations, very few claims go to arbitration or to the courts.

Stage 4: Claim Payment

Once claims are liquidated and the claimant accepts the offer, claims are paid according to the FIFO payment queue and according to three other important rules.[22] Individual trusts may not have sufficient funds to pay every claim the full, liquidated value that could have been recovered through the tort system. Ever since the reorganization of the Manville Trust, asbestos PI trusts have wrestled with the question of how to pay future claims out of the limited pool of assets. Although the number of current claims is fixed and knowable, there is substantial uncertainty over the number of claims that will be filed in the future. If predictions are too low, trusts run the risk of insolvency (as was the case with the Manville Trust).

To manage this problem, the trusts require mechanisms for allocating trust assets so money will be available for future claimants. To this end, TAs and TDPs allow the trustees (with the consent of the TAC and FCR) to establish a system of pro rata discounts to the value of a claim offered to a current claimant. This pro rata share is known as the *payment percentage*.

Payment percentages are a percentage of a claim's liquidated value. After a claim's liquidated value is established (whether by individual review, expedited review, arbitration, or litigation), it will be multiplied by the trust's payment percentage to calculate the actual payment the claimant will receive.[23] For example, a trust processing a mesothelioma claim liquidated at $110,000 with a payment percentage of 20 percent would pay a claimant $22,000.

As is discussed in Chapter Four, the payment percentage varies a great deal across trusts and can change over time. Some trusts have been forced to adopt very low payment percentages in light of a flood of claims. The UNR Asbestos-Disease Claims Trust (2009), for example, applies a 1.1 percent payment percentage. In 1995, Manville, which initially paid 100 percent

---

[20] The fact that trusts have special procedures for extraordinary claims suggests that trusts recognize the likelihood of claimants filing with multiple trusts or filing suit in the tort system.

[21] Some trusts call this a *settlement*. Section 524(g) considers this a payment. While, on its face, the difference seems semantic, there are rules pertaining to the confidentiality of settlements that may come into play in the discovery process in related litigation depending on whether the trust payment is a settlement.

[22] The payment queue, like the processing queue, operates under the FIFO rule, with one notable exception. Exigent-hardship claims make up a class of claims that triggers flexibility in the trust's processing and payment queues. Designation as an exigent case assigns the claim to an early position in the FIFO queue. Each trust establishes qualifications for exigent-hardship claims. Many trusts limit exigent cases to malignant diseases and severe asbestosis. Furthermore, trusts condition such claims on a claimant's immediate financial need that resulted from the claimant's asbestos-related disease. At least one trust (NGC) considers all living mesothelioma claimants to have exigent-hardship claims.

[23] As shown in Appendix B, the payment percentage may not apply to all disease levels at a particular trust.

of a claim, renegotiated the payment percentage to 10 percent. However, even that reduced amount was too much of a strain on trust assets; in 2001, Manville reduced the payment percentage to 5 percent. More recently, it increased the payment percentage to 7.5 percent.[24]

The two remaining rules that govern payment processing are rules that govern when a claimant will receive his or her compensation, rather than how much compensation will be paid. These two rules are the maximum annual payment (MAP) and the claim ratio.

The MAP is the annually determined upper limit on the amount of money the trust can pay to claimants in the aggregate for that year. The purpose of the limit is to preserve trust assets for future claimants. The MAP affects the FIFO payment queue. If there are too many claimants in a given year, then those who were at the end of the payment queue will be placed first in line in the next year's payment queue. Hence, because of a backlog of claims, a claimant who received an offer of settlement may have to wait a year or even several years before payment is received.

The MAP is divvied up by disease severity according to the claim ratio (sometimes called the *claim payment ratio*). This ratio sets annual limits on the proportion of the MAP that will be paid to claimants with malignancies or severe asbestosis versus those with less severe claims. For example, the Kaiser trust allocates 70 percent of the MAP to claimants with malignancies or severe asbestosis (Kaiser Aluminum and Chemical Corporation, 2007, p. 10). For all trusts that use a claim ratio, a majority of the MAP is slated for the most-severe diseases, although the actual percentage varies.

The claimant is responsible for paying the fees of his or her attorney from the award made by the trusts. The Manville Trust limits attorneys' fees to 25 percent of the award, although we have not been able to assess what methods are used to enforce this limit or how vigorously it is enforced. Knowledgeable parties interviewed during the course of this project believed that attorneys' fees of 25 percent are typical.

Indirect Personal-Injury Claims

The foregoing discussion traces the process for an asbestos victim seeking payment through the trust mechanism. There are, however, times when someone other than the claimant (or, in the case of a deceased claimant, the claimant's estate) seeks a monetary payment from an asbestos PI trust. These cases are known in the TDPs as *indirect PI claims*. In essence, these are claims filed under a theory of contribution.

An indirect PI claim is a claim filed against the trust by parties other than the asbestos claimholder (the individual claimholder is considered the *direct claimant*). These claims arise when a third party pays the direct claimant a sum of money that includes the trust's share of liability. The payment can be the result of a legal judgment or a settlement. Because the third party paid a sum of money for which the trust is responsible, the third party seeks to recover the sum from the trust. To do so, the third party files a claim with the trust (thus becoming an indirect claimant) and describes to the trust the conditions under which it paid the asbestos claimant (and spelling out the legal theory that justifies its claim against the trust—e.g., theories of contribution or indemnification). For valid indirect claims, the TDPs direct the trust to

---

[24] When a trust increases the payment percentage, it typically makes additional payments to claimants who have already settled with the trust at the lower payment percentage.

reimburse the indirect claimant for the payments it made in satisfaction of the trust's liability, subject to the payment percentage and FIFO queue.

Generally, to establish an indirect claim, the indirect claimant needs to provide evidence that, pursuant to a final legal judgment or binding settlement, the trust's liability was fixed, liquidated, and fully paid by the indirect claimant pursuant to a final legal judgment or binding settlement. In the case of a settlement, the indirect claimant must furnish evidence that both the direct and indirect claimants have fully released the trust from all future liability for asbestos PI harms. There is some scholarly speculation as to whether this is a reasonable expectation (Shelley, Cohn, and Arnold, 2008, p. 271).

Conclusion

This chapter has outlined the major players in the trusts' administration and outlined the general process by which claims are reviewed, liquidated, and paid. These elements are contained in the two main trust documents, the TA and the TDP. Chapter Four turns from trust structure and processes to trust finances and annual payment activities.

Overview of Trust Activity

A considerable amount of information is available about the asbestos bankruptcy trusts that have been established. This information is contained in the asbestos TAs and TDPs that must be approved by bankruptcy courts, as well as other documents filed with the court during bankruptcy proceedings. Trusts typically must also file annual reports with the bankruptcy court that contain specified information. While these reports and documents are publicly available, the data have not been assembled in a readily accessible source. In this chapter, we describe the information we have assembled on the trusts and provide an overview of trust activity. Detailed reports on 26 of the largest active trusts and the three largest proposed trusts are presented in Appendix B.

Data and Methods

Data on the trusts were abstracted from publicly available sources, including bankruptcy documents, trust websites, trust annual reports, and U.S. Securities and Exchange Commission (SEC) filings.[1] Data were available on an annual basis for each trust as a whole but not on the payments made to individual claimants. Thus, neither the variation of a given trust's payments across claimants nor payments by multiple trusts to the same claimant could be examined.

To verify the accuracy of the data, detailed reports for each of the 26 largest active trusts (the method for selecting the trust is described later) were assembled and then submitted to the relevant trusts for review. Twenty-three of the trusts were able to review the data, and the data were updated accordingly.[2]

Parties that follow asbestos litigation closely have identified 96 companies that have filed for bankruptcy in which liability for asbestos tort cases was addressed. A list of the companies filing for bankruptcy, the date the case was filed with the bankruptcy court, the date the court confirmed the reorganization plan, and the name of the trust established, if any, is provided in Appendix A.

Table 4.1 alphabetically lists the 63 trusts that have been established or are proposed. We divide trusts into three groups:

---

[1] Bates White is an economic consulting firm that has been collecting publicly available information on asbestos trusts for many years. We purchased this information from Bates White and used it as the starting point for our database. The data were reviewed for accuracy and gaps filled after consulting trust documents and websites.

[2] The following three trusts did not respond to review the information compiled on their trusts: the API, Inc. Asbestos Settlement Trust, the NGC Bodily Injury Trust, and the Swan Asbestos and Silica Settlement Trust.

Table 4.1
Trusts Established, in Alphabetical Order

Trust Name	Year Established	Estimate of Initial Assets ($ millions)	Claim Payments Through 2008 ($ millions)	Selected for Study Sample
Active trusts				
A&I Corporation Asbestos Bodily Injury Trust	2005	13	n.a.	No
A-Best Asbestos Settlement Trust	2004	18	5	No
AC&S Asbestos Settlement Trust	2008	528	185	Yes
API, Inc. Asbestos Settlement Trust	2006	94	43	Yes
Armstrong World Industries Asbestos Personal Injury Settlement Trust	2006	2,062	149	Yes
ARTRA 524(g) Asbestos Trust	2007	74	11	No
ASARCO LLC Asbestos Personal Injury Settlement Trust	2009	830	0	Yes
Babcock and Wilcox Company Asbestos Personal Injury Settlement Trust	2006	1,845	694	Yes
Bartells Asbestos Settlement Trust	2001	20	15	No
Brauer 524(g) Asbestos Trust	2007	1	0	No
Burns and Roe Asbestos Personal Injury Settlement Trust	2009	172	0	Yes
C. E. Thurston and Sons Asbestos Trust	2006	53	1	No
Celotex Asbestos Settlement Trust	1997	1,246	844	Yes
Combustion Engineering 524(g) Asbestos Personal Injury Trust	2006	1,243	176	Yes
DII Industries, LLC Asbestos Personal Injury Trust	2005	2,514	221	Yes
Eagle-Picher Industries Personal Injury Settlement Trust	1996	730	525	Yes
Federal Mogul U.S. Asbestos Personal Injury Trust, Fel-Pro Subfund	2007	n.a.	0	No
Federal Mogul U.S. Asbestos Personal Injury Trust, FMP Subfund	2007	55	0	No
Federal Mogul U.S. Asbestos Personal Injury Trust, T&N Subfund	2007	635	0	Yes
Federal Mogul U.S. Asbestos Personal Injury Trust, Vellumoid Subfund	2007	n.a.	0	No
G-1 Asbestos Settlement Trust	2009	770	0	Yes
H. K. Porter Asbestos Trust	1998	n.a.	77	Yes
J. T. Thorpe Company Successor Trust	2004	233	95	Yes
J. T. Thorpe Settlement Trust	2006	154	55	Yes
Kaiser Asbestos Personal Injury Trust	2006	1,218	116	Yes

Table 4.1—Continued

Trust Name	Year Established	Estimate of Initial Assets ($ millions)	Claim Payments Through 2008 ($ millions)	Selected for Study Sample
Keene Creditors Trust	1996	45	4	No
Lummus 524(g) Asbestos Personal Injury Trust	2006	38	1	No
Lykes Tort Claims Trust	1997	n.a.	0	No
Manville Personal Injury Settlement Trust	1988	2,500	3,881	Yes
NGC Bodily Injury Trust	1993	446	203	Yes
Owens Corning Fibreboard Asbestos Personal Injury Trust, Fibreboard Subfund	2006	1,556	361	Yes
Owens Corning Fibreboard Asbestos Personal Injury Trust, Owens Corning Subfund	2006	3,423	1,096	Yes
Plibrico Asbestos Trust	2006	206	69	Yes
Porter Hayden Bodily Injury Trust	2006	0	1	No
Raytech Corporation Asbestos Personal Injury Settlement Trust	2000	n.a.	0	No
Shook and Fletcher Asbestos Settlement Trust	2002	109	n.a.	No
Stone and Webster Asbestos Trust	2004	6	n.a.	No
Swan Asbestos and Silica Settlement Trust	2003	120	101	Yes
T. H. Agriculture and Nutrition, LLC Industries Asbestos Personal Injury Trust	2009	901	0	Yes
United States Gypsum Asbestos Personal Injury Settlement Trust	2006	3,957	612	Yes
United States Mineral Products Company Asbestos Personal Injury Settlement Trust	2005	8	0.4	No
UNR Asbestos-Disease Claims Trust	1990	n.a.	261	Yes
Utex Industries, Inc. Successor Trust	2004	10	4	No
Western Asbestos Settlement Trust	2004	2,000	1,092	Yes
Inactive trusts				
Amatex Asbestos Disease Trust Fund	1990	16	n.a.	No
Forty-Eight Insulations Qualified Settlement Trust	1995	n.a.	n.a.	No
Fuller-Austin Asbestos Settlement Trust	1998	n.a.	n.a.	No
M. H. Detrick Company Asbestos Trust	2002	3	0.3	No
Muralo Trust	2007	n.a.	n.a.	No
PLI Disbursement Trust	1989	n.a.	n.a.	No
Rock Wool Manufacturing Company Asbestos Trust	1999	n.a.	n.a.	No

Table 4.1—Continued

Trust Name	Year Established	Estimate of Initial Assets ($ millions)	Claim Payments Through 2008 ($ millions)	Selected for Study Sample
Rutland Fire Clay Company Asbestos Trust	2000	8	0.7	No
United States Lines, Inc. and United States Lines (S.A.) Inc. Reorganization Trust	1989	n.a.	0.6	No
Wallace and Gale Company Asbestos Settlement Trust	1998	0.8	n.a.	No
Proposed trusts				
APG Asbestos Trust	—	333	0	No
Congoleum Plan Trust	—	270	0	No
Flintkote Company and Flintkote Mines Limited Asbestos Personal Injury Trust	—	214	0	No
North American Refractories Company Asbestos Personal Injury Settlement Trust	—	6,320	0	Yes
Pittsburgh Corning Corporation Asbestos PI Trust	—	3,407	0	Yes
Quigley Company, Inc. Asbestos PI Trust	—	569	0	No
Skinner Engine Co. Asbestos Trust	—	n.a.	0	No
Thorpe Insulation Company Asbestos Personal Injury Settlement Trust	—	389	0	No
W. R. Grace and Co. Asbestos Personal Injury Settlement Trust	—	2,978	0	Yes
All trusts	—	44,341	10,900	—

NOTE: n.a. = not available.

- 44 active trusts: those that are still paying claims
- ten inactive trusts: those that have been established but no longer appear to be paying claims
- nine proposed trusts: those that are being considered as part of ongoing bankruptcy proceedings or trusts established by a bankruptcy plan that is under appeal.

In addition to the year in which the trust was established, Table 4.1 reports claim payments through 2008. These figures are drawn from the annual financial statements that trusts file with bankruptcy courts. Data on claim payments could not be located for some trusts (indicated by "n.a." in the table), particularly for trusts that appear to be inactive. The figures that are reported appear to be complete except for two trusts that were established prior to 1999.[3] Table 4.1 also provides an estimate of the initial funding for the trust. As explained in Chapter Two, sources of this funding include cash or stock from the debtor and insurance settlements.[4] In some cases, contributions to the trust are paid over time, but the data in Table 4.1

---

[3] The two trusts are the H. K. Porter Asbestos Trust and the NGC Bodily Injury Trust. A complete set of financial reports could not be established for these trusts.

[4] These insurance settlements are payments on insurance policies held by the debtor.

do not discount future contributions back to the establishment date. Insurance disputes can also be settled subsequent to trust establishment, but resulting settlements are not included in these figures. The figures on initial trust assets are rough estimates and intended to provide only a general idea of the size of the trust. They were used to select the trusts for detailed review but were not used in subsequent analysis.

Figure 4.1 shows the number of bankruptcies filed and number of trusts established by year, and Figure 4.2 shows the cumulative number of bankruptcies filed and trusts established. After an uptick in the 1980s, the number of bankruptcies filed remained modest in the 1990s. The bankruptcies surged in the first part of the 2000s, peaking at 15 in 2002. Trends in the number of trusts formed reflect the lag between bankruptcy filing and the confirmation of the bankruptcy plan. Based on the 78 filings that have been confirmed, the average time from filing to confirmation is 3.9 years, and the average may increase somewhat as the longest-running bankruptcy cases are finally resolved.[5] As illustrated in Figure 4.2, 54 trusts have been established as of June 2010, with a considerable acceleration in the total number of trusts in the second half of the 2000s. Nine more trusts are in the pipeline, and there are undoubtedly more to come.[6]

Limits on the time and resources available to complete this report did not allow us to assemble and verify detailed information for all 54 trusts that have been established. We thus

Figure 4.1
Number of Bankruptcies Filed and Number of Trusts Established, by Year, as of June 2010

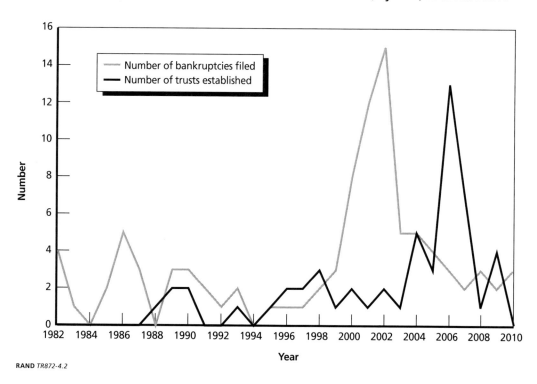

RAND *TR872-4.2*

---

[5] The longest-running bankruptcy case still open has been open for 12.9 years.

[6] For example, an FCR has been appointed in the General Motors bankruptcy, suggesting that an asbestos trust will be established. In addition, trusts will likely emerge from the recent bankruptcies of Bondex International and Garlock Sealing Technologies.

Figure 4.2
Cumulative Number of Bankruptcies Filed and Trusts Established as of June 2010

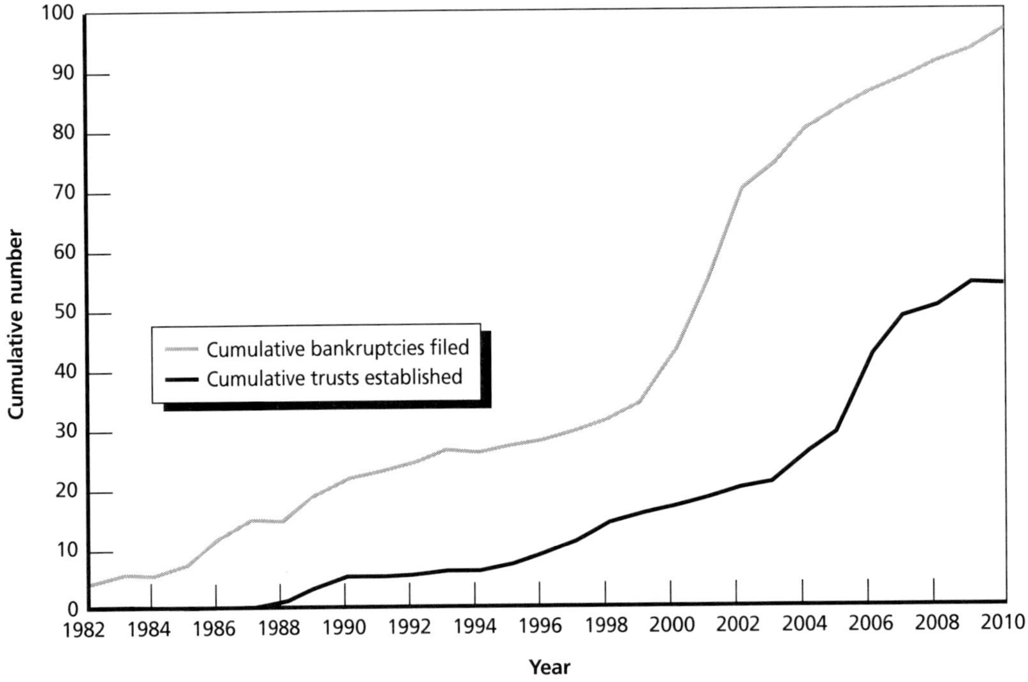

limited our attention to active and inactive trusts that had either (1) at least $100 million in initial assets or (2) at least $20 million in claim payments through 2008. Twenty-six of the 44 active trusts and none of the ten inactive trusts met these selection criteria. The last column of Table 4.1 indicates which trusts were selected.

The analysis in the remainder of this chapter is restricted to the 26 active trusts meeting the selection criteria. While the data from the smaller trusts are not included in the statistics in the next section, it is not likely that the error due to excluding these trusts is large relative to overall trust activity.[7]

The projected assets of the nine trusts that have been proposed but not yet established are large. As can be calculated from the bottom set of rows in Table 4.1, the projected initial assets at eight trusts for which estimates could be developed total $14.5 billion. To provide some insight on the largest trusts that may soon be established, Appendix B also presents information about the three proposed trusts with projected initial assets of at least $500 million.

---

[7] The 26 active trusts account for more than 99 percent of the $10.9 billion in claim payments for the active and inactive trusts that we could identify through 2008 and for 98 percent of the $29.9 billion in initial trust assets. Claim payment data are missing for some trusts, but the missing payments are likely small relative to the total accounted for.

Overview of Trust Activity

In this section, we provide an overview of the following aspects of asbestos trust operations:

- aggregate claim activity
- breakdown of claim payments by injury type
- trust assets and expenses
- claim valuation schedules
- composition of trust governing bodies.

We address each topic in turn. The data on which the figures and tables in this section are based are reported by trust in Appendix B.

Aggregate Claim Activity

Figures 4.3 and 4.4 display the number of claims paid and the value of claim payments for the 26 selected trusts. Data for the years prior to 2006 are aggregated because we were not able to break down pre-2006 figures by year for some trusts. As mentioned earlier, data on pre-2006 claim payments for two trusts are incomplete because complete records could not be located for these older trusts. Also, it appears that data on the number of paid claims are incomplete for three of the 26 trusts. Thus, the data in Figures 4.3 and 4.4 provide lower bounds on the number of claims paid and the value of claim payments.[8] Plaintiffs' attorneys' fees must be removed from claim payments in order to determine the amount received by claimants.

Reflecting the influx of new trusts in 2006 and 2007, both the number of claims paid and the value of claim payments surged in 2007 and 2008 from 2006 levels. Approximately 575,000 claims were paid, for a total of $3.3 billion in 2008, with the number of claims paid and claim payments totaling 2.4 million and $10.9 billion through 2008, respectively. To put these numbers in perspective, the 2005 RAND report estimated that asbestos defendants paid $7.1 billion (not including asbestos trusts) in compensation in 2002 and that compensation (not including asbestos trusts) totaled $49 billion through 2002 (Carroll, Hensler, et al., 2005, p. 92).[9] Comprehensive data on which to base more-current estimates of tort compensation are not available.

Breakdown of Payments, by Injury Type

The compensation of claimants with more-severe diseases relative to those with less severe diseases has been an ongoing issue in asbestos litigation. We now turn to the experience of the trusts in this regard. Ten of the 26 active trusts provide separate figures on malignant and non-

---

[8] Data on the number of claims filed by year are reported for some trusts in Appendix B. These data are quite incomplete, however, and do not merit reporting in aggregate form.

[9] The $7.1 billion figure excludes defense costs. Carroll, Hensler, et al. (2005, p. 71) also report that approximately 55,000 individuals brought asbestos-related PI claims against defendants and PI trusts in 2002 and that 730,000 individuals brought asbestos-related claims through 2002 (note that these figures do not reflect the number of individuals filing court cases—not all claims result in court filings). Even considering the lag between the dates when claims are filed and when they are paid, these figures are not readily comparable to the number of claims paid by trusts because the trust figures on the number of claims paid do not net out payments by multiple trusts to the same individual.

Figure 4.3
The Number of Claims Paid and the Value of Claim Payments, by Year, for the Selected Trusts

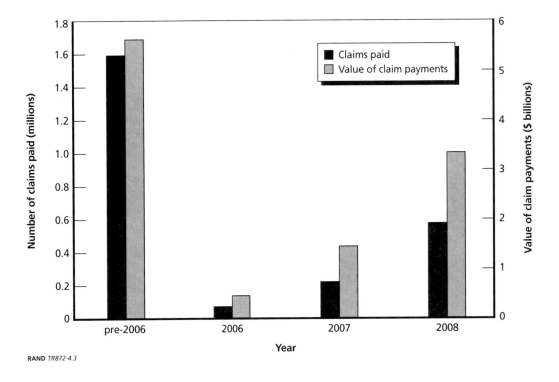

RAND *TR872-4.3*

Figure 4.4
Cumulative Claims Paid and Claim Payments at the Selected Trusts

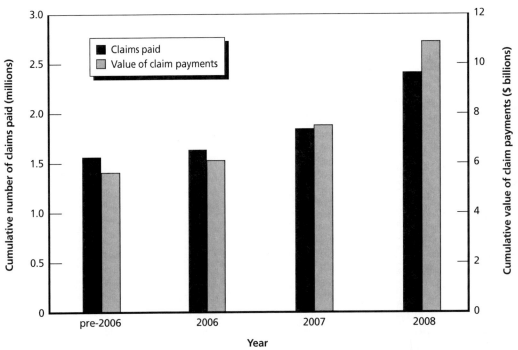

RAND *TR872-4.4*

malignant claims for 2007 and 2008.[10] These ten trusts account for 57 percent and 72 percent of the claims paid and claim payments by all 26 selected trusts in 2008, respectively. *Malignant claims*, by and large, refers to claims involving mesothelioma, lung cancer, and other cancers. *Nonmalignant claims* refers to claims involving severe asbestosis, asbestosis and pleural disease, or other asbestos-related diseases.[11]

As shown in Table 4.2, malignant claims accounted for a modest proportion of the number of claims paid but the bulk of the value of claim payments in 2007 and 2008. Average payment per malignant claim grew from $21,700 in 2007 to $34,100 in 2008. In contrast, nonmalignant claims accounted for more than 85 percent of claims in both years but received much less per claim. Payment per claim averaged $2,700 in 2007 and $3,000 in 2008. The relatively modest payments per claim meant that nonmalignant claims accounted for 45 percent and 34 percent of the total value of claim payments at these ten trusts in 2007 and 2008, respectively.

While the number of nonmalignant claims paid as a percentage of total claims paid remains high, the proportion of trust payments that go to nonmalignant claims is down from estimates for both the trust and the tort system in earlier years. Estimates in Carroll, Hensler, et al. (2005, p. 99) for the percentage of tort payments that went to nonmalignant claims between 1998 and 2002 run from 47 percent to 61 percent. Carroll, Hensler, et al. (2005, p. 99) also report that Tillinghast (a unit of Towers Perrin) found that 64 percent of tort payments between 1991 and 2000 were for nonmalignant claims and that 64 percent of payments by the Manville trust between 1995 and 2000 were on nonmalignant claims.[12] The one trust

Table 4.2
Breakdown of Claim Payments by Injury Type for Trusts that Separately Report Data on Malignant and Nonmalignant Claims

Item	2007	2008
Number of claims paid (thousands)	158	327
Malignant claims (percentage)	13	14
Nonmalignant claims (percentage)	87	86
Value of claim payments ($ millions)	809	2,405
Malignant claims (percentage)	55	66
Nonmalignant claims (percentage)	45	34
Average value of claim payment ($/claim paid)		
Malignant claims	21,700	34,100
Nonmalignant claims	2,700	3,000
Number of trusts reporting	10	10

[10] Results are reported only for 2007 and 2008 because only a few trusts reported payments separately for malignant and nonmalignant claims prior to 2007.

[11] Some trusts include severe asbestosis in the malignant category, but none of the ten trusts considered here does so.

[12] Carroll, Hensler, et al. (2005, p. 99) estimated that 92 percent of claimants brought claims for nonmalignant injuries between 1998 and 2002. They also reported that 88 percent of claims to the Manville Trust between 1995 and 2000 were for nonmalignant injuries.

in our sample of 26 trusts that separated malignant from nonmalignant claim payments prior to 2004 (the H. K. Porter Trust) reported that nonmalignant claims accounted for 72 percent of claim payments between 2001 and 2003 and for 43 percent of claim payment between 2006 and 2008.[13]

Comprehensive data on the current breakdown of tort payments between malignant and nonmalignant claims are not available. However, there are indications of a decline in the share of tort payments for nonmalignant claims. Based on their work with asbestos defendants, Bates and Mullin estimate that nonmalignant claims account for less than 10 percent of all tort compensation (Bates and Mullin, 2006, p. 2). Drawing on the SEC Form 10-K filings of 150 asbestos defendants, Allen and Stern (2009, p. 2) report that the average number of claim filings per defendant dropped considerably between 2003 and 2008 and attribute the decline to a drop in nonmalignant filings.

A decline in fraction of tort payments on nonmalignant claims is consistent with the expected effects of a number of legislative reforms and judicial decisions that were adopted in the first half of the 2000s. Some states barred unimpaired claims (which are a subset of nonmalignant claims) or assigned them to deferred dockets. Other states barred out-of-state claims with out-of state exposures. Also, U.S. District Court judge Janice Jack challenged diagnoses from doctors frequently used to support claims for nonmalignant injuries (see Carroll, Dixon, et al., 2009, p. 17).

While it has become increasingly difficult to obtain compensation for nonmalignant injuries in the tort system, the large number of nonmalignant claims paid by trusts indicates that the trust system remains a source of compensation for such injuries. How the total compensation a claimant might receive for nonmalignant injuries from the trusts has changed in the past ten years, however, is uncertain. On the one hand, Manville, the oldest and largest trust, cut its payments for the least serious nonmalignant claims in 2004 (Carroll, Dixon, et al., 2009, p. 17). On the other hand, an increase in the number of trusts means that a claimant may be able to obtain compensation for nonmalignant claims from more trusts.

Trust Assets and Expenses

The financial statements that trusts file annually with the bankruptcy court contain information on trust income, expenditures, assets, and liabilities. Of the 26 selected trusts, 22 reported financial data for at least one year up through 2008. The remaining four trusts have not yet filed financial statements because they were formed only recently.[14]

The top rows in Table 4.3 show the combined debits from 2006 through 2008 for the reporting trusts. The number of trusts reporting (see the last row of the table) increased over the period as additional trusts began to file annual reports. Trust expenses include

- claim-processing costs
- costs of managing the trust's investment portfolio
- fees and expenses of trustees, TAC members, and the FCR
- fees for the trust counsel, TAC counsel, FCR counsel, and other legal and other professional fees

---

[13] The Manville Trust does not break out malignant from nonmalignant claims in its publicly available reports.

[14] The trusts are not required to follow generally accepted accounting principles (GAAPs) in preparing financial statements. Trust financial statements vary in format, and care was taken in aggregating information across trusts.

Table 4.3
Overview of Trust Assets, Claim Payments, and Expenses

Item	2006	2007	2008
Balance-sheet debits ($ millions)			
Trust expenses	89	125	149
Claim payments	461	1,442	3,340
Taxes	71	75	−105
Other deductions	25	9	47
Gross claimant compensation as a percentage of trust expenditures			
Lower bound	71	87	94
Upper bound	75	88	96
Year-end trust assets ($ billions)	20.9	22.7	18.2
Number of trusts reporting	19	20	22

- general administrative expenses
- cost of purchasing insurance.

Data for claim payments and taxes follow trust expenses. Other deductions include payments on property-damage claims (or amounts set aside for such payments), costs related to stock or other asset sales, increases in outstanding claim offers, and amounts payable on indirect claims. Of these, payment on property-damage claims is the largest component.[15]

Table 4.3 provides an estimate of gross claimant compensation as a percentage of trust expenditures. The claimant compensation is gross in the sense that it includes any fees the claimant pays to his or her attorney for services related to the recovery.[16] Because the publicly available data do not allow us to fully determine whether outlays in the other deductions category are made to claimants, we calculate upper and lower bounds for the gross claimant-compensation percentage. In the lower-bound estimate, none of the payments in the other deductible category is assumed to go to claimants. In the upper-bound estimate, they all are.[17] As can be seen in the table, there is not a great deal of difference between the two estimates.

As claim payments rose rapidly between 2006 and 2008, the gross claimant-compensation percentage rose from between 71 and 75 percent to approximately 95 percent. These levels compare favorably to estimates of gross compensation as a percentage of defendant expenditures in the tort system. Carroll, Hensler, et al. (2005, p. xxvi) estimated that claimant compensation through 2002 amounted to 69 percent of total spending by defendants and insurers. It should be noted, however, that the gross compensation percentages in Table 4.3 do not include the legal and other transaction costs incurred in negotiating the terms for the trust during the bankruptcy proceedings.

---

[15] Some trusts pay for asbestos removal and other asbestos-related property damage.

[16] Informed parties indicated that plaintiffs' attorneys' fees typically run about 25 percent of the award.

[17] Negative taxes (tax refunds) are set to zero in calculating gross compensation as a percentage of trust expenditures.

Trust assets provide a measure of the resources available to pay claims. The penultimate row of Table 4.3 provides the year-end assets of the reporting trusts in 2006, 2007, and 2008. Despite the $4.8 billion in claim payments in 2007 and 2008, year-end assets only declined from $20.9 billion to $18.2 billion between 2006 and 2008, due in part to the initial reporting by three newly formed trusts. The assets at the end of 2008 are an indicator of the substantial claim payments yet to be made by the bankruptcy trusts.

Claim Valuation Schedules

Table 4.4 reports the scheduled and average values for mesothelioma claims, the payment percentage, and the scheduled and average values after the payment percentage has been applied. As discussed in Chapter Three, a claimant who selects expedited review and meets the relevant criteria will be offered the scheduled value for the specified disease, subject to the payment percentage. For most trusts, the average value is the trust's target value for all paid claims in a particular disease category, including claims that go through either expedited or individual review.[18] The payment percentage must then be applied to this figure to determine the average amount paid to claimants. We have not evaluated the extent to which the average value after payment percentage is a good approximation of the actual average award in a disease category.

A number of trusts set different scheduled values for the separate classes of claims they accept. For example, the Western Asbestos Trust posts separate scheduled values for claims involving exposure at Minnesota facilities and claims involving exposure at North Dakota facilities. We consider each of these trust-claim-class combinations separately.

As shown in the first row of Table 4.4, the scheduled value for mesothelioma claims varies from $7,000 to $1.2 million across the 30 trust-claim-class combinations, with a median of $126,000. The median of the average value for mesothelioma claims is $180,000, again with a large spread, across the somewhat fewer trust-claim-class combinations that report average values for mesothelioma claims.[19] The wide spread in both the scheduled and average values reflects, in part, the difference in payments made by companies through the tort system before they filed for bankruptcy.

The payment percentage runs from 1.1 to 100 percent, with a median of 25 percent. The current payment percentages for the 29 trust-claim-class combinations reporting are provided in Figure 4.5. As can be seen, the payment percentage is less than 25 percent for a sizable group of trusts and between roughly 40 and 60 percent for another sizable group of trusts. Only one trust (THAN) has a payment percentage higher than 60 percent, although that trust had not paid any claims through 2008. As can be seen, the assets available to some trusts allow them to pay only a very small proportion of the value assigned to the claim while other trusts are able to pay a much higher proportion.[20]

---

[18] For a few trusts, the reported average value considers only claims that go through individual review.

[19] The sum of the scheduled values after payment percentage for the 28 trust-claim-class combinations is $1.34 million. A mesothelioma claimant could, in principle, receive this amount from these trusts. However, it is exceedingly unlikely that a claimant would be eligible for payment from all trusts and for multiple payments from trusts that have more than one claim class. The sum of the average values after payment percentage for the 21 trust-claim-class combinations reporting is $1.44 million.

[20] As discussed in Chapter Three, it is important to consider the scheduled or average value when interpreting the payment percentage. A low payment percentage applied to an artificially high value can result in the same ultimate payment as a high payment percentage applied to a lower value.

Table 4.4
Mesothelioma Claim Values

Item	Minimum	Percentile			Maximum
		20th	50th	80th	
Prior to applying payment percentage					
Scheduled value ($ thousands) (30 trust-claim-class combinations)	7	59	126	203	1,200
Average value ($ thousands) (23 trust-claim-class combinations)	45	99	180	262	524
Payment percentage (29 trust-claim-class combinations)	1.1	9.4	25.0	46.3	100.0
After applying payment percentage					
Scheduled value ($ thousands) (28 trust-claim-class combinations)	1	13	27	68	240
Average value ($ thousands) (21 trust-claim-class combinations)	13	23	41	101	238

The bottom rows in Table 4.4 summarize the distribution of the scheduled and average values for mesothelioma claims once the payment percentage has been applied. As indicated in Appendix B, not all trusts apply the payment percentage to every disease level, and the scheduled and average values after payment percentage are calculated accordingly. The resulting medians for the scheduled and average values are $27,000 and $41,000, respectively. The individual values are graphed in Figures 4.6 and 4.7. Scheduled values net of payment percentage are typically under $50,000, although they range between $50,000 and $238,000 for a number of trusts. Average values net of payment percentage for mesothelioma claims range from $13,000 to $238,000 across the trust-claim-class combinations reporting (see Figure 4.7).

Trusts recognize various disease levels, and the scheduled and average values are usually set for each. While mesothelioma is always considered a separate disease level, the number of other disease levels varies by trust. It is most common to set up seven or eight standard disease levels, and 15 of the 26 selected trusts do so. In presenting figures on the average and scheduled values for the nonmesothelioma disease levels, we restrict our attention to these 15 trusts, because the disease level used by other trusts often do not map cleanly into the most commonly used levels. We also report the mesothelioma values for this subset of trusts to facilitate comparison across disease levels.

Table 4.5 summarizes the distributions of the scheduled and average values by disease level for the trust-claim-class combinations at the 15 trusts for which data are available. For reasons discussed in Chapter Three, expedited review is generally not allowed for claims alleging lung cancer 2; consequently, trusts do not set a scheduled value for this disease level. Following mesothelioma, the median scheduled value and median average value are highest for lung cancer 1 and severe asbestosis. The medians of both the scheduled and average values are considerably lower for the other disease categories.

Table 4.6 summarizes the distribution of the scheduled and average values after the payment percentage has been applied, if appropriate. At $38,000, the median of the average value for the set of trusts with comparable disease levels is considerably higher for mesothelioma than for other disease levels. Again, there is wide variation across trusts.

Figure 4.5
Payment Percentage

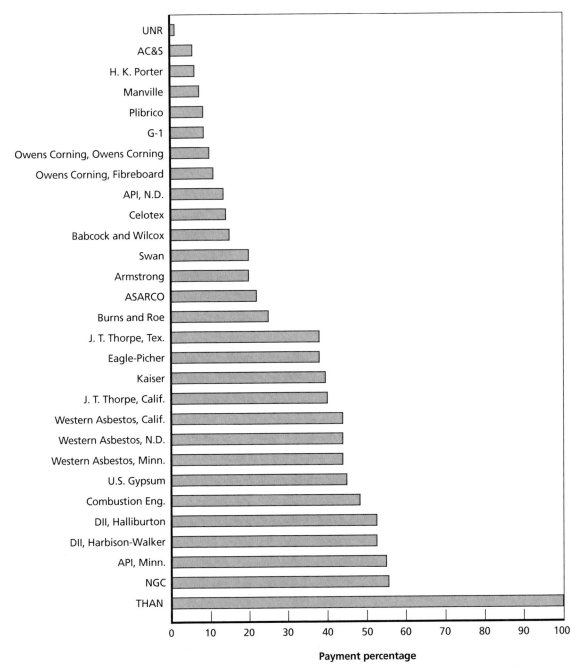

Composition of Trust Governing Bodies

Members of the same organization are frequently represented on the governing and advisory bodies of different trusts. At the 26 selected trusts, we identified a total of 255 different positions for trustees, TAC members, FCRs, trust counsel, TAC counsel, and FCR counsel. There were 122 different individuals filling these 255 positions, representing 83 different organizations. While the lists assembled for trustees, TAC members, and FCRs are fairly complete, the

Figure 4.6
Scheduled Value for Mesothelioma Claims After Applying Payment Percentage

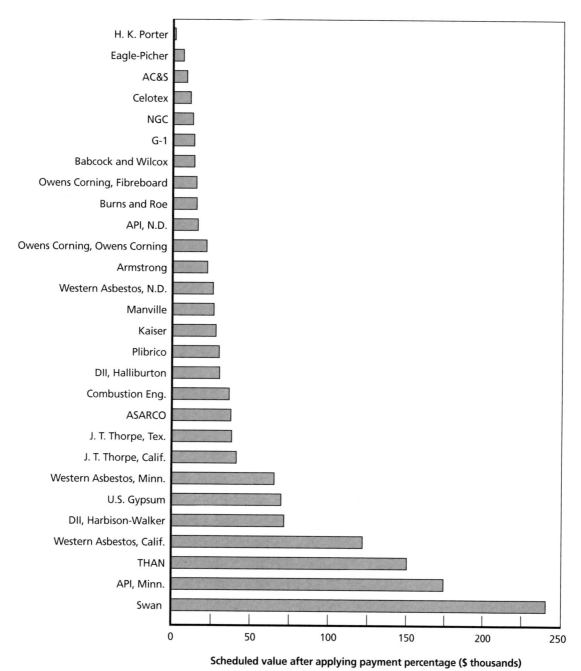

Scheduled value after applying payment percentage ($ thousands)

lists for trust counsel, TAC counsel, and FCR counsel are less complete because it is more difficult to obtain the information on who is serving in these capacities.

Table 4.7 shows the organizations represented at more than five different trusts. The Kazan firm is represented at more than half of the 26 trusts, and the other firms are represented at sizable percentages. These organizations tend to be represented at the larger trusts (see Table 4.7): The combined assets of the trusts at which a firm is represented as a percentage of total year-end 2008 assets of the selected trusts is larger than the percentage of trusts at which

Figure 4.7
Average Value for Mesothelioma Claims After Applying Payment Percentage

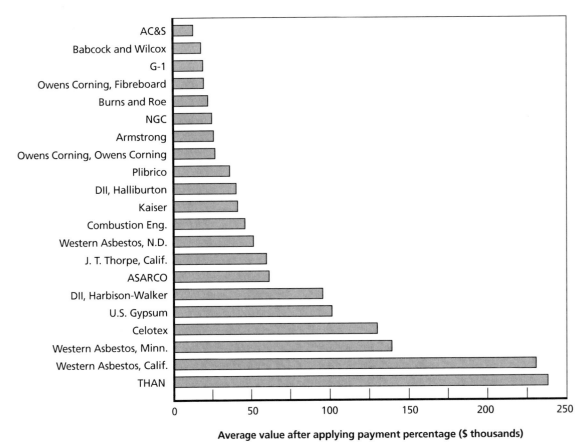

Average value after applying payment percentage ($ thousands)

RAND *TR872-4.7*

the organization is represented. The involvement of all of these firms and sizable share of the selected trusts reflect the leading role that they play in asbestos litigation or in the bankruptcy process and the creation of asbestos trusts.

Table 4.8 indicates that the most–frequently represented organizations specialize in the roles they take on at the different trusts. Seven of the nine organizations are represented on TACs and assume other roles at the trust. These seven organizations are all plaintiffs' law firms. The other two firms, Campbell and Levine and Caplin and Drysdale, are trust counsel and TAC counsel, respectively, at multiple trusts.

Table 4.5
Scheduled and Average Values, by Disease Level, at Trusts with Seven or Eight Disease Levels ($ thousands)

Value	Minimum	Percentile			Maximum
		20th	50th	80th	
Scheduled values ($ thousands)					
Mesothelioma (20 trust-claim-class combinations)	11	68	136	176	350
Lung cancer 1 (20 trust-claim-class combinations)	3	25	41	52	120
Lung cancer 2 (1 trust-claim-class combination)	—	—	—	—	—
Other cancer (20 trust-claim-class combinations)	2	10	15	22	65
Severe asbestosis (19 trust-claim-class combinations)	9	25	30	46	120
Asbestosis/pleural disease 1 (20 trust-claim-class combinations)	1	5	8	12	25
Asbestosis/pleural disease 2 (20 trust-claim-class combinations)	1	1	3	5	12
Other asbestos disease (16 trust-claim-class combinations)	0.1	0.2	0.3	0.4	0.6
Average values ($ thousands)					
Mesothelioma (18 trust-claim-class combinations)	63	99	181	245	425
Lung cancer 1 (18 trust-claim-class combinations)	12	35	53	59	135
Lung cancer 2 (19 trust-claim-class combinations)	3	12	15	20	45
Other cancer (18 trust-claim-class combinations)	5	15	19	28	70
Severe asbestosis (18 trust-claim-class combinations)	10	28	36	53	135
Asbestosis/pleural disease 1 (9 trust-claim-class combinations)	3	7	10	15	20
Asbestosis/pleural disease 2 (8 trust-claim-class combinations)	1	3	5	7	9
Other asbestos disease (no trust-claim-class combinations)	—	—	—	—	—

Table 4.6
Scheduled and Average Values, by Disease Level, at Trusts with Seven or Eight Disease Levels, After Payment Percentage Applied ($ thousands)

Value	Minimum	Percentile			Maximum
		20th	50th	80th	
Scheduled values					
Mesothelioma (18 trust-claim-class combinations)	9	14	27	38	150
Lung cancer 1 (18 trust-claim-class combinations)	3	4	8	13	65
Lung cancer 2 (1 trust-claim-class combination)	—	—	—	—	—
Other cancer (18 trust-claim-class combinations)	1	2	4	5	30
Severe asbestosis (17 trust-claim-class combinations)	2	4	8	12	60
Asbestosis/pleural disease 1 (18 trust-claim-class combinations)	0.4	1	2	3	8
Asbestosis/pleural disease 2 (18 trust-claim-class combinations)	0.1	0.4	1	1	4
Other asbestos disease (16 trust-claim-class combinations)	0.1	0.2	0.3	0.4	0.6
Average values					
Mesothelioma (16 trust-claim-class combinations)	13	20	38	96	238
Lung cancer 1 (16 trust-claim-class combinations)	3	5	11	25	90
Lung cancer 2 (19 trust-claim-class combinations)	3	12	15	20	45
Other cancer (16 trust-claim-class combinations)	1	3	5	8	50
Severe asbestosis (16 trust-claim-class combinations)	3	5	9	16	68
Asbestosis/pleural disease 1 (7 trust-claim-class combinations)	1	1	2	7	16
Asbestosis/pleural disease 2 (6 trust-claim-class combinations)	0.6	0.6	0.9	4	8
Other asbestos disease (no trust-claim-class combinations)	—	—	—	—	—

Table 4.7
Organizations Most Frequently Represented at the 26 Selected Trusts

Organization	Number of Trusts at Which Firm Was Represented		2008 Assets of Trusts at Which Firm Was Represented	
	Number	Percentage of Selected Trusts	Assets ($ billions)	Percentage of Assets of Selected Trusts
Kazan, McClain, Abrams, Lyons, Greenwood and Harley	15	58	11.6	64
Baron and Budd	11	42	11.5	63
Cooney and Conway	11	42	13.3	73
Weitz and Luxenberg	11	42	13.4	74
Motley Rice	8	31	9.4	52
Bergman Draper and Frockt	6	23	5.5	30
Campbell and Levine	6	23	8.0	44
Caplin and Drysdale	6	23	10.4	57
Goldberg Persky White	6	23	10.3	57

Table 4.8
Positions of the Most Frequently Represented Organizations

Organization	Trustee	TAC Member	FCR	Counsel Trust	Counsel TAC	Counsel FCR
Kazan, McClain, Abrams, Lyons, Greenwood and Harley		x				
Baron and Budd		x				
Cooney and Conway		x				
Weitz and Luxenberg		x				
Motley Rice		x				
Bergman Draper and Frockt		x				
Campbell and Levine				x		
Caplin and Drysdale					x	
Goldberg Persky White		x				

CHAPTER FIVE

Conclusion

The publicly available information on asbestos bankruptcy trusts is a useful resource and provides an overview of trust practices and activity. However, it is limited in many important ways. Data on important variables, such as the number of claims filed, are incomplete, and it is difficult to locate information for the early years of the older trusts. Data by disease level are uneven, with less than half of the selected 26 trusts breaking out information for malignant and nonmalignant claims. Only a few trusts report data by disease level beyond the malignant/nonmalignant breakdown. In addition, disease-level categories vary across trusts, adding to the challenges of comparing claim valuations and payments by disease level across trusts. Trusts do not follow a common set of accounting principles when preparing financial statements, which makes it difficult to compare financial performance across trusts and develop measures of gross claimant compensation as a percentage of trust expenditures.

From the perspective of trying to understand the role of the trusts in the compensation for asbestos-related injuries, perhaps the most-significant limitation of the publicly available data is the inability to link payments across trusts to the same individual. It is not possible to use trust-level data to determine the number of trusts providing payments to the same individual or the amount the trusts together pay to an individual claimant. This lack of information makes it difficult or perhaps impossible to evaluate the trusts' effect on the overall compensation provided to individual claimants and on the compensation paid by solvent defendants.

Information on individual settlements is very difficult to obtain from solvent defendants and from plaintiffs' attorneys. In the past, researchers have had success obtaining individual settlement data from a number of solvent defendants on a confidential basis (see, for example, Carroll, Hensler, et al., 2005). Researchers have likewise been able to obtain individual data from the Manville Trust in the past, although, in recent years, the Manville Trust has declined to make these data available for research purposes. Researchers have also not been successful in obtaining individual asbestos compensation data from plaintiffs' attorneys.

The ability to understand the trusts' effects on overall claimant compensation and the compensation paid by solvent defendants will depend to a large extent on whether solvent defendants, trusts, and plaintiffs' attorneys are willing to release individual compensation information on a confidential basis for research purposes.

List of Bankruptcies with at Least Some Asbestos Liability

Table A.1 lists 96 companies that have declared bankruptcy with some asbestos liability, by filing date. Asbestos liability was the main cause of bankruptcy in some cases but only a peripheral cause in others. The table reports the date bankruptcy was filed and the date the reorganization plan was confirmed. Also listed is the name of the asbestos bankruptcy trust that was established, if any. The status of the trust is listed in the last column.

Table A.1
Chronological List of Bankruptcies with Some Asbestos Liability

Company Name	Date Bankruptcy Filed	Date Reorganization Confirmed	Trust Established	Trust Status
UNR Industries	July 29, 1982	June 2, 1989	UNR Asbestos-Disease Claims Trust	Active
Unarco	July 29, 1982	June 2, 1989	UNR Asbestos-Disease Claims Trust	Active
Johns-Manville Corp.	August 1, 1982	July 15, 1987	Manville Personal Injury Settlement Trust	Active
Amatex Corp.	November 1, 1982	April 25, 1990	Amatex Asbestos Disease Trust Fund	Inactive
Waterman Steamship Corp.	December 1, 1983	June 19, 1986	—	—
Forty-Eight Insulations	April 19, 1985	May 16, 1995	Forty-Eight Insulations Qualified Settlement Trust	Inactive
Wallace and Gale Co.	November 16, 1985	June 27, 1998	Wallace and Gale Company Asbestos Settlement Trust	Inactive
Philadelphia Asbestos Corp. (Pacor)	July 1, 1986	November 30, 1989	Manville Personal Injury Settlement Trust	Active
Standard Insulations, Inc.	August 1, 1986	October 26, 1992	—	—
Prudential Lines, Inc.	November 4, 1986	December 15, 1989	PLI Disbursement Trust	Inactive

Table A.1—Continued

Company Name	Date Bankruptcy Filed	Date Reorganization Confirmed	Trust Established	Trust Status
McLean Industries	November 24, 1986	May 16, 1989	United States Lines, Inc. and United States Lines (S.A.) Inc. Reorganization Trust	Inactive
United States Lines	November 24, 1986	May 16, 1989	United States Lines, Inc. and United States Lines (S.A.) Inc. Reorganization Trust	Inactive
Gatke Corp.	March 2, 1987	August 9, 1991	—	—
Nicolet, Inc.	July 17, 1987	September 21, 1989	—	—
Todd Shipyards	August 17, 1987	Unknown	—	—
Raymark Corp./ Raytech Corp.	March 10, 1989	August 31, 2000	Raytech Corporation Asbestos Personal Injury Settlement Trust	Active
Delaware Insulations	May 22, 1989	September 9, 1992	—	—
Hillsborough Holding Co.	December 27, 1989	March 2, 1995	—	—
Celotex Corp.	October 12, 1990	December 6, 1996	Celotex Asbestos Settlement Trust	Active
Carey Canada, Inc.	October 12, 1990	October 6, 1996	Celotex Asbestos Settlement Trust	Active
National Gypsum	October 28, 1990	March 9, 1993	NGC Bodily Injury Trust	Active
Eagle-Picher Industries	January 7, 1991	November 18, 1996	Eagle-Picher Industries Inc. Personal Injury Settlement Trust	Active
H. K. Porter Co.	February 15, 1991	June 25, 1998	H. K. Porter Asbestos Trust	Active
Kentile Floors	November 20, 1992	December 10, 1998	—	—
American Shipbuilding, Inc.	November 4, 1993	October 11, 1994	—	—
Keene Corp.	December 3, 1993	June 13, 1996	Keene Creditors Trust	Active
Lykes Bros. Steamship	October 11, 1995	April 15, 1997	Lykes Tort Claims Trust	Active
Rock Wool Manufacturing	November 18, 1996	December 3, 1999	Rock Wool Mfg Company Asbestos Trust	Inactive
Brunswick Fabricators	November 30, 1997	Unknown	—	—

Table A.1—Continued

Company Name	Date Bankruptcy Filed	Date Reorganization Confirmed	Trust Established	Trust Status
M. H. Detrick	January 13, 1998	August 21, 2002	M. H. Detrick Company Asbestos Trust	Inactive
Fuller-Austin	September 4, 1998	November 13, 1998	Fuller-Austin Asbestos Settlement Trust	Inactive
Harnischfeger Corp.	June 7, 1999	May 18, 2001	—	—
Rutland Fire Clay	October 13, 1999	November 17, 2000	Rutland Fire Clay Company Asbestos Trust	Inactive
Asbestos and Insulation Corporation (A&I Corporation)	November 5, 1999	June 17, 2005	A&I Corporation Asbestos Bodily Injury Trust	Active
Babcock and Wilcox Co.	February 22, 2000	January 17, 2006	Babcock and Wilcox Company Asbestos Personal Injury Settlement Trust	Active
Pittsburgh Corning	April 16, 2000	n.y.c.	Pittsburgh Corning Corporation Asbestos PI Trust	Proposed
Stone and Webster Engineering	June 2, 2000	January 16, 2004	Stone and Webster Asbestos Trust	Active
Owens Corning Corp.	October 5, 2000	October 31, 2006	Owens Corning Fibreboard Asbestos Personal Injury Trust—Owens Corning Subfund	Active
Owens Corning Fibreboard	October 5, 2000	October 31, 2006	Owens Corning Fibreboard Asbestos Personal Injury Trust, Fibreboard Subfund	Active
E. J. Bartells	October 20, 2000	February 14, 2001	Bartells Asbestos Settlement Trust	Active
Burns and Roe Enterprises, Inc.	December 4, 2000	February 20, 2009	Burns and Roe Asbestos Personal Injury Settlement Trust	Active
Armstrong World Industries	December 6, 2000	August 18, 2006	Armstrong World Industries Asbestos Personal Injury Settlement Trust	Active
G-1 Holdings, Inc.	January 5, 2001	November 12, 2009	G-1 Asbestos Personal Injury Settlement Trust	Active
Murphy Marine Services	March 21, 2001	July 25, 2002	—	—

Table A.1—Continued

Company Name	Date Bankruptcy Filed	Date Reorganization Confirmed	Trust Established	Trust Status
W. R. Grace	April 1, 2001	n.y.c.	W. R. Grace and Co. Asbestos Personal Injury Settlement Trust	Proposed
Skinner Engine Co.	April 16, 2001	n.y.c.	Skinner Engine Co. Asbestos Trust	Proposed
United States Mineral Products	June 23, 2001	November 30, 2005	United States Mineral Products Company Asbestos Personal Injury Settlement Trust	Active
USG Corp.	June 25, 2001	June 15, 2006	United States Gypsum Asbestos Personal Injury Settlement Trust	Active
Insul Co.	September 4, 2001	June 7, 2005	—	—
Federal Mogul (Turner & Newall, Flexitallic, Ferodo)	October 1, 2001	November 13, 2007	Federal Mogul U.S. Asbestos Personal Injury Trust, Turner & Newall Subfund	Active
Federal Mogul (Federal Mogul Products/Wagner)	October 1, 2001	November 13, 2007	Federal Mogul U.S. Asbestos Personal Injury Trust, FMP Subfund	Active
Federal Mogul (Federal Mogul Corporation/ Vellumoid)	October 1, 2001	November 13, 2007	Federal Mogul U.S. Asbestos Personal Injury Trust, Vellumoid Subfund	Active
Federal Mogul (Felt Products Manufacturing)	October 1, 2001	November 13, 2007	Federal Mogul U.S. Asbestos Personal Injury Trust, Fel-Pro Subfund	Active
Swan Transportation Co.	December 20, 2001	July 21, 2003	Swan Asbestos and Silica Settlement Trust	Active
North American Refractories Corp. (NARCO)	January 4, 2002	July 25, 2008	North American Refractories Company Asbestos Personal Injury Settlement Trust	Proposed
Kaiser Aluminum	February 12, 2002	May 11, 2006	Kaiser Aluminum & Chemical Corporation Asbestos Personal Injury Trust	Active
J. T. Thorpe, Inc.	February 12, 2002	January 19, 2006	J. T. Thorpe Settlement Trust	Active
Global Industrial Technologies (Harbison-Walker)	February 14, 2002	November 13, 2007	DII Industries, LLC Asbestos PI Trust	Active
A. P. Green	February 14, 2002	December 16, 2003	APG Asbestos Trust	Proposed

Table A.1—Continued

Company Name	Date Bankruptcy Filed	Date Reorganization Confirmed	Trust Established	Trust Status
Plibrico Co.	March 13, 2002	January 30, 2006	Plibrico 524(g) Trust	Active
Porter-Hayden Co.	March 15, 2002	July 5, 2006	Porter Hayden Bodily Injury Trust	Active
Special Metals Corp.	March 27, 2002	September 29, 2003	—	—
Shook and Fletcher	April 8, 2002	October 29, 2002	Shook and Fletcher Asbestos Settlement Trust	Active
ARTRA Group, Inc.	June 3, 2002	January 25, 2007	ARTRA 524(g) Asbestos Trust	Active
Asbestos Claims Management Corp. (ACMC)	August 19, 2002	June 5, 2003	NGC Bodily Injury Trust	Active
AC&S	September 16, 2002	May 6, 2008	ACandS Asbestos Settlement Trust	Active
A-Best Products	September 20, 2002	June 7, 2004	A-Best Asbestos Settlement Trust	Active
J. T. Thorpe Co.	October 1, 2002	March 3, 2004	J. T. Thorpe Company Successor Trust	Active
Western MacArthur/ Western Asbestos	November 22, 2002	January 27, 2004	Western Asbestos Trust	Active
Combustion Engineering	February 17, 2003	March 1, 2006	Combustion Engineering 524(g) Asbestos PI Trust	Active
Muralo Co.	May 20, 2003	December 21, 2007	Muralo Trust	Inactive
C. E. Thurston	August 18, 2003	March 30, 2006	C. E. Thurston and Sons Asbestos Trust	Active
Congoleum Corp.	December 1, 2003	June 8, 2010	Congoleum Plan Trust	Active
Mid-Valley, Inc. (Halliburton)	December 16, 2003	July 21, 2004	DII Industries, LLC Asbestos PI Trust	Active
Oglebay Norton Co. (ONCO)	February 23, 2004	November 7, 2004	—	—
Utex Industries	March 26, 2004	June 16, 2004	Utex Industries, Inc. Successor Trust	Active
Special Electric	April 15, 2004	December 21, 2006	—	—
Flintkote Co./ Flintkote Mines	May 1, 2004	n.y.c.	Flintkote Company and Flintkote Mines Limited Asbestos Personal Injury Trust	Proposed
Quigley Co. (Pfizer)	September 3, 2004	n.y.c.	Quigley Company, Inc. Asbestos PI Trust	Proposed
API, Inc.	January 6, 2005	May 25, 2006	API, Inc. Asbestos Settlement Trust	Active

Table A.1—Continued

Company Name	Date Bankruptcy Filed	Date Reorganization Confirmed	Trust Established	Trust Status
Lake Asbestos of Quebec, Ltd.	August 9, 2005	Unknown	ASARCO LLC Asbestos Personal Injury Settlement Trust	Active
ASARCO, LLC	August 9, 2005	November 13, 2009	ASARCO LLC Asbestos Personal Injury Settlement Trust	Active
Brauer Supply Co.	August 22, 2005	January 5, 2007	Brauer 524(g) Asbestos Trust	Active
Dana Corporation	March 3, 2006	December 26, 2007	—	—
ABB Lummus Global	April 21, 2006	July 21, 2006	Lummus 524(g) Asbestos PI Trust	Active
Lloyd E. Mitchell Co.	June 6, 2006	Unknown	—	—
Thorpe Insulation Co.	October 15, 2007	n.y.c.	Thorpe Insulation Company Asbestos Personal Injury Settlement Trust	Proposed
Pacific Insulation Co.	October 31, 2007	n.y.c.	Thorpe Insulation Company Asbestos Personal Injury Settlement Trust	Proposed
Hercules Chemical Co.	September 18, 2008	December 23, 2009	—	—
Christy Refractories Co. LLC	October 29, 2008	n.y.c.	—	—
T. H. Agriculture and Nutrition, LLC (THAN)	November 24, 2008	October 26, 2009	T. H. Agriculture and Nutrition, LLC Asbestos Personal Injury Trust	Active
Plant Insulation Co.	March 13, 2009	n.y.c.	—	—
General Motors Corp.	June 1, 2009	n.y.c.	Whether a trust will be established is uncertain	—
Durabla Manufacturing Co.	April 12, 2010	n.y.c	Whether a trust will be established is uncertain	—
Bondex International Inc./ Specialty Products Holding Corp.	May 31, 2010	n.y.c.	Trust not yet named	—
Garlock Sealing Technologies, LLC	June 5, 2010	n.y.c.	Trust not yet named	—

SOURCES: Plevin, Davis, and Bloomberg (2009); bankruptcy documents.

NOTE: n.y.c. = not yet confirmed.

Detailed Reports on Largest Trusts

This appendix contains detailed reports on 26 of the largest active trusts and three of the largest proposed trusts. Each report contains a number of different sections. Table B.1 lists the sections in the order presented for each trust with notes on the terms and definitions used. The reader should also consult the glossary definitions.

The following notations are used for missing data:

- Not available (n.a.) is used to indicate that the item is relevant to the trust but the trust either does not do the calculation or does not publicly release the information.
- Not applicable (n.appl.) is used to indicate that the item is not relevant to the trust (e.g., when a trust does not use a claim payment ratio).

Table B.1
Notes on Individual Trust Reports

Section	Notes
Bankruptcy court and trust administrative information	Each of the claim classes accepted by the trust is listed. These classes typically refer to different business divisions of the debtor or to claims from different geographic locations.
Trustees and advisers	—
Estimated initial funding of the trust	Insurance settlements exclude potential recoveries by the trust from the debtor's insurers after the trust is established.
Trust financial statement	*Investment fees* refers to the professional and other fees related to managing the trust's investment portfolio. Other deductions include payments on property-damage claims (or amounts set aside for such payments), costs related to stock or other asset sales, increases in outstanding claim offers, and amounts payable on contribution and indemnity claims. Of these, payment on property-damage claims is the largest component. Gross claimant compensation as a percentage of deductions is calculated as follows: Lower bound = (claim payments) × 100/(trust expenses + taxes + other deductions + claim payments). Upper bound = (claim payments + other deductions) × 100/(trust expenses + taxes + other deductions + claim payments). Negative taxes and other deductions are set to zero.
Claim valuation	If the values differ by claim class, separate tables are included.
Claim activity	—
Claim activity by disease level	Included for only those trusts that break down claim data by disease levels. Few trusts provide such a breakdown.
Claim-approval criteria	If the criteria vary by claim class, separate tables are included. The disease levels in this table match those in the claim valuation table. Exposure criterion of one day means that some exposure is required but there is no requirement on the amount.

ACandS Asbestos Settlement Trust

ACandS Asbestos Settlement Trust

Bankruptcy Court and Trust Administrative Information

Debtor(s)	AC&S		
Bankruptcy filing date	9/16/02	Confirmation date	5/6/08
Bankruptcy court	Bankr. D. Del.	Bankruptcy judge	Judith Fitzgerald

Trust status	Active
Date trust established	7/31/08
Classes of claims processed	ACandS claims
Claim administrator	Verus Claims Services
Trust website	www.acandsasbestostrust.com

Trustees and Advisors

Position	Name	Affiliation
Trustee	Alfred Wolin	Saiber LLC
FCR	Lawrence Fitzpatrick	Asbestos Claims Facility
TAC Member	Armand Volta	Peter G. Angelos
TAC Member	Bryan Blevins	Provost Umphrey LLC
TAC Member	John Cooney	Cooney & Conway
TAC Member	Joseph Rice	Motley Rice, LLC
TAC Member	Matthew Bergman	Bergman Draper & Frockt, PLLC
TAC Member	Perry Weitz	Weitz & Luxenburg
TAC Member	Steven Kazan	Kazan, McClain, Abrams, Fernandez, Lyons, Farrise & Greenwood, P.C.
Trust Counsel	Carl Kunz	Morris James LLP
Trust Counsel	Kevin E. Irwin	Keating Muething & Klekamp PLL
Trust Counsel	Sue A. Erhart	Keating Muething & Klekamp PLL

Estimated Initial Funding of Trust ($millions)

	Funding for Claims Paid Through Trust	Funding for Claims Paid Outside Trust
Cash from debtor(s)	0	0
Stock from debtors(s)	5.3	0
Insurance settlements	522.3	0
Other assets	0	0
Total	527.6	0

ACandS Asbestos Settlement Trust (continued)

Trust Financial Statement ($)

	Pre-2006	2006	2007	2008
Beginning trust assets	0	0	0	0
Additions				
Cash from debtors	0	0	0	0
Stock from debtors	0	0	0	5,286,000
Insurance settlements	0	0	0	522,310,991
Investment gains	0	0	0	127,728
Investment income	0	0	0	2,930,991
Other additions	0	0	0	0
Deductions				
Trust expenses	0	0	0	715,702
Claim processing costs	0	0	0	30,000
Investment fees	0	0	0	109,805
All other expenses	0	0	0	575,897
Taxes	0	0	0	0
Claim payments	0	0	0	184,823,525
Other deductions	0	0	0	44,900,000
Ending trust assets	0	0	0	300,216,483

Gross claimant compensation as a percentage of deductions				
Lower bound	–	–	–	80.2%
Upper bound	–	–	–	99.7%

Claim Valuation for — ACandS claims

Disease level	Scheduled Value	Average Value	Maximum Value
Mesothelioma	150,000	220,000	550,000
Lung Cancer 1	50,000	55,000	125,000
Lung Cancer 2	n.appl.	12,000	50,000
Other Cancer	14,000	15,000	50,000
Severe Asbestosis	40,000	45,000	100,000
Asbestosis / Pleural Disease II	7,500	n.appl.	n.appl.
Asbestosis / Pleural Disease I	3,000	n.appl.	n.appl.

Payment percentage	
Initial payment percentage	5.8%
Current payment percentage	5.8%

Claim payment ratio	
Malignancies and severe asbestosis	82.9%
Asbestosis and pleural disease	17.1%

ACandS Asbestos Settlement Trust (continued)

Claim Activity

	Pre-2006	2006	2007	2008	Total
Pre-petition pending and post-petition claims					
Claims filed					
Malignant	0	0	0	0	0
Non-malignant	0	0	0	0	0
Not specified	0	0	0	0	0
All disease types	0	0	0	0	0
Claims paid					
Malignant	0	0	0	0	0
Non-malignant	0	0	0	0	0
Not specified	0	0	0	0	0
All disease types	0	0	0	0	0
Claim payments ($)					
Malignant	0	0	0	0	0
Non-malignant	0	0	0	0	0
Not specified	0	0	0	0	0
All disease types	0	0	0	0	0
Average payment per claim ($)					
Malignant	–	–	–	–	–
Non-malignant	–	–	–	–	–
Not specified	–	–	–	–	–
All disease types	–	–	–	–	–
Claims settled but not paid pre-petition					
Claims filed					
Malignant	0	0	0	n.a.	n.a.
Non-malignant	0	0	0	n.a.	n.a.
Not specified	0	0	0	217,500	217,500
All disease types	0	0	0	217,500	217,500
Claims paid					
Malignant	0	0	0	n.a.	n.a.
Non-malignant	0	0	0	n.a.	n.a.
Not specified	0	0	0	199,855	199,855
All disease types	0	0	0	199,855	199,855
Claim payments ($)					
Malignant	0	0	0	n.a.	n.a.
Non-malignant	0	0	0	n.a.	n.a.
Not specified	0	0	0	184,797,996	184,797,996
All disease types	0	0	0	184,797,996	184,797,996
Average payment per claim ($)					
Malignant	–	–	–	–	–
Non-malignant	–	–	–	–	–
Not specified	–	–	–	925	925
All disease types	–	–	–	925	925

ACandS Asbestos Settlement Trust (continued)

Claim Approval Criteria for	ACandS claims						
	Meso	LC1	LC2	OC	SA	AP2	AP1
1. Diagnosis requirement (one or more of checked items satisfies requirement)							
a. Physical exam	✔	✔	✔	✔	✔	✔	✔
b. Pathology	✔	✔	✔	✔	✔	✔	✔
c. Medical document review							
2. ILO or x-ray requirement							
a. ILO reading		1/0		1/0	2/1	1/0	1/0
OR b. X-ray, CT scan, or pathology showing one or more of the checked conditions							
(1) Bilateral interstitial fibrosis		✔		✔		✔	✔
(2) Bilateral pleural plaques		✔		✔		✔	✔
(3) Bilateral pleural thickening		✔		✔		✔	✔
(4) Bilateral pleural calcification		✔		✔		✔	✔
3. Pulmonary function test requirement							
a. TLC < (% of normal)					65	80	
AND FEV1/FVC ratio >							
OR b. DLCO < (% of normal)							
AND FEV1/FVC ratio >							
OR c. FVC < (% of normal)					65	80	
AND FEV1/FVC ratio >					0.65	0.65	
4. Causation statement requirement	No	Yes	Yes	Yes	Yes	Yes	No
5. Latency and exposure requirements							
a. Latency	10 yr	10 yr	10 yr	10 yr	10 yr	10 yr	10 yr
b. Company exposure prior to 1983	1 day	6 mo	1 day	6 mo	6 mo	6 mo	6 mo
c. Occupational exposure							
(1) Total		5 yr		5 yr	5 yr	5 yr	5 yr
(2) Prior to 1983	1 day	2 yr	1 day	2 yr	2 yr	2 yr	6 mo

API, Inc. Asbestos Settlement Trust

API, Inc. Asbestos Settlement Trust

Bankruptcy Court and Trust Administrative Information

Debtor(s)	API, Inc.		
Bankruptcy filing date	1/6/05	Confirmation date	5/25/06
Bankruptcy court	Bankr. D. Minn.	Bankruptcy judge	Gregory Kishel

Trust status	Active
Date trust established	2006
Classes of claims processed	API, Inc. claims - Minnesota
	API, Inc. claims - North Dakota
Claim administrator	Brownson & Ballou Attorneys and Counselors, PLLP
Trust website	www.apiincasbestossettlementtrust.com

Trustees and Advisors

Position	Name	Affiliation
Trustee	Robert Brownson	Brownson & Ballou, PLLP
FCR	Thomas Carey	Retired Minnesota state judge
TAC Member	Michael Polk	Sieben Polk

Estimated Initial Funding of Trust ($ millions)

	Funding for Claims Paid Through Trust	Funding for Claims Paid Outside Trust
Cash from debtor(s)	41.0	0
Stock from debtors(s)	0	0
Insurance settlements	53.0	0
Other assets	0	0
Total	94.0	0

API, Inc. Asbestos Settlement Trust (continued)

Trust Financial Statement ($)

	Pre-2006	2006	2007	2008
Beginning trust assets	0	0	0	82,940,662
Additions				
Cash from debtors	0	0	15,000,000	0
Stock from debtors	0	0	0	0
Insurance settlements	0	0	53,112,972	24,536
Investment gains	0	0	0	-552,358
Investment income	0	0	215,524	690,833
Other additions	0	0	26,000,000	3,300
Deductions				
Trust expenses	0	0	3,084,814	488,701
Claim processing costs	0	0	n.a.	n.a.
Investment fees	0	0	n.a.	40,270
All other expenses	0	0	n.a.	n.a.
Taxes	0	0	0	0
Claim payments	0	0	8,303,020	34,809,852
Other deductions	0	0	0	0
Ending trust assets	0	0	82,940,662	47,808,420
Gross claimant compensation as a percentage of deductions				
Lower bound	–	–	72.9%	98.6%
Upper bound	–	–	72.9%	98.6%

Claim Valuation for — API, Inc. claims - Minnesota

Disease level	Scheduled Value	Average Value	Maximum Value
Mesothelioma	316,250	n.appl.	n.appl.
Lung Cancer	137,050	n.appl.	n.appl.
Other Cancer	73,800	n.appl.	n.appl.
Asbestosis	57,200	n.appl.	n.appl.
Pleural	30,150	n.appl.	n.appl.

Payment percentage

Initial payment percentage	13.5%
Current payment percentage	55.0%

Claim payment ratio

Malignancies and severe asbestosis	n.appl.
Asbestosis and pleural disease	n.appl.

Claim Valuation for — API, Inc. claims - North Dakota

Disease level	Scheduled Value	Average Value	Maximum Value
Mesothelioma	117,087	n.appl.	n.appl.
Lung Cancer	44,777	n.appl.	n.appl.
Other Cancer	16,884	n.appl.	n.appl.
Asbestosis	16,500	n.appl.	n.appl.
Pleural	12,000	n.appl.	n.appl.

Payment percentage

Initial payment percentage	13.5%
Current payment percentage	13.5%

Claim payment ratio

Malignancies and severe asbestosis	n.appl.
Asbestosis and pleural disease	n.appl.

API, Inc. Asbestos Settlement Trust (continued)

Claim Activity

	Pre-2006	2006	2007	2008	Total
Pre-petition pending and post-petition claims					
Claims filed [a]					
Malignant	0	0	36	n.a.	n.a.
Non-malignant	0	0	13	n.a.	n.a.
Not specified	0	0	0	n.a.	n.a.
All disease types	0	0	49	n.a.	n.a.
Claims paid					
Malignant	0	0	5	70	75
Non-malignant	0	0	0	65	65
Not specified	0	0	0	0	0
All disease types	0	0	5	135	140
Claim payments ($)					
Malignant	0	0	212,836	11,635,179	11,848,016
Non-malignant	0	0	0	1,660,205	1,660,205
Not specified	0	0	0	0	0
All disease types	0	0	212,836	13,295,384	13,508,221
Average payment per claim ($)					
Malignant	–	–	42,567	166,217	157,974
Non-malignant	–	–	–	25,542	25,542
Not specified	–	–	–	–	–
All disease types	–	–	42,567	98,484	96,487
Claims settled but not paid pre-petition					
Claims filed [a]					
Malignant	0	0	n.a.	n.a.	n.a.
Non-malignant	0	0	n.a.	n.a.	n.a.
Not specified	0	0	n.a.	n.a.	n.a.
All disease types	0	0	n.a.	n.a.	n.a.
Claims paid					
Malignant	0	0	64	64	128
Non-malignant	0	0	621	623	1,244
Not specified	0	0	1	1	2
All disease types	0	0	686	688	1,374
Claim payments ($)					
Malignant	0	0	2,535,082	6,993,006	9,528,088
Non-malignant	0	0	5,119,675	13,674,245	18,793,920
Not specified	0	0	94,297	255,703	350,000
All disease types	0	0	7,749,054	20,922,954	28,672,008
Average payment per claim ($)					
Malignant	–	–	39,611	109,266	74,438
Non-malignant	–	–	8,244	21,949	15,108
Not specified	–	–	94,297	255,703	175,000
All disease types	–	–	11,296	30,411	20,868

[a] Claims filed data are not complete

API, Inc. Asbestos Settlement Trust (continued)

Claim Activity by Disease Level

	2006	2007	2008	Total
Pre-petition pending and post-petition claims				
Claims paid				
Mesothelioma	0	49	99	148
Lung cancer	0	18	33	51
Other cancer	0	2	2	4
Asbestosis	0	397	444	841
Pleural	0	224	244	468
Unknown	0	1	1	2
Claims payments ($)				
Mesothelioma	0	2,318,807	16,411,469	18,730,276
Lung cancer	0	406,808	2,156,236	2,563,044
Other cancer	0	22,303	60,480	82,783
Asbestosis	0	3,862,030	11,857,656	15,719,686
Pleural	0	1,257,646	3,476,794	4,734,439
Unknown	0	94,297	255,703	350,000
Average payment per claim ($)				
Mesothelioma	–	47,323	165,772	126,556
Lung cancer	–	22,600	65,340	50,256
Other cancer	–	11,152	30,240	20,696
Asbestosis	–	9,728	26,706	18,692
Pleural	–	5,614	14,249	10,116
Unknown	–	94,297	255,703	175,000

API, Inc. Asbestos Settlement Trust (continued)

Claim Approval Criteria for	API, Inc. claims - Minnesota and North Dak				
	Meso	LC	OC	AB	PL
1. Diagnosis requirement (one or more of checked items satisfies requirement)					
a. Physical exam					
b. Pathology					✔
c. Medical document review					
2. ILO or x-ray requirement					
a. ILO reading					
OR b. X-ray, CT scan, or pathology showing one or more of the checked conditions					
(1) Bilateral interstitial fibrosis			✔		
(2) Bilateral pleural plaques			✔		✔
(3) Bilateral pleural thickening			✔		✔
(4) Bilateral pleural calcification					
3. Pulmonary function test requirement					
a. TLC < (% of normal)					
AND FEV1/FVC ratio >					
OR b. DLCO < (% of normal)					
AND FEV1/FVC ratio >					
OR c. FVC < (% of normal)					
AND FEV1/FVC ratio >					
4. Causation statement requirement	Yes	Yes	Yes	Yes	Yes
5. Latency and exposure requirements					
a. Latency	10 yr	10 yr	10 yr	10 yr	10 yr
b. Company exposure prior to 1983	1 day	1 day	1 day	1 day	1 day
c. Occupational exposure					
(1) Total					
(2) Prior to 1983					

Armstrong World Industries Asbestos Personal Injury Settlement Trust

Armstrong World Industries Asbestos Personal Injury Settlement Trust

Bankruptcy Court and Trust Administrative Information

Debtor(s)	Armstrong World Industries		
Bankruptcy filing date	12/6/00	Confirmation date	8/18/06
Bankruptcy court	Bankr. D. Del.	Bankruptcy judge	Judith Fitzgerald

Trust status	Active
Date trust established	10/2/06
Classes of claims processed	Armstrong World Industries claims
Executive director	Thomas Florence
Claim administrator	Delaware Claims Processing Facility
Trust website	www.armstrongworldasbestostrust.com

Trustees and Advisors

Position	Name	Affiliation
Trustee	Anne Ferazzi	unknown
Trustee	Harry Huge	Harry Huge Law Firm, LLP
Trustee	Richard Neville	JAMS
FCR	Dean Trafelet	Retired Cook County Circuit Court Judge
TAC Member	John Cooney	Cooney & Conway
TAC Member	Joseph Rice	Motley Rice, LLC
TAC Member	Perry Weitz	Weitz & Luxenburg
TAC Member	Russell Budd	Baron & Budd, P.C.
TAC Member	Steven Kazan	Kazan, McClain, Abrams, Fernandez, Lyons, Farrise & Greenwood, P.C.
Trust Counsel	Carl Kunz	Morris James LLP
Trust Counsel	Kevin E. Irwin	Keating Muething & Klekamp PLL
Trust Counsel	Sue A. Erhart	Keating Muething & Klekamp PLL
Trust Counsel	Jennifer Morales	Keating Muething & Klekamp PLL

Estimated Initial Funding of Trust ($ millions)

	Funding for Claims Paid Through Trust	Funding for Claims Paid Outside Trust
Cash from debtor(s)	738.5	0
Stock from debtors(s)	1,323.1	0
Insurance settlements	0.0	0
Other assets	0.0	0
Total	2,061.6	0

Armstrong World Industries Asbestos Personal Injury Settlement Trust (continued)

Trust Financial Statement ($)

	Pre-2006	2006 [a]	2007	2008
Beginning trust assets	0	0	2,308,676,202	2,235,068,939
Additions				
Cash from debtors	0	n.a.	0	0
Stock from debtors	0	n.a.	0	0
Insurance settlements	0	n.a.	0	0
Investment gains	0	n.a.	-75,021,580	-767,109,978
Investment income	0	n.a.	26,550,958	27,117,624
Other additions	0	n.a.	0	166,416,660
Deductions		n.a.		
Trust expenses	0	n.a.	12,329,548	17,933,038
Claim processing costs	0	n.a.	3,069,070	7,484,240
Investment fees	0	n.a.	1,625,351	3,064,159
All other expenses	0	n.a.	7,635,127	7,384,639
Taxes	0	n.a.	0	19,339,059
Claim payments	0	0	12,807,093	135,999,706
Other deductions	0	n.a.	0	0
Ending trust assets	0	2,308,676,202	2,235,068,939	1,488,221,442
Gross claimant compensation as a percentage of deductions				
Lower bound	–	0.0%	50.9%	78.5%
Upper bound	–	0.0%	50.9%	78.5%

[a] Financial statements for 2006 were restated, but restated figures not available.

Claim Valuation for Armstrong World Industries claims

Disease level	Scheduled Value	Average Value	Maximum Value
Mesothelioma	110,000	130,500	400,000
Lung Cancer 1	42,500	43,800	150,000
Lung Cancer 2	n.appl.	15,000	50,000
Other Cancer	21,500	21,800	75,000
Severe Asbestosis	42,500	44,300	140,000
Asbestosis / Pleural Disease II	9,700	10,100	20,000
Asbestosis / Pleural Disease I	3,700	4,200	10,000
Other Asbestos Disease	400 *	n.appl.	n.appl.

Payment percentage	
Initial payment percentage	20.0%
Current payment percentage	20.0%

Claim payment ratio	
Malignancies and severe asbestosis	65.0%
Asbestosis and pleural disease	35.0%

*Payment percentage does not apply

Armstrong World Industries Asbestos Personal Injury Settlement Trust (continued)

Claim Activity

	Pre-2006	2006	2007	2008	Total
Pre-petition pending and post-petition claims					
Claims filed					
Malignant	0	0	18,891	16,488	35,379
Non-malignant	0	0	106,349	81,422	187,771
Not specified	0	0	83	0	83
All disease types	0	0	125,323	97,910	223,233
Claims paid					
Malignant	0	0	139	4,374	4,513
Non-malignant	0	0	1,834	33,795	35,629
Not specified	0	0	0	0	0
All disease types	0	0	1,973	38,169	40,142
Claim payments ($)					
Malignant	0	0	2,143,641	73,146,762	75,290,403
Non-malignant	0	0	2,663,452	51,433,773	54,097,225
Not specified	0	0	0	0	0
All disease types	0	0	4,807,093	124,580,535	129,387,628
Average payment per claim ($)					
Malignant	–	–	15,422	16,723	16,683
Non-malignant	–	–	1,452	1,522	1,518
Not specified	–	–	–	–	–
All disease types	–	–	2,436	3,264	3,223
Claims settled but not paid pre-petition					
Claims filed					
Malignant	0	0	0	0	0
Non-malignant	0	0	0	0	0
Not specified	0	0	0	0	0
All disease types	0	0	0	0	0
Claims paid					
Malignant	0	0	0	0	0
Non-malignant	0	0	0	0	0
Not specified	0	0	0	0	0
All disease types	0	0	0	0	0
Claim payments ($)					
Malignant	0	0	0	0	0
Non-malignant	0	0	0	0	0
Not specified	0	0	0	0	0
All disease types	0	0	0	0	0
Average payment per claim ($)					
Malignant	–	–	–	–	–
Non-malignant	–	–	–	–	–
Not specified	–	–	–	–	–
All disease types	–	–	–	–	–

Armstrong World Industries Asbestos Personal Injury Settlement Trust (continued)

Claim Activity by Disease Level

	2006	2007	2008	Total
Pre-petition pending and post-petition claims				
Claims paid				
Mesothelioma	0	52	n.a.	n.a.
Lung cancer 1	0	52	n.a.	n.a.
Lung cancer 2	0	0	n.a.	n.a.
Other cancer	0	35	n.a.	n.a.
Severe asbestosis	0	6	n.a.	n.a.
Asbestosis/pleural disease 1	0	536	n.a.	n.a.
Asbestosis/pleural disease 2	0	1,289	n.a.	n.a.
Other	0	3	n.a.	n.a.
Unknown	0	0	38,169	38,169
Claims payments ($)				
Mesothelioma	0	1,376,005	n.a.	n.a.
Lung cancer 1	0	567,161	n.a.	n.a.
Lung cancer 2	0	0	n.a.	n.a.
Other cancer	0	200,474	n.a.	n.a.
Severe asbestosis	0	68,139	n.a.	n.a.
Asbestosis/pleural disease 1	0	1,346,233	n.a.	n.a.
Asbestosis/pleural disease 2	0	1,247,880	n.a.	n.a.
Other	0	1,200	n.a.	n.a.
Unknown	0	0	124,579,935	124,579,935
Average payment per claim ($)				
Mesothelioma	–	26,462	–	–
Lung cancer 1	–	10,907	–	–
Lung cancer 2	–	–	–	–
Other cancer	–	5,728	–	–
Severe asbestosis	–	11,356	–	–
Asbestosis/pleural disease 1	–	2,512	–	–
Asbestosis/pleural disease 2	–	968	–	–
Other	–	400	–	–
Unknown	–	–	3,264	3,264

Armstrong World Industries Asbestos Personal Injury Settlement Trust (continued)

Claim Approval Criteria for	Armstrong World Industries claims							
	Meso	LC1	LC2	OC	SA	AP1	AP2	OAD
1. Diagnosis requirement (one or more of checked items satisfies requirement)								
a. Physical exam	✔	✔	✔	✔	✔	✔	✔	✔
b. Pathology	✔	✔	✔	✔	✔	✔	✔	✔
c. Medical document review								
2. ILO or x-ray requirement								
a. ILO reading		1/0		1/0	2/1	1/0	1/0	1/0
OR b. X-ray, CT scan, or pathology showing one or more of the checked conditions								
(1) Bilateral interstitial fibrosis		✔		✔		✔	✔	✔
(2) Bilateral pleural plaques		✔		✔		✔	✔	✔
(3) Bilateral pleural thickening		✔		✔		✔	✔	✔
(4) Bilateral pleural calcification		✔		✔		✔	✔	✔
3. Pulmonary function test requirement								
a. TLC < (% of normal)					65	80		
AND FEV1/FVC ratio >								
OR b. DLCO < (% of normal)								
AND FEV1/FVC ratio >								
OR c. FVC < (% of normal)					65	80		
AND FEV1/FVC ratio >					0.65	0.65		
4. Causation statement requirement	No	Yes	Yes	Yes	Yes	Yes	No	No
5. Latency and exposure requirements								
a. Latency	10 yr	10 yr	10 yr	10 yr	10 yr	10 yr	10 yr	10 yr
b. Company exposure prior to 1983	1 day	6 mo	1 day	6 mo	6 mo	6 mo	6 mo	1 day
c. Occupational exposure								
(1) Total		5 yr		5 yr	5 yr	5 yr	5 yr	
(2) Prior to 1983	1 day	2 yr	1 day	2 yr	2 yr	2 yr	6 mo	1 day

ASARCO LLC Asbestos Personal Injury Settlement Trust

ASARCO LLC Asbestos Personal Injury Settlement Trust

Bankruptcy Court and Trust Administrative Information

Debtor(s)	ASARCO, LLC		
	Lake Asbestos of Quebec, Ltd.		
Bankruptcy filing date	8/9/05	Confirmation date	11/13/09
Bankruptcy court	Bankr. S.D. Tex.	Bankruptcy judge	Richard Schmidt
Trust status	Active - Pending Claims Processing		
Date trust established	2009		
Classes of claims processed	ASARCO claims		
Claim administrator	Unknown		
Trust website	Unknown		

Trustees and Advisors

Position	Name	Affiliation
FCR	Robert Pate	Law Office of Robert C. Pate
Trust Counsel	Sander Esserman	Stutzman, Bromberg, Esserman & Plifka
TAC Counsel	Steven Felsenthal	Stutzman, Bromberg, Esserman & Plifka

Estimated Initial Funding of Trust ($ millions)

	Funding for Claims Paid Through Trust	Funding for Claims Paid Outside Trust
Cash from debtor(s)	527.5	0
Stock from debtors(s)	0.0	0
Insurance settlements	22.8	0
Other assets	280.0	0
Total	830.3	0

ASARCO LLC Asbestos Personal Injury Settlement Trust (continued)

Trust Financial Statement ($)	Pre-2006	2006	2007	2008
Beginning trust assets				
Additions				
Cash from debtors				
Stock from debtors				
Insurance settlements				
Investment gains				
Investment income				
Other additions				
Deductions	TRUST NOT ESTABLISHED UNTIL 2009			
Trust expenses				
Claim processing costs				
Investment fees				
All other expenses				
Taxes				
Claim payments				
Other deductions				
Ending trust assets				
Gross claimant compensation as a percentage of deductions				
Lower bound	–	–	–	–
Upper bound	–	–	–	–

Claim Valuation for	ASARCO claims		
	Scheduled	Average	Maximum
Disease level	Value	Value	Value
Mesothelioma	170,000	280,000	900,000
Lung Cancer 1	60,000	90,000	150,000
Lung Cancer 2	n.appl.	15,000	35,000
Other Cancer	20,000	32,000	75,000
Severe Asbestosis	50,000	70,000	125,000
Asbestosis / Pleural Disease II	7,500	8,000	25,000
Asbestosis / Pleural Disease I	3,000	n.appl.	n.appl.
Other Asbestos Disease	400	n.appl.	n.appl.

Payment percentage	
Initial payment percentage	22.0%
Current payment percentage	22.0%

Claim payment ratio	
Malignancies and severe asbestosis	90.0%
Asbestosis and pleural disease	10.0%

ASARCO LLC Asbestos Personal Injury Settlement Trust (continued)

Claim Activity

	Pre-2006	2006	2007	2008	Total
Pre-petition pending and post-petition claims					
Claims filed					
Malignant					
Non-malignant					
Not specified					
All disease types					
Claims paid					
Malignant					
Non-malignant					
Not specified					
All disease types					
Claim payments ($)					
Malignant					
Non-malignant					
Not specified					
All disease types					
Average payment per claim ($)					
Malignant					
Non-malignant					
Not specified					
All disease types					
		TRUST NOT ESTABLISHED UNTIL 2009			
Claims settled but not paid pre-petition					
Claims filed					
Malignant					
Non-malignant					
Not specified					
All disease types					
Claims paid					
Malignant					
Non-malignant					
Not specified					
All disease types					
Claim payments ($)					
Malignant					
Non-malignant					
Not specified					
All disease types					
Average payment per claim ($)					
Malignant					
Non-malignant					
Not specified					
All disease types					

ASARCO LLC Asbestos Personal Injury Settlement Trust (continued)

Claim Approval Criteria for	ASARCO							
	Meso	LC1	LC2	OC	SA	AP1	AP2	Other
1. Diagnosis requirement (one or more of checked items satisfies requirement)								
a. Physical exam	✔	✔	✔	✔	✔	✔	✔	✔
b. Pathology	✔	✔	✔	✔	✔	✔	✔	✔
c. Medical document review								
2. ILO or x-ray requirement								
a. ILO reading	0	1/0	0	1/0	2/1	1/0	1/0	1/0
OR b. X-ray, CT scan, or pathology showing one or more of the checked conditions								
(1) Bilateral interstitial fibrosis		✔		✔		✔	✔	✔
(2) Bilateral pleural plaques		✔		✔		✔	✔	✔
(3) Bilateral pleural thickening		✔		✔		✔	✔	✔
(4) Bilateral pleural calcification		✔		✔		✔	✔	✔
3. Pulmonary function test requirement								
a. TLC < (% of normal)					65	80		
AND FEV1/FVC ratio >								
OR b. DLCO < (% of normal)								
AND FEV1/FVC ratio >								
OR c. FVC < (% of normal)					65	80		
AND FEV1/FVC ratio >					0.65	0.65		
4. Causation statement requirement	No	Yes	Yes	Yes	Yes	Yes	No	No
5. Latency and exposure requirements								
a. Latency	10 yr	10 yr	10 yr	10 yr	10 yr	10 yr	10 yr	10 yr
b. Company exposure prior to 1983	1 day	6 mo	1 day	6 mo	6 mo	6 mo	6 mo	1 day
c. Occupational exposure								
(1) Total		5 yr		5 yr	5 yr	5 yr	5 yr	
(2) Prior to 1983								

Babcock & Wilcox Company Asbestos Personal Injury Settlement Trust

Babcock & Wilcox Company Asbestos Personal Injury Settlement Trust

Bankruptcy Court and Trust Administrative Information

Debtor(s)	Babcock & Wilcox Co.		
Bankruptcy filing date	2/22/00	Confirmation date	1/17/06
Bankruptcy court	Bankr. E.D. La.	Bankruptcy judge	Jerry Brown
Trust status	Active		
Date trust established	2/22/06		
Classes of claims processed	Babcock & Wilcox Company claims		
Claim administrator	Delaware Claims Processing Facility		
Trust website	www.bwasbestostrust.com		

Trustees and Advisors

Position	Name	Affiliation
Managing Trustee	James McMonagle	Vorys, Sater, Seymour and Pease LLP
Trustee	Jack Marionneaux	Retired Louisiana state judge
Trustee	Philip Pahigian	Retired from Wilentz, Goldman & Spitzer
FCR	Eric Green	Resolutions, LLC
TAC Member	J. Burton Leblanc	LeBlanc & Waddell
TAC Member	Joseph Rice	Motley Rice, LLC
TAC Member	Mark Meyer	Goldberg, Persky & White, P.C.
TAC Member	Perry Weitz	Weitz & Luxenburg
TAC Member	Peter Kraus	Waters & Kraus, LLP
TAC Member	Russell Budd	Baron & Budd, P.C.
TAC Member	Steven Kazan	Kazan, McClain, Abrams, Fernandez, Lyons, Farrise & Greenwood, P.C.
Trust Counsel	Douglas A. Campbell	Campbell & Levine, LLC
Trust Counsel	Philip E. Milch	Campbell & Levine, LLC
Trust Counsel	Marla R. Eskin	Campbell & Levine, LLC
TAC Counsel	Elihu Inselbuch	Caplin & Drysdale, Chartered
FCR Counsel	Jim Patton	Young Conaway Stargatt & Taylor, LLP

Estimated Initial Funding of Trust ($ millions)

	Funding for Claims Paid Through Trust	Funding for Claims Paid Outside Trust
Cash from debtor(s)	955.0	0
Stock from debtors(s)	0.0	0
Insurance settlements	890.0	0
Other assets	0.0	0
Total	1,845.0	0

Babcock & Wilcox Company Asbestos Personal Injury Settlement Trust (continued)

Trust Financial Statement ($)

	Pre-2006	2006	2007	2008
Beginning trust assets	0	0	1,638,859,492	1,589,295,140
Additions				
Cash from debtors	0	955,000,000	0	0
Stock from debtors	0	0	0	0
Insurance settlements	0	710,534,312	136,879,441	61,327,500
Investment gains	0	4,489,477	30,935,297	-142,463,875
Investment income	0	36,283,723	62,354,130	47,195,394
Other additions	0	19,974	0	0
Deductions				
Trust expenses	0	8,076,564	15,704,642	13,736,870
Claim processing costs	0	1,922,264	7,546,757	6,372,630
Investment fees	0	685,766	3,503,983	2,493,258
All other expenses	0	6,154,300	8,157,885	4,870,982
Taxes	0	9,484,867	-307	-3,207,995
Claim payments	0	48,206,563	264,028,885	381,657,122
Other deductions	0	1,700,000	0	0
Ending trust assets	0	1,638,859,492	1,589,295,140	1,163,168,162
Gross claimant compensation as a percentage of deductions				
Lower bound	–	71.5%	94.4%	96.5%
Upper bound	–	74.0%	94.4%	96.5%

Claim Valuation for Babcock & Wilcox Company claims

Disease level	Scheduled Value	Average Value	Maximum Value
Mesothelioma	90,000	120,000	400,000
Lung Cancer 1	35,000	45,000	150,000
Lung Cancer 2	n.appl.	15,000	50,000
Other Cancer	18,500	22,500	75,000
Severe Asbestosis	35,000	37,000	15,000
Asbestosis / Pleural Disease II	10,000	n.appl.	n.appl.
Asbestosis / Pleural Disease I	5,000	n.appl.	n.appl.
Other Asbestos Disease	250 *	n.appl.	n.appl.

Payment percentage	
Initial payment percentage	34.0%
Current payment percentage	15.0%

Claim payment ratio	
Malignancies and severe asbestosis	62.0%
Asbestosis and pleural disease	38.0%

*Payment percentage does not apply

Babcock & Wilcox Company Asbestos Personal Injury Settlement Trust (continued)

Claim Activity					
	Pre-2006	2006	2007	2008	Total
Pre-petition pending and post-petition claims					
Claims filed					
Malignant	0	n.a.	n.a.	n.a.	n.a.
Non-malignant	0	n.a.	n.a.	n.a.	n.a.
Not specified	0	103,017	79,698	58,387	241,102
All disease types	0	103,017	79,698	58,387	241,102
Claims paid					
Malignant	0	63	5,098	11,081	16,242
Non-malignant	0	1,009	30,382	36,647	68,038
Not specified	0	0	0	0	0
All disease types	0	1,072	35,480	47,728	84,280
Claim payments ($)					
Malignant	0	1,974,000	83,528,970	285,345,000	370,847,970
Non-malignant	0	2,726,000	146,175,698	95,115,000	244,016,698
Not specified	0	0	0	0	0
All disease types	0	4,700,000	229,704,668	380,460,000	614,864,668
Average payment per claim ($)					
Malignant	–	31,333	16,385	25,751	22,833
Non-malignant	–	2,702	4,811	2,595	3,586
Not specified	–	–	–	–	–
All disease types	–	4,384	6,474	7,971	7,295
Claims settled but not paid pre-petition					
Claims filed					
Malignant	0	n.a.	0	0	n.a.
Non-malignant	0	n.a.	0	0	n.a.
Not specified	0	7,380	0	0	7,380
All disease types	0	7,380	0	0	7,380
Claims paid					
Malignant	0	419	285	31	735
Non-malignant	0	5,570	2,662	138	8,370
Not specified	0	0	0	0	0
All disease types	0	5,989	2,947	169	9,105
Claim payments ($)					
Malignant	0	16,995,000	11,900,000	793,000	29,688,000
Non-malignant	0	13,905,000	11,900,000	397,000	26,202,000
Not specified	0	0	0	0	0
All disease types	0	30,900,000	23,800,000	1,190,000	55,890,000
Average payment per claim ($)					
Malignant	–	40,561	41,754	25,581	40,392
Non-malignant	–	2,496	4,470	2,877	3,130
Not specified	–	–	–	–	–
All disease types	–	5,159	8,076	7,041	6,138

Babcock & Wilcox Company Asbestos Personal Injury Settlement Trust (continued)

Claim Approval Criteria for	Babcock & Wilcox Company claims							
	Meso	LC1	LC2	OC	SA	AP1	AP2	OAD
1. Diagnosis requirement (one or more of checked items satisfies requirement)								
a. Physical exam	✔	✔	✔	✔	✔	✔	✔	✔
b. Pathology	✔	✔	✔	✔	✔	✔	✔	✔
c. Medical document review								
2. ILO or x-ray requirement								
a. ILO reading		1/0		1/0	2/1	1/0	1/0	1/0
OR b. X-ray, CT scan, or pathology showing one or more of the checked conditions								
(1) Bilateral interstitial fibrosis		✔		✔		✔	✔	✔
(2) Bilateral pleural plaques		✔		✔		✔	✔	✔
(3) Bilateral pleural thickening		✔		✔		✔	✔	✔
(4) Bilateral pleural calcification		✔		✔		✔	✔	✔
3. Pulmonary function test requirement								
a. TLC < (% of normal)					65	80		
AND FEV1/FVC ratio >								
OR b. DLCO < (% of normal)								
AND FEV1/FVC ratio >								
OR c. FVC < (% of normal)					65	80		
AND FEV1/FVC ratio >					0.65	0.65		
4. Causation statement requirement	No	Yes	Yes	Yes	Yes	No	Yes	No
5. Latency and exposure requirements								
a. Latency	10 yr	10 yr	10 yr	10 yr	10 yr	10 yr	10 yr	10 yr
b. Company exposure prior to 1983	1 day	6 mo	1 day	6 mo	6 mo	6 mo	6 mo	1 day
c. Occupational exposure								
(1) Total		5 yr		5 yr	5 yr	5 yr	5 yr	
(2) Prior to 1983	1 day	2 yr	1 day	2 yr	2 yr	2 yr	6 mo	1 day

Burns and Roe Asbestos Personal Injury Settlement Trust

Burns and Roe Asbestos Personal Injury Settlement Trust

Bankruptcy Court and Trust Administrative Information

Debtor(s)	Burns and Roe Enterprises, Inc.
	Burns and Roe Construction Group, Inc.
Bankruptcy filing date	12/4/00 for Burns and Roe Enterprises
	10/12/05 for Burns and Roe Construction Group
Confirmation date	2/20/09
Bankruptcy court	Bankr. D. N.J.
Bankruptcy judge	Rosemary Gambardella
Trust status	Active
Date trust established	7/16/09
Classes of claims processed	Burns and Roe claims
Claim administrator	Unknown
Trust website	Unknown

Trustees and Advisors

Position	Name	Affiliation
Trustee	Alfred Wolin	Saiber LLC
FCR	Anthony Calascibetta	Wiss & Company, LLP
TAC Member	Deirdre Woulfe Pacheco	Wilentz, Goldman & Spitzer
TAC Member	Lisa Busch	Weitz & Luxenburg
Trust Counsel	Frances Gecker	Frank/Gecker LLP

Estimated Initial Funding of Trust ($ millions)

	Funding for Claims Paid Through Trust	Funding for Claims Paid Outside Trust
Cash from debtor(s)	0.0	0
Stock from debtors(s)	0.0	0
Insurance settlements	162.8	0
Other assets	9.3	0
Total	172.1	0

Burns and Roe Asbestos Personal Injury Settlement Trust (continued)

Trust Financial Statement ($)

	Pre-2006	2006	2007	2008
Beginning trust assets				
Additions				
Cash from debtors				
Stock from debtors				
Insurance settlements				
Investment gains				
Investment income				
Other additions				
Deductions		TRUST NOT ESTABLISHED UNTIL 2009		
Trust expenses				
Claim processing costs				
Investment fees				
All other expenses				
Taxes				
Claim payments				
Other deductions				
Ending trust assets				
Gross claimant compensation as a percentage of deductions				
Lower bound	–	–	–	–
Upper bound	–	–	–	–

Claim Valuation for Burns and Roe claims

Disease level	Scheduled Value	Average Value	Maximum Value
Mesothelioma	60,000	90,000	500,000
Lung Cancer 1	30,000	40,000	200,000
Lung Cancer 2	n.appl.	15,000	50,000
Other Cancer	15,000	18,500	50,000
Severe Asbestosis	25,000	27,000	125,000
Asbestosis / Plueral Disease II	5,000	5,400	15,000
Asbestosis / Plueral Disease I	2,000	2,300	8,000
Other Asbestos Disease	200 *	n.appl.	n.appl.

Payment percentage	
Initial payment percentage	25.0%
Current payment percentage	25.0%

Claim payment ratio	
Malignancies and severe asbestosis	60.0%
Asbestosis and pleural disease	40.0%

*Payment percentage does not apply

Burns and Roe Asbestos Personal Injury Settlement Trust (continued)

Claim Activity

	Pre-2006	2006	2007	2008	Total
Pre-petition pending and post-petition claims					
Claims filed					
Malignant					
Non-malignant					
Not specified					
All disease types					
Claims paid					
Malignant					
Non-malignant					
Not specified					
All disease types					
Claim payments ($)					
Malignant					
Non-malignant					
Not specified					
All disease types					
Average payment per claim ($)					
Malignant					
Non-malignant					
Not specified					
All disease types					

TRUST NOT ESTABLISHED UNTIL 2009

Claims settled but not paid pre-petition					
Claims filed					
Malignant					
Non-malignant					
Not specified					
All disease types					
Claims paid					
Malignant					
Non-malignant					
Not specified					
All disease types					
Claim payments ($)					
Malignant					
Non-malignant					
Not specified					
All disease types					
Average payment per claim ($)					
Malignant					
Non-malignant					
Not specified					
All disease types					

Burns and Roe Asbestos Personal Injury Settlement Trust (continued)

Claim Approval Criteria for	Burns and Roe claims							
	Meso	LC1	LC2	OC	SA	AP2	AP1	OAD
1. Diagnosis requirement (one or more of checked items satisfies requirement)								
a. Physical exam	✔	✔	✔	✔	✔	✔	✔	✔
b. Pathology	✔	✔	✔	✔	✔	✔	✔	✔
c. Medical document review								
2. ILO or x-ray requirement								
a. ILO reading		1/0		1/0	2/1	1/0	1/0	1/0
OR b. X-ray, CT scan, or pathology showing one or more of the checked conditions								
(1) Bilateral interstitial fibrosis		✔		✔		✔	✔	✔
(2) Bilateral pleural plaques		✔		✔		✔	✔	✔
(3) Bilateral pleural thickening		✔		✔		✔	✔	✔
(4) Bilateral pleural calcification		✔		✔		✔	✔	✔
3. Pulmonary function test requirement								
a. TLC < (% of normal)					65	80		
AND FEV1/FVC ratio >								
OR b. DLCO < (% of normal)								
AND FEV1/FVC ratio >								
OR c. FVC < (% of normal)					65	80		
AND FEV1/FVC ratio >					0.65	0.65		
4. Causation statement requirement	No	Yes	Yes	Yes	Yes	Yes	No	No
5. Latency and exposure requirements								
a. Latency	10 yr	10 yr	10 yr	10 yr	10 yr	10 yr	10 yr	10 yr
b. Company exposure prior to 1983	1 day	6 mo	1 day	6 mo	6 mo	6 mo	6 mo	1 day
c. Occupational exposure								
(1) Total		5 yr		5 yr	5 yr	5 yr	5 yr	
(2) Prior to 1983	1 day	2 yr	1 day	2 yr	2 yr	2 yr	6 mo	1 day

Celotex Asbestos Settlement Trust

Celotex Asbestos Settlement Trust

Bankruptcy Court and Trust Administrative Information

Debtor(s)	Celotex Corp.		
	Carey Canada, Inc.		
Bankruptcy filing date	10/12/90	Confirmation date	12/6/96
Bankruptcy court	Bankr. M.D. Fla.	Bankruptcy judge	Paul Glenn

Trust status	Active
Date trust established	5/30/97
Classes of claims processed	Celotex claims
Executive Director	Thomas Florence
Claim administrator	Delaware Claims Processing Facility
Trust website	www.celotextrust.com

Trustees and Advisors

Position	Name	Affiliation
Trustee	Frank Andrews	Retired Texas state judge
Trustee	James Stevens	Self employed
Trustee	Sharon Meadows	Credit Suisse
FCR	James Patton	Young Conaway Stargatt & Taylor LLP
TAC Member	Joseph Rice	Motley Rice, LLC
TAC Member	Russell Budd	Baron & Budd, P.C.
TAC Member	Steven Kazan	Kazan, McClain, Abrams, Fernandez, Lyons, Farrise & Greenwood, P.C.
TAC Member	Gary Kendall	Michie Hamlett Lowry Rasmussen & Tweel PLLC
Trust Counsel	Kevin Irwin	Keating Muething & Klekamp PLL

Estimated Initial Funding of Trust ($ millions)

	Funding for Claims Paid Through Trust	Funding for Claims Paid Outside Trust
Cash from debtor(s)	221.5	0
Stock from debtors(s)	526.8	0
Insurance settlements	141.2	0
Other assets	356.1	0
Total	1,245.6	0

Celotex Asbestos Settlement Trust (continued)

Trust Financial Statement ($)

	Pre-2006	2006	2007	2008
Beginning trust assets	0	706,258,685	705,846,896	654,761,806
Additions				
Cash from debtors	277,812,074	0	0	0
Stock from debtors	526,797,000	0	0	0
Insurance settlements	469,159,555	63,828,432	31,242,206	15,489,901
Investment gains	-120,877,428	21,109,186	10,192,239	-79,104,447
Investment income	163,962,952	32,061,592	29,735,870	22,324,671
Other additions	356,682,373	1,995,433	3,398,335	3,701
Deductions				
Trust expenses	147,054,208	16,030,186	9,948,079	8,733,376
Claim processing costs	42,756,824	3,858,700	3,200,895	2,874,420
Investment fees	10,576,567	2,128,930	2,132,523	1,727,530
All other expenses	93,720,817	10,042,556	4,614,661	4,131,426
Taxes	147,732	-426,782	0	0
Claim payments	566,850,491	98,942,480	108,276,558	69,923,986
Other deductions	246,697,260	4,860,548	7,429,103	-2,484,443
Ending trust assets	706,258,685	705,846,896	654,761,806	537,302,713
Gross claimant compensation as a percentage of deductions				
Lower bound	59.0%	82.9%	86.2%	88.9%
Upper bound	84.7%	86.9%	92.1%	88.9%

Claim Valuation for Celotex claims

Disease level	Scheduled Value	Average [a] Value	Maximum Value
Mesothelioma	11,000 *	130,000	325,000
Lung Cancer 2	3,200 *	58,000	260,000
Lung Cancer 1	n.appl.	39,000	260,000
Other Cancer	1,900 *	26,000	130,000
Disabling Bilateral Interstitial Lung Disease	n.appl.	32,000	192,000
Nondisabling Bilateral Interstitial Lung Disec	1,300 *	16,000	25,600
Bilateral Pleural Disease	650 *	8,000	20,000

Payment percentage	
Initial payment percentage	12.0%
Current payment percentage	14.1%

Claim payment ratio	
Malignancies and severe asbestosis	n.appl.
Asbestosis and pleural disease	n.appl.

*Payment percentage does not apply

[a] Considers only claims that go through the individual review process.

Celotex Asbestos Settlement Trust (continued)

Claim Activity					
	Pre-2006	2006	2007	2008	Total
Pre-petition pending and post-petition claims					
Claims filed					
Malignant	n.a.	n.a.	n.a.	n.a.	n.a.
Non-malignant	n.a.	n.a.	n.a.	n.a.	n.a.
Not specified	625,000	14,185	12,114	8,000	659,299
All disease types	625,000	14,185	12,114	8,000	659,299
Claims paid					
Malignant	n.a.	n.a.	n.a.	n.a.	n.a.
Non-malignant	n.a.	n.a.	n.a.	n.a.	n.a.
Not specified	280,256	28,658	18,147	18,778	345,839
All disease types	280,256	28,658	18,147	18,778	345,839
Claim payments ($)					
Malignant	n.a.	n.a.	n.a.	n.a.	n.a.
Non-malignant	n.a.	n.a.	n.a.	n.a.	n.a.
Not specified	462,965,576	112,559,550	85,657,668	111,328,609 [a]	772,511,403
All disease types	462,965,576	112,559,550	85,657,668	111,328,609	772,511,403
Average payment per claim ($)					
Malignant	–	–	–	–	–
Non-malignant	–	–	–	–	–
Not specified	1,652	3,928	4,720	4,278 [b]	2,234
All disease types	1,652	3,928	4,720	4,278	2,234
Claims settled but not paid pre-petition					
Claims filed					
Malignant	n.a.	n.a.	n.a.	n.a.	n.a.
Non-malignant	n.a.	n.a.	n.a.	n.a.	n.a.
Not specified	n.a.	n.a.	n.a.	n.a.	n.a.
All disease types	n.a.	n.a.	n.a.	n.a.	n.a.
Claims paid					
Malignant	n.a.	n.a.	n.a.	n.a.	n.a.
Non-malignant	n.a.	n.a.	n.a.	n.a.	n.a.
Not specified	1,859	0	1	0	1,860
All disease types	1,859	0	1	0	1,860
Claim payments ($)					
Malignant	n.a.	n.a.	n.a.	n.a.	n.a.
Non-malignant	n.a.	n.a.	n.a.	n.a.	n.a.
Not specified	2,566,267	0	12,973	0	2,579,240
All disease types	2,566,267	0	12,973	0	2,579,240
Average payment per claim ($)					
Malignant	–	–	–	–	–
Non-malignant	–	–	–	–	–
Not specified	1,380	–	12,973	–	1,387
All disease types	1,380	–	12,973	–	1,387

[a] Includes $31.0 million in payments on pre-2008 claims
[b] Excludes $31.0 million in payments for past claims

Celotex Asbestos Settlement Trust (continued)

Claim Approval Criteria for	Celotex claims						
	Meso	LC1	LC2	OC	DBILD	NDBILD	BPD
1. Diagnosis requirement (one or more of checked items satisfies requirement)							
a. Physical exam	✔	✔	✔	✔	✔	✔	✔
b. Pathology	✔	✔	✔	✔	✔	✔	✔
c. Medical document review							
2. ILO or x-ray requirement							
a. ILO reading							
OR b. X-ray, CT scan, or pathology showing one or more of the checked conditions							
(1) Bilateral interstitial fibrosis		✔		✔	✔	✔	
(2) Bilateral pleural plaques		✔		✔			✔
(3) Bilateral pleural thickening		✔		✔			✔
(4) Bilateral pleural calcification							
3. Pulmonary function test requirement							
a. TLC < (% of normal)					80		
AND FEV1/FVC ratio >							
OR b. DLCO < (% of normal)					80		
AND FEV1/FVC ratio >							
OR c. FVC < (% of normal)					80		
AND FEV1/FVC ratio >							
4. Causation statement requirement	No	No	No	No	Yes	Yes	No
5. Latency and exposure requirements							
a. Latency	10 yr	10 yr	10 yr	10 yr	10 yr	10 yr	10 yr
b. Company exposure prior to 1983	1 day	1 day	1 day	1 day	1 day	1 day	1 day
c. Occupational exposure							
(1) Total		3 yr	15 yr	3 yr			
(2) Prior to 1983							

Combustion Engineering 524(g) Asbestos PI Trust

Combustion Engineering 524(g) Asbestos PI Trust

Bankruptcy Court and Trust Administrative Information

Debtor(s)	Combustion Engineering		
Bankruptcy filing date	2/17/03	Confirmation date	3/1/06
Bankruptcy court	Bankr. D. Del.	Bankruptcy judge	Judith Fitzgerald

Trust status	Active
Date trust established	2006
Classes of claims processed	Combustion Engineering claims
Claim administrator	Verus Claims Services
Trust website	www.cetrust.org

Trustees and Advisors

Position	Name	Affiliation
Managing Trustee	Richard Neville	Retired Illinois state judge
Trustee	Ken Kawaichi	Retired California state judge
Trustee	Ellen Pryor	Southern Methodist University, Dedman School of Law
FCR	David Austern	Claims Resolution Management Corporation
TAC Member	Brent Coon	Brent Coon & Associates
TAC Member	John Cooney	Cooney & Conway
TAC Member	Matthew Bergman	Bergman Draper & Frockt, PLLC
TAC Member	Russell Budd	Baron & Budd, P.C.
TAC Member	Steven Kazan	Kazan, McClain, Abrams, Fernandez, Lyons, Farrise & Greenwood, P.C.
TAC Counsel	Joseph Frank	Frank Gecker, LLP
TAC Counsel	Frances Gecker	Frank Gecker, LLP
Trust Counsel	Sander Esserman	Stutzman, Bromberg, Esserman & Plifka
Trust Counsel	Steven Felsenthal	Stutzman, Bromberg, Esserman & Plifka
Trust Counsel	Daniel Hogan	The Hogan Firm
FCR Counsel	Roger Frankel	Orrick, Herrington & Sutcliffe LLP
FCR Counsel	Richard H. Wyron	Orrick, Herrington & Sutcliffe LLP

Estimated Initial Funding of Trust ($ millions)

	Funding for Claims Paid Through Trust	Funding for Claims Paid Outside Trust
Cash from debtor(s)	574.0	507.0
Stock from debtors(s)	402.6	0.0
Insurance settlements	266.6	0.0
Other assets	0.0	0.0
Total	1,243.2	507.0

Combustion Engineering 524(g) Asbestos PI Trust (continued)

Trust Financial Statement ($)

	Pre-2006	2006	2007	2008
Beginning trust assets	0	0	1,261,773,054	1,113,744,608
Additions				
Cash from debtors	0	224,000,000	0	0
Stock from debtors	0	402,569,537	0	0
Insurance settlements	0	266,644,237	-47,782,000	13,160,048
Investment gains	0	24,464,758	6,087,983	-120,423,359
Investment income	0	18,298,599	30,196,969	41,236,528
Other additions	0	350,000,000	0	0
Deductions				
Trust expenses	0	6,303,594	9,509,001	5,111,335
Claim processing costs	0	149,731	848,103	746,596
Investment fees	0	874,022	1,630,407	1,920,640
All other expenses	0	5,279,841	7,030,491	2,444,099
Taxes	0	1,847,647	0	0
Claim payments	0	16,052,836	127,022,397	33,268,055
Other deductions	0	0	0	0
Ending trust assets	0	1,261,773,054	1,113,744,608	1,009,338,435
Gross claimant compensation as a percentage of deductions				
Lower bound	–	66.3%	93.0%	86.7%
Upper bound	–	66.3%	93.0%	86.7%

Claim Valuation for — Combustion Engineering claims

Disease level	Scheduled Value	Average Value	Maximum Value
Mesothelioma	75,000	95,000	400,000
Lung Cancer 1	25,000	35,000	150,000
Lung Cancer 2	n.appl.	15,000	50,000
Other Cancer	6,000	9,000	75,000
Severe Asbestosis	25,000	40,000	150,000
Asbestosis / Pleural Disease II	4,800	n.appl.	n.appl.
Asbestosis / Pleural Disease I	1,800	n.appl.	n.appl.
Other Asbestos Disease	250 *	n.appl.	n.appl.

Payment percentage	
Initial payment percentage	48.3%
Current payment percentage	48.3%

Claim payment ratio	
Malignancies and severe asbestosis	87.0%
Asbestosis and pleural disease	13.0%

*Payment percentage does not apply

Combustion Engineering 524(g) Asbestos PI Trust (continued)

Claim Activity

	Pre-2006	2006	2007	2008	Total
Pre-petition pending and post-petition claims					
Claims filed					
Malignant [a]	0	n.a.	n.a.	n.a.	n.a.
Non-malignant	0	n.a.	n.a.	n.a.	n.a.
Not specified	0	8,331	77,115	18,582	104,028
All disease types	0	8,331	77,115	18,582	104,028
Claims paid					
Malignant	0	n.a.	n.a.	n.a.	n.a.
Non-malignant	0	n.a.	n.a.	n.a.	n.a.
Not specified	0	1,444	18,723	9,106	29,273
All disease types	0	1,444	18,723	9,106	29,273
Claim payments ($)					
Malignant	0	14,935,907	99,994,057	29,743,249	144,673,213
Non-malignant	0	1,116,933	18,384,739	9,749,541	29,251,213
Not specified	0	0	0	0	0
All disease types	0	16,052,840	118,378,796	39,492,790	173,924,426
Average payment per claim ($)					
Malignant	–	–	–	–	–
Non-malignant	–	–	–	–	–
Not specified	–	0	0	0	0
All disease types	–	11,117	6,323	4,337	5,941
Claims settled but not paid pre-petition					
Claims filed					
Malignant	0	0	0	0	0
Non-malignant	0	0	0	0	0
Not specified	0	0	0	0	0
All disease types	0	0	0	0	0
Claims paid					
Malignant	0	0	0	0	0
Non-malignant	0	0	0	0	0
Not specified	0	0	0	0	0
All disease types	0	0	0	0	0
Claim payments ($)					
Malignant	0	0	0	0	0
Non-malignant	0	0	0	0	0
Not specified	0	0	0	0	0
All disease types	0	0	0	0	0
Average payment per claim ($)					
Malignant	–	–	–	–	–
Non-malignant	–	–	–	–	–
Not specified	–	–	–	–	–
All disease types	–	–	–	–	–

[a] Malignant claims for this trust include severe asbestosis claims.

Combustion Engineering 524(g) Asbestos PI Trust (continued)

Claim Approval Criteria for	Combustion Engineering claims							
	Meso	LC1	LC2	OC	SA	AP1	AP2	OAD
1. Diagnosis requirement (one or more of checked items satisfies requirement)								
a. Physical exam	✔	✔	✔	✔	✔	✔	✔	✔
b. Pathology	✔	✔	✔	✔	✔	✔	✔	✔
c. Medical document review								
2. ILO or x-ray requirement								
a. ILO reading		1/0		1/0	2/1	1/0	1/0	1/0
OR b. X-ray, CT scan, or pathology showing one or more of the checked conditions								
(1) Bilateral interstitial fibrosis		✔		✔			✔	✔
(2) Bilateral pleural plaques		✔		✔			✔	✔
(3) Bilateral pleural thickening		✔		✔			✔	✔
(4) Bilateral pleural calcification		✔		✔			✔	✔
3. Pulmonary function test requirement								
a. TLC < (% of normal)					65	80		
AND FEV1/FVC ratio >								
OR b. DLCO < (% of normal)								
AND FEV1/FVC ratio >								
OR c. FVC < (% of normal)					65	80		
AND FEV1/FVC ratio >					0.65	0.65		
4. Causation statement requirement	No	Yes	Yes	Yes	Yes	Yes	No	No
5. Latency and exposure requirements								
a. Latency	10 yr	10 yr	10 yr	10 yr	10 yr	10 yr	10 yr	10 yr
b. Company exposure prior to 1983	1 day	6 mo	1 day	6 mo	6 mo	6 mo	6 mo	1 day
c. Occupational exposure								
(1) Total		5 yr		5 yr	5 yr	5 yr	5 yr	
(2) Prior to 1983								

DII Industries, LLC Asbestos PI Trust

DII Industries, LLC Asbestos PI Trust

Bankruptcy Court and Trust Administrative Information

Debtor(s)	Global Industrial Technologies, Inc., et al. (Harbison-Walker)		
	Mid-Valley, Inc, et al. (Halliburton)		

Bankruptcy filing date		Confirmation date	
Harbison-Walker	2/14/02	Harbison-Walker	11/13/07
Halliburton	12/16/03	Halliburton	7/21/04
Bankruptcy court	Bankr. W.D. Pa.	Bankruptcy judge	Judith Fitzgerald

Trust status	Active
Date trust established	1/20/05
Classes of claims processed	Harbison-Walker claims
	Non-Harbison-Walker (Halliburton) claims
Executive director	Marcellene Malouf
Claim administrator	Delaware Claims Processing Facility
Trust website	www.diiasbestostrust.org

Trustees and Advisors

Position	Name	Affiliation
Managing Trustee	Alan Kahn	Self employed
Trustee	Mark Gleason	Gleason & Associates, P.C.
Trustee	Robert Parker	Parker, Bunt & Ainsworth, P.C.
FCR	Eric Green	Resolutions, LLC
TAC Member	John Cooney	Cooney & Conway
TAC Member	Joseph Rice	Motley Rice, LLC
TAC Member	Marc Meyer	Goldberg, Persky & White, P.C.
TAC Member	Perry Weitz	Weitz & Luxenburg
TAC Member	Steven Baron	Silber Pearlman, LLP
TAC Member	Steven Kazan	Kazan, McClain, Abrams, Fernandez, Lyons, Farrise & Greenwood, P.C.
TAC Member	Glen Morgan	Reaud, Morgan & Quinn
TAC Member	Thomas Wilson	Kelley & Ferraro, LLC
TAC Counsel	Ann McMillan	Caplin & Drysdale, Chartered
TAC Counsel	Elihu Inselbuch	Caplin & Drysdale, Chartered
Trust Counsel	Gregg McHugh	General Counsel at DII Industries, LLC Asbestos PI Trust

Estimated Initial Funding of Trust ($ millions)

	Funding for Claims Paid Through Trust	Funding for Claims Paid Outside Trust
Cash from debtor(s)	31.6	2,775.0
Stock from debtors(s)	2,482.0	0.0
Insurance settlements	0.0	0.0
Other assets	0.0	0.0
Total	2,513.6	2,775.0

DII Industries, LLC Asbestos PI Trust (continued)

Trust Financial Statement ($)

	Pre-2006	2006	2007	2008
Beginning trust assets [a]	0	2,570,659,885	2,683,034,003	2,753,589,177
Additions				
Cash from debtors	31,692,628	0	0	0
Stock from debtors	0	0	0	0
Insurance settlements	0	0	0	0
Investment gains	-7,354,491	90,479,768	43,598,051	-228,984,313
Investment income	50,972,444	81,553,634	120,098,685	87,725,228
Other additions	0	0	0	0
Deductions				
Trust expenses	9,303,196	12,247,819	13,090,030	12,716,938
Claim processing costs	n.a.	n.a.	n.a.	n.a.
Investment fees	n.a.	n.a.	n.a.	n.a.
All other expenses	n.a.	n.a.	n.a.	n.a.
Taxes	0	26,233,527	22,888,635	-76,272,667
Claim payments	0	21,177,938	57,162,897	142,579,967
Other deductions	0	0	0	0
Ending trust assets [a]	2,570,659,885	2,683,034,003	2,753,589,177	2,533,305,854
Gross claimant compensation as a percentage of deductions				
Lower bound	0.0%	35.5%	61.4%	91.8%
Upper bound	0.0%	35.5%	61.4%	91.8%

[a] Referred to as net claimants' equity by the trust.

Claim Valuation for Harbison-Walker claims

Disease level	Scheduled Value	Average Value	Maximum Value
Mesothelioma	136,500	182,000	610,000
Lung Cancer 1	44,900	57,700	192,200
Lung Cancer 2	n.appl.	19,200	64,000
Other Cancer	24,000	29,000	96,500
Severe Asbestosis	29,500	31,000	125,600
Level III	7,200	n.appl.	n.appl.
Level II	3,800	n.appl.	n.appl.
Level I	300 *	n.appl.	n.appl.

Payment percentage	
Initial payment percentage	100.0%
Current payment percentage	52.5%

Claim payment ratio	
Malignancies and severe asbestosis	60.0%
Asbestosis and pleural disease	40.0%

*Payment percentage does not apply

Claim Valuation for Halliburton claims

Disease level	Scheduled Value	Average Value	Maximum Value
Mesothelioma	57,200	76,400	256,000
Lung Cancer 1	9,300	12,000	39,900
Lung Cancer 2	n.appl.	4,000	13,300
Other Cancer	8,000	9,800	32,700
Severe Asbestosis	9,400	9,900	40,100
Level III	2,400	n.appl.	n.appl.
Level II	1,100	n.appl.	n.appl.
Level I	100 *	n.appl.	n.appl.

Payment percentage	
Initial payment percentage	100.0%
Current payment percentage	52.5%

Claim payment ratio	
Malignancies and severe asbestosis	60.0%
Asbestosis and pleural disease	40.0%

*Payment percentage does not apply

DII Industries, LLC Asbestos PI Trust (continued)

Claim Activity

	Pre-2006	2006	2007	2008	Total
Pre-petition pending and post-petition claims					
Claims filed					
Malignant	0	0	0	0	0
Non-malignant	0	0	0	0	0
Not specified	315	23,140	54,042	134,264	211,761
All disease types	315	23,140	54,042	134,264	211,761
Claims paid					
Malignant	0	845	2,206	3,671	6,722
Non-malignant	0	1,867	7,592	16,495	25,954
Not specified	0	0	0	0	0
All disease types	0	2,712	9,798	20,166	32,676
Claim payments ($)					
Malignant	0	18,833,549	47,395,648	106,898,239	173,127,437
Non-malignant	0	2,353,700	9,724,508	19,574,514	31,652,722
Not specified	0	0	0	0	0
All disease types	0	21,187,249	57,120,156	126,472,753	204,780,159
Average payment per claim ($)					
Malignant	–	22,288	21,485	29,120	25,755
Non-malignant	–	1,261	1,281	1,187	1,220
Not specified	–	–	–	–	–
All disease types	–	7,812	5,830	6,272	6,267
Claims settled but not paid pre-petition					
Claims filed					
Malignant	0	0	0	0	0
Non-malignant	0	0	0	0	0
Not specified	0	0	0	0	0
All disease types	0	0	0	0	0
Claims paid					
Malignant	0	0	0	0	0
Non-malignant	0	0	0	0	0
Not specified	0	0	0	0	0
All disease types	0	0	0	0	0
Claim payments ($)					
Malignant	0	0	0	0	0
Non-malignant	0	0	0	0	0
Not specified	0	0	0	0	0
All disease types	0	0	0	0	0
Average payment per claim ($)					
Malignant	–	–	–	–	–
Non-malignant	–	–	–	–	–
Not specified	–	–	–	–	–
All disease types	–	–	–	–	–

DII Industries, LLC Asbestos PI Trust (continued)

Claim Activity by Disease Level

	2006	2007	2008	Total
Pre-petition pending and post-petition claims				
Claims paid				
Mesothelioma	390	682	1,954	3,026
Lung Cancer 1	328	889	1,086	2,303
Lung Cancer 2	8	238	256	502
Other Cancer	119	397	375	891
Severe Asbestosis	11	64	125	200
Level III	650	2,771	4,696	8,117
Level II	1,204	4,728	11,590	17,522
Level I	2	29	84	115
Unknown	0	0	0	0
Claims payments ($)				
Mesothelioma	14,620,029	34,813,753	92,429,146	141,862,928
Lung Cancer 1	3,447,941	9,565,320	11,418,605	24,431,866
Lung Cancer 2	15,332	592,366	774,979	1,382,676
Other Cancer	750,247	2,424,210	2,275,510	5,449,967
Severe Asbestosis	106,000	520,908	908,114	1,535,022
Level III	1,237,000	5,349,100	8,368,200	14,954,300
Level II	1,010,300	3,849,200	10,283,800	15,143,300
Level I	400	5,300	14,400	20,100
Unknown	0	0	0	0
Average payment per claim ($)				
Mesothelioma	37,487	51,047	47,303	46,881
Lung Cancer 1	10,512	10,760	10,514	10,609
Lung Cancer 2	1,917	2,489	3,027	2,754
Other Cancer	6,305	6,106	6,068	6,117
Severe Asbestosis	9,636	8,139	7,265	7,675
Level III	1,903	1,930	1,782	1,842
Level II	839	814	887	864
Level I	200	183	171	175
Unknown	–	–	–	–

DII Industries, LLC Asbestos PI Trust (continued)

Claim Approval Criteria for	Halliburton and Harbison-Walker claims							
	Meso	LC1	LC2	OC	SA	L.III	L.II	L.I
1. Diagnosis requirement (one or more of checked items satisfies requirement)								
a. Physical exam	✔	✔	✔	✔	✔	✔	✔	✔
b. Pathology	✔	✔	✔	✔	✔	✔	✔	✔
c. Medical document review								
2. ILO or x-ray requirement								
a. ILO reading		1/0		1/0	2/1	1/0	1/0	1/0
OR b. X-ray, CT scan, or pathology showing one or more of the checked conditions								
(1) Bilateral interstitial fibrosis	✔			✔		✔	✔	✔
(2) Bilateral pleural plaques	✔			✔		✔	✔	✔
(3) Bilateral pleural thickening	✔			✔		✔	✔	✔
(4) Bilateral pleural calcification	✔			✔		✔	✔	✔
3. Pulmonary function test requirement								
a. TLC < (% of normal)					65	80		
AND FEV1/FVC ratio >								
OR b. DLCO < (% of normal)								
AND FEV1/FVC ratio >								
OR c. FVC < (% of normal)					65	65		
AND FEV1/FVC ratio >					0.65	0.65		
4. Causation statement requirement	No	Yes	Yes	Yes	Yes	Yes	No	No
5. Latency and exposure requirements								
a. Latency	10 yr	10 yr	10 yr	10 yr	10 yr	10 yr	10 yr	10 yr
b. Company exposure prior to 1983	1 day	6 mo	1 day	6 mo	6 mo	6 mo	6 mo	1 day
c. Occupational exposure								
(1) Total		5 yr		5 yr	5 yr	5 yr	5 yr	
(2) Prior to 1983	1 day	2 yr	1 day	2 yr	2 yr	2 yr	6 mo	1 day

Eagle-Picher Industries Inc. Personal Injury Settlement Trust

Eagle-Picher Industries Inc. Personal Injury Settlement Trust

Bankruptcy Court and Trust Administrative Information

Debtor(s)	Eagle-Picher Industries		
Bankruptcy filing date	1/7/91	Confirmation date	11/18/96
Bankruptcy court	Bankr. S.D. Ohio	Bankruptcy judge	Burton Perlman

Trust status	Active
Date trust established	11/29/96
Classes of claims processed	Eagle-Picher Industries claims
Executive Director	William Nurre
Claim administrator	Claims Processing Facility
Trust website	www.cpf-inc.com

Trustees and Advisors

Position	Name	Affiliation
Managing Trustee	Ruth McMullin	Chairperson, Eagle-Picher Personal Injury Settlement Trust
Trustee	David McLean	PricewaterhouseCoopers LLP
Trustee	James McMonagle	Vorys, Sater, Seymour and Pease LLP
TAC Member	Gene Locks	Locks Law Firm, LLC
TAC Member	Robert Steinberg	Rose, Klein and Marias, LLP
Trust Counsel	Theodore V.H. Mayer	Hughes Hubbard & Reed LLP
Trust Counsel	Christopher Kiplok	Hughes Hubbard & Reed LLP

Estimated Initial Funding of Trust ($ millions)

	Funding for Claims Paid Through Trust	Funding for Claims Paid Outside Trust
Cash from debtor(s)	388.5	0
Stock from debtors(s)	341.8	0
Insurance settlements	0.0	0
Other assets	0.0	0
Total	730.3	0

Eagle-Picher Industries Inc. Personal Injury Settlement Trust (continued)

Trust Financial Statement ($)

	Pre-2006	2006	2007	2008
Beginning trust assets	0	492,808,001	492,863,862	495,798,513
Additions				
Cash from debtors	394,989,000	0	0	0
Stock from debtors	341,807,000	0	0	0
Insurance settlements	0	0	0	0
Investment gains	110,781,467	16,808,303	7,416,257	-78,053,586
Investment income	199,827,189	18,992,188	19,107,861	17,501,405
Other additions	399,925	0	380,301	0
Deductions				
Trust expenses	56,869,598	7,111,888	5,694,791	4,971,834
Claim processing costs	39,878,130	5,364,803	3,884,550	3,431,501
Investment fees	7,974,816	807,133	800,352	798,960
All other expenses	9,016,652	939,952	1,009,889	741,373
Taxes	42,497,474	5,282,428	2,264,745	-27,743,368
Claim payments	465,988,414	23,350,314	16,019,232	19,321,572
Other deductions	6,853,235	0	0	0
Ending trust assets	492,808,001	492,863,862	495,789,513	438,696,294
Gross claimant compensation as a percentage of deductions				
Lower bound	81.4%	65.3%	66.8%	79.5%
Upper bound	82.6%	65.3%	66.8%	79.5%

Claim Valuation for — Eagle-Picher Industries claims

Disease level	Scheduled Value [a]	Average Value	Maximum Value
Mesothelioma	6,500 *	n.appl.	n.appl.
Lung Cancer	2,000 *	n.appl.	n.appl.
Other Cancer	1,000 *	n.appl.	n.appl.
Non-malignancy	400 *	n.appl.	n.appl.

Payment percentage [b]			
Initial payment percentage	31.9%		
Current payment percentage	38.0%		

Claim payment ratio			
Malignancies and severe asbestosis	n.appl.		
Asbestosis and pleural disease	n.appl.		

*Payment percentage does not apply

[a] Values for the discounted claim payment option

[b] Applied to individual review claims only

Eagle-Picher Industries Inc. Personal Injury Settlement Trust (continued)

Claim Activity

Pre-petition pending and post-petition claims	Pre-2006	2006	2007	2008	Total
Claims filed					
Malignant	6,490	2,750	2,969	2,221	14,430
Non-malignant	31,158	5,501	3,771	2,910	43,340
Not specified	0	0	0	0	0
All disease types	37,648	8,251	6,740	5,131	57,770
Claims paid					
Malignant	0	0	0	0	0
Non-malignant	0	0	0	0	0
Not specified	0	0	0	0	0
All disease types	0	0	0	0	0
Claim payments ($)					
Malignant	23,749,000	11,842,000	10,561,000	13,604,000	59,756,000
Non-malignant	31,151,000	7,258,000	7,339,000	4,296,000	50,044,000
Not specified	409,965,405	0	0	0	409,965,405
All disease types	464,865,405	19,100,000	17,900,000	17,900,000	519,765,405
Average payment per claim ($)					
Malignant	-	-	-	-	-
Non-malignant	-	-	-	-	-
Not specified	-	-	-	-	-
All disease types	-	-	-	-	-
Claims settled but not paid pre-petition					
Claims filed					
Malignant	0	0	0	0	0
Non-malignant	0	0	0	0	0
Not specified	0	0	0	0	0
All disease types	0	0	0	0	0
Claims paid					
Malignant	0	0	0	0	0
Non-malignant	0	0	0	0	0
Not specified	0	0	0	0	0
All disease types	0	0	0	0	0
Claim payments ($)					
Malignant	0	0	0	0	0
Non-malignant	0	0	0	0	0
Not specified	0	0	0	0	0
All disease types	0	0	0	0	0
Average payment per claim ($)					
Malignant	-	-	-	-	-
Non-malignant	-	-	-	-	-
Not specified	-	-	-	-	-
All disease types	-	-	-	-	-

Eagle-Picher Industries Personal Injury Settlement Trust (continued)

Claim Approval Criteria

"In order to establish a valid Asbestos Personal Injury Claim, a claimant must (a) make a conclusive demonstration of exposure to an Eagle-Picher asbestos-containing product and (b) submit a medical report from a qualified physician that (i) results from a physical examination by that physician and (ii) contains a diagnosis of an asbestos-related injury. The PI Trust may require the submission of evidence of exposure to an Eagle-Picher asbestos-containing product, x-rays, laboratory tests, medical examinations or reviews, other medical evidence, or any other evidence to support such Asbestos Personal Injury Claims and require that medical evidence submitted comply with recognized medical standards regarding equipment, testing methods, and procedures to assure that such evidence is reliable." (Excerpted from EPI Claims Resolution Procedures)

Federal Mogul Asbestos Personal Injury Trust—Turner & Newall Subfund

Federal Mogul Asbestos Personal Injury Trust - Turner & Newall Subfund

Bankruptcy Court and Trust Administrative Information

Debtor(s)	Federal Mogul (Turner & Newall, Flexitallic, Ferodo)		
Bankruptcy filing date	10/1/01	Confirmation date	11/13/07
Bankruptcy court	Bankr. D. Del.	Bankruptcy judge	n/a
Trust status	Active		
Date trust established	12/27/07		
Classes of claims processed	Federal Mogul (Turner & Newall, Flexitallic, Ferodo)		
Claim administrator	n.a.		
Trust website	www.federalmogulasbestostrust.com		

Trustees and Advisors

Position	Name	Affiliation
Trustee	Ken Kawaichi	Retired California state judge
Trustee	Edward Robertson	Bartimus, Fickleton, Robertson & Gorny, P.C.
Trustee	Kirk Watson	Member of Texas State Senate
FCR	Eric Green	Resolutions, LLC
TAC Member	Joseph Rice	Motley Rice, LLC
TAC Member	Perry Weitz	Weitz & Luxenburg
TAC Member	Russell Budd	Baron & Budd, P.C.
TAC Member	Steven Kazan	Kazan, McClain, Abrams, Fernandez, Lyons, Farrise & Greenwood, P.C.
TAC Member	John Cooney	Cooney & Conway
Trust Counsel	Douglas A. Campbell	Campbell & Levine, LLC
Trust Counsel	Stanley E. Levine	Campbell & Levine, LLC
Trust Counsel	Kathleen Campbell Davis	Campbell & Levine, LLC
FCR Counsel	Edwin Harron	Young Conaway Stargatt & Taylor, LLP
TAC Counsel	Elihu Inselbuch	Caplin & Drysdale

Estimated Initial Funding of Trust ($ millions)

	Funding for Claims Paid Through Trust	Funding for Claims Paid Outside Trust
Cash from debtor(s)	635.0	0
Stock from debtors(s)	0.0	0
Insurance settlements	0.0	0
Other assets	0.0	0
Total	635.0	0

Federal Mogul Asbestos Personal Injury Trust - Turner & Newall Subfund (continued)

Trust Financial Statement ($)

	Pre-2006	2006	2007	2008
Beginning trust assets	0	0	0	0
Additions				
Cash from debtors	0	0	0	235,000,000
Stock from debtors	0	0	0	0
Insurance settlements	0	0	0	0
Investment gains	0	0	0	3,584,537
Investment income	0	0	0	18,017,115
Other additions	0	0	0	0
Deductions				
Trust expenses	0	0	0	9,703,645
Claim processing costs	0	0	0	66,469
Investment fees	0	0	0	330,355
All other expenses	0	0	0	9,306,821
Taxes	0	0	0	0
Claim payments	0	0	0	0
Other deductions	0	0	0	0
Ending trust assets	0	0	0	246,898,007
Gross claimant compensation as a percentage of deductions				
Lower bound	–	–	–	0.0%
Upper bound	–	–	–	0.0%

Claim Valuation for — Flexitallic and Ferodo Claims

Disease level	Scheduled Value	Average Value	Maximum Value
Mesothelioma	50,000	62,500	150,000
Lung Cancer 1	10,625	15,000	31,250
Lung Cancer 2	n.appl.	3,000	10,000
Other Cancer	3,700	4,900	22,500
Severe Asbestosis	10,625	13,625	31,250
Asbestosis / Pleural Disease II	3,175	3,375	6,250
Asbestosis / Pleural Disease I	1,425	1,450	2,000
Other Asbestos Disease	100 *	n.appl.	n.appl.

Payment percentage
Initial payment percentage   n.a.
Current payment percentage   n.a.

Claim payment ratio
Malignancies and severe asbestosis   60.0%
Asbestosis and pleural disease   40.0%

*Payment percentage does not apply

Claim Valuation for — Turner & Newall claims

Disease level	Scheduled Value	Average Value	Maximum Value
Mesothelioma	200,000	250,000	600,000
Lung Cancer 1	42,500	60,000	125,000
Lung Cancer 2	n.appl.	12,000	40,000
Other Cancer	14,750	19,500	90,000
Severe Asbestosis	42,500	54,500	125,000
Asbestosis / Pleural Disease II	12,700	13,500	25,000
Asbestosis / Pleural Disease I	5,700	5,800	8,000
Other Asbestos Disease	400 *	n.appl.	n.appl.

Payment percentage
Initial payment percentage   n.a.
Current payment percentage   n.a.

Claim payment ratio
Malignancies and severe asbestosis   60.0%
Asbestosis and pleural disease   40.0%

*Payment percentage does not apply

Federal Mogul Asbestos Personal Injury Trust - Turner & Newall Subfund (continued)

Claim Activity					
	Pre-2006	_2006_	_2007_	_2008_	_Total_
Pre-petition pending and post-petition claims					
Claims filed					
Malignant					
Non-malignant					
Not specified					
All disease types					
Claims paid					
Malignant					
Non-malignant					
Not specified					
All disease types					
Claim payments ($)					
Malignant					
Non-malignant					
Not specified					
All disease types					
Average payment per claim ($)					
Malignant					
Non-malignant					
Not specified					
All disease types					

NO CLAIMS PAID THROUGH 2008

Claims settled but not paid pre-petition					
Claims filed					
Malignant					
Non-malignant					
Not specified					
All disease types					
Claims paid					
Malignant					
Non-malignant					
Not specified					
All disease types					
Claim payments ($)					
Malignant					
Non-malignant					
Not specified					
All disease types					
Average payment per claim ($)					
Malignant					
Non-malignant					
Not specified					
All disease types					

Federal Mogul Asbestos Personal Injury Trust - Turner & Newall Subfund (continued)

Claim Approval Criteria for	Flexitallic and Ferodo Claims							
	Meso	_LC1_	_LC2_	_OC_	_SA_	_AP1_	_AP2_	_OAD_
1. Diagnosis requirement (one or more of checked items satisfies requirement)								
a. Physical exam	✔	✔	✔	✔	✔	✔	✔	✔
b. Pathology	✔	✔	✔	✔	✔	✔	✔	✔
c. Medical document review								
2. ILO or x-ray requirement								
a. ILO reading		1/0		1/0	2/1	1/0	1/0	1/0
OR b. X-ray, CT scan, or pathology showing one or more of the checked conditions								
(1) Bilateral interstitial fibrosis		✔		✔		✔	✔	✔
(2) Bilateral pleural plaques		✔		✔		✔	✔	✔
(3) Bilateral pleural thickening		✔		✔		✔	✔	✔
(4) Bilateral pleural calcification		✔		✔		✔	✔	✔
3. Pulmonary function test requirement								
a. TLC < (% of normal)					65	80		
AND FEV1/FVC ratio >								
OR b. DLCO < (% of normal)								
AND FEV1/FVC ratio >								
OR c. FVC < (% of normal)					65	80		
AND FEV1/FVC ratio >					0.65	0.65		
4. Causation statement requirement	No	Yes	Yes	Yes	Yes	Yes	No	No
5. Latency and exposure requirements								
a. Latency	10 yr	10 yr	10 yr	10 yr	10 yr	10 yr	10 yr	10 yr
b. Company exposure prior to 1983	1 day	6 mo	1 day	6 mo	6 mo	6 mo	6 mo	1 day
c. Occupational exposure								
(1) Total		5 yr		5 yr	5 yr	5 yr	5 yr	
(2) Prior to 1983	1 day	2 yr	1 day	2 yr	2 yr	2 yr	6 mo	1 day

G-1 Holdings Inc. Asbestos Personal Injury Settlement Trust

G-1 Holdings Inc. Asbestos Personal Injury Settlement Trust

Bankruptcy Court and Trust Administrative Information

Debtor(s)	G-1 Holdings Inc. ACI Inc.		
Bankruptcy filing date	1/5/01	Confirmation date	11/12/09
Bankruptcy court	Bankr. D. N.J.	Bankruptcy judge	Rosemary Gambardella

Trust status	Active
Date trust established	11/17/09
Classes of claims processed	G-1 claims
Claim administrator	Not selected
Trust website	None

Trustees and Advisors

Position	Name	Affiliation
Trustee	Stephen M. Snyder	Snyder Miller & Orton LLP.
Trustee	Alan B. Rich	Formerly at Baron & Budd, P.C.
Trustee	Marina Corodemus	Corodemus & Corodemus LLC. (retired NJ state judge)
FCR	C. Judson Hamlin	Purcell, Ries, Shannon, Mulcahy & O'Neill
Trust Counsel	Frances Gecker	Frank/Gecker, LLP

Estimated Initial Funding of Trust ($ millions)

	Funding for Claims Paid Through Trust	Funding for Claims Paid Outside Trust
Cash from debtor(s)	770.1	0
Stock from debtors(s)	0.0	0
Insurance settlements	0.0	0
Other assets	0.0	0
Total	770.1	0

G-1 Holdings Inc. Asbestos Personal Injury Settlement Trust (continued)

Trust Financial Statement ($)

	Pre-2006	2006	2007	2008
Beginning trust assets				
Additions				
Cash from debtors				
Stock from debtors				
Insurance settlements				
Investment gains				
Investment income		DATA NOT AVAILABLE		
Other additions				
Deductions				
Trust expenses				
Claim processing costs				
Investment fees				
All other expenses				
Taxes				
Claim payments				
Other deductions				
Ending trust assets				
Gross claimant compensation as a percentage of deductions				
Lower bound	–	–	–	–
Upper bound	–	–	–	–

Claim Valuation for   G-1 claims

Disease level	Scheduled Value	Average Value	Maximum Value
Mesothelioma	155,000	225,000	450,000
Lung Cancer 1	45,000	55,000	100,000
Lung Cancer 2	n.appl.	15,000	35,000
Other Cancer	15,000	18,000	35,000
Severe Asbestosis	30,000	35,000	50,000
Asbestosis / Pleural Disease II	8,300	n.appl.	n.appl.
Asbestosis / Pleural Disease I	2,625	n.appl.	n.appl.
Other Asbestos Disease	225 *	n.appl.	n.appl.

Payment percentage			
Initial payment percentage	8.6% [a]		
Current payment percentage	8.6% [a]		

Claim payment ratio			
Malignancies and severe asbestosis	85.0%		
Asbestosis and pleural disease	15.0%		

*Payment percentage does not apply

[a] 4.3 percent paid up front with the remaining 4.3 percent paid when it is determined that adequate funds are available.

G-1 Holdings Inc. Asbestos Personal Injury Settlement Trust (continued)

Claim Activity					
	Pre-2006	_2006_	_2007_	_2008_	_Total_
Pre-petition pending and post-petition claims					
Claims filed					
Malignant					
Non-malignant					
Not specified					
All disease types					
Claims paid					
Malignant					
Non-malignant					
Not specified					
All disease types					
Claim payments ($)					
Malignant					
Non-malignant					
Not specified					
All disease types					
Average payment per claim ($)					
Malignant					
Non-malignant					
Not specified					
All disease types					
		TRUST HAS NOT YET BEGUN TO ACCEPT OR PROCESS CLAIMS			
Claims settled but not paid pre-petition					
Claims filed					
Malignant					
Non-malignant					
Not specified					
All disease types					
Claims paid					
Malignant					
Non-malignant					
Not specified					
All disease types					
Claim payments ($)					
Malignant					
Non-malignant					
Not specified					
All disease types					
Average payment per claim ($)					
Malignant					
Non-malignant					
Not specified					
All disease types					

G-1 Holdings Inc. Asbestos Personal Injury Settlement Trust (continued)

Claim Approval Criteria for	G-1 claims							
	Meso	LC1	LC2	OC	SA	AP2	AP1	OAD
1. Diagnosis requirement (one or more of checked items satisfies requirement)								
a. Physical exam	✔	✔	✔	✔	✔	✔	✔	✔
b. Pathology	✔	✔	✔	✔	✔	✔	✔	✔
c. Medical document review								
2. ILO or x-ray requirement								
a. ILO reading		1/0		1/0	2/1	1/0	1/0	1/0
OR b. X-ray, CT scan, or pathology showing one or more of the checked conditions								
(1) Bilateral interstitial fibrosis		✔		✔		✔	✔	✔
(2) Bilateral pleural plaques		✔		✔		✔	✔	✔
(3) Bilateral pleural thickening		✔		✔		✔	✔	✔
(4) Bilateral pleural calcification		✔		✔		✔	✔	✔
3. Pulmonary function test requirement								
a. TLC < (% of normal)					65	80		
AND FEV1/FVC ratio >								
OR b. DLCO < (% of normal)								
AND FEV1/FVC ratio >								
OR c. FVC < (% of normal)					65	80		
AND FEV1/FVC ratio >					0.65	0.65		
4. Causation statement requirement	No	Yes	Yes	Yes	Yes	Yes	No	No
5. Latency and exposure requirements								
a. Latency	10 yr	10 yr	10 yr	10 yr	10 yr	10 yr	10 yr	10 yr
b. Company exposure prior to 1983	1 day	6 mo	1 day	6 mo	6 mo	6 mo	6 mo	1 day
c. Occupational exposure								
(1) Total		5 yr		5 yr	5 yr	5 yr	5 yr	
(2) Prior to 1983	1 day	2 yr	1 day	2 yr	2 yr	2 yr	6 mo	1 day

H. K. Porter Asbestos Trust

H. K. Porter Asbestos Trust

Bankruptcy Court and Trust Administrative Information

Debtor(s)	H.K. Porter Company, Inc.		
Bankruptcy filing date	2/15/91	Confirmation date	6/25/98
Bankruptcy court	Bankr. W.D. Pa.	Bankruptcy judge	Warren Bentz

Trust status	Active
Date trust established	1998
Classes of claims processed	H. K. Porter claims
Claim administrator	Verus Claims Services
Trust website	www.hkporterasbestostrust.org

Trustees and Advisors

Position	Name	Affiliation
Trustee	Mark Gleason	Gleason & Associates, P.C.
TAC Member	Perry Weitz	Weitz & Luxenburg
TAC Member	Philip Pahigian	Retired from Wilentz, Goldman & Spitzer
TAC Member	Brent Rosenthal	Baron & Budd
Trust Counsel	David A. Campbell	Campbell & Levine, LLC
Trust Counsel	Philip E. Milch	Campbell & Levine, LLC
FCR	George Cass	Buchanan Ingersoll & Rooney PC
FCR Counsel	George Cass	Buchanan Ingersoll & Rooney PC

Estimated Initial Funding of Trust ($ millions)

	Funding for Claims Paid Through Trust	Funding for Claims Paid Outside Trust
Cash from debtor(s)		
Stock from debtors(s)		
Insurance settlements		
Other assets	DATA NOT AVAILABLE	
Total		

H. K. Porter Asbestos Trust (continued)

Trust Financial Statement ($)

	Pre-2006 [a]	2006	2007	2008
Beginning trust assets	0	77,200,115	77,205,466	78,110,766
Additions				
Cash from debtors	26,484,989	4,156,106	5,677,116	2,136,194
Stock from debtors	0	0	0	0
Insurance settlements	1,231,338	0	0	0
Investment gains	6,433,512	1,621,054	-362,672	-4,855,828
Investment income	2,364,885	41,295	36,136	14,317
Other additions	0	0	0	0
Deductions				
Trust expenses	6,673,322	864,760	811,367	896,950
Claim processing costs	3,579,380	243,088	235,041	161,794
Investment fees	n.a.	n.a.	n.a.	n.a.
All other expenses	n.a.	n.a.	n.a.	n.a.
Taxes	0	0	0	0
Claim payments	68,472,149	4,948,344	3,633,913	381,282
Other deductions	0	0	0	0
Ending trust assets	77,200,115	77,205,466	78,110,766	74,127,217
Gross claimant compensation as a percentage of deductions				
Lower bound	91.1%	85.1%	81.7%	29.8%
Upper bound	91.1%	85.1%	81.7%	29.8%

[a] Data for pre-2006 period incomplete

Claim Valuation for H. K. Porter claims

Disease level	Scheduled Value	Average Value	Maximum Value
Mesothelioma	20,000	n.appl.	40,000
Lung Cancer	12,000	n.appl.	24,000
Other Cancer	7,500	n.appl.	15,000
Non-malignancy	3,750	n.appl.	7,500

Payment percentage			
Initial payment percentage	4.6%		
Current payment percentage	6.3%		

Claim payment ratio			
Malignancies and severe asbestosis	n.appl.		
Asbestosis and pleural disease	n.appl.		

H. K. Porter Asbestos Trust (continued)

Claim Activity

	Pre-2006	2006	2007	2008	Total
Pre-petition pending and post-petition claims					
Claims filed [a]					
Malignant	37,853	2,709	2,371	1,187	44,120
Non-malignant	274,106	4,036	4,046	2,459	284,647
Not specified	6,215	0	0	0	6,215
All disease types	318,174	6,745	6,417	3,646	334,982
Claims paid					
Malignant	35,315	4,502	3,314	438 0	43,569
Non-malignant	269,872	13,332	10,124	584 0	293,912
Not specified	0	0	0	0 0	0
All disease types	305,187	17,834	13,438	1,022	337,481
Claim payments ($)					
Malignant	21,903,025	2,746,556	2,070,139	280,752	27,000,472
Non-malignant	46,551,790	2,195,440	1,570,122	100,531	50,417,883
Not specified	0	0	0	0	0
All disease types	68,454,815	4,941,996	3,640,261	381,283	77,418,355
Average payment per claim ($)					
Malignant	620	610	625	641	620
Non-malignant	172	165	155	172	172
Not specified	–	–	–	–	–
All disease types	224	277	271	373	229
Claims settled but not paid pre-petition					
Claims filed					
Malignant	0	0	0	0	0
Non-malignant	0	0	0	0	0
Not specified	0	0	0	0	0
All disease types	0	0	0	0	0
Claims paid					
Malignant	0	0	0	0	0
Non-malignant	0	0	0	0	0
Not specified	0	0	0	0	0
All disease types	0	0	0	0	0
Claim payments ($)					
Malignant	0	0	0	0	0
Non-malignant	0	0	0	0	0
Not specified	0	0	0	0	0
All disease types	0	0	0	0	0
Average payment per claim ($)					
Malignant	–	–	–	–	–
Non-malignant	–	–	–	–	–
Not specified	–	–	–	–	–
All disease types	–	–	–	–	–

[a] Claims filed data are incomplete

H. K. Porter Asbestos Trust (continued)

Claim Activity by Disease Level

	2006	2007	2008	Total
Pre-petition pending and post-petition claims				
Claims paid				
Mesothelioma	1,296	999	124	2,419
Lung cancer	2,270	1,669	244	4,183
Other cancer	936	646	70	1,652
Non-malignancy	13,332	10,124	584	24,040
Unknown	0	0	0	0
Claims payments ($)				
Mesothelioma	1,207,012	998,046	122,220	2,327,278
Lung cancer	1,222,441	863,291	134,382	2,220,114
Other cancer	317,103	208,802	24,150	550,055
Non-malignancy	2,195,440	1,570,122	100,531	3,866,093
Unknown	0	0	0	0
Average payment per claim ($)				
Mesothelioma	931	999	986	962
Lung cancer	539	517	551	531
Other cancer	339	323	345	333
Non-malignancy	165	155	172	161
Unknown	–	–	–	–

H. K. Porter Asbestos Trust (continued)

Claim Approval Criteria

	Meso	LC	OC	NM

1. Diagnosis requirement (one or more of checked items satisfies requirement)
   a. Physical exam
   b. Pathology
   c. Medical document review
2. ILO or x-ray requirement
   a. ILO reading
OR b. X-ray, CT scan, or pathology showing one or more of the checked conditions
   (1) Bilateral interstitial fibrosis
   (2) Bilateral pleural plaques
   (3) Bilateral pleural thickening
   (4) Bilateral pleural calcification
3. Pulmonary function test requirement   DATA NOT AVAILABLE
   a. TLC < (% of normal)
        AND FEV1/FVC ratio >
OR b. DLCO < (% of normal)
        AND FEV1/FVC ratio >
OR c. FVC < (% of normal)
        AND FEV1/FVC ratio >
4. Causation statement requirement
5. Latency and exposure requirements
   a. Latency
   b. Company exposure prior to 1983
   c. Occupational exposure
      (1) Total
      (2) Prior to 1983

J.T. Thorpe Company Successor Trust

J.T. Thorpe Company Successor Trust

Bankruptcy Court and Trust Administrative Information

Debtor(s)	JT Thorpe Co. (S.D. Tex.)		
Bankruptcy filing date	10/1/02	Confirmation date	3/3/04
Bankruptcy court	Bankr. S.D. Tex.	Bankruptcy judge	Karen Brown

Trust status	Active
Date trust established	2004
Classes of claims processed	JT Thorpe claims
Claim administrator	MFR Claims Processing, Inc.
Trust website	mfrclaims.com/html/jt_thorpe.html

Trustees and Advisors

Position	Name	Affiliation
Trustee	Joseph Ashmore	Ashmore Law Firm, P.C.
Trustee	Robert Pendergraft	Pendergraft & Simon L.L.P.
Trustee	Dan Lain	unknown
FCR	Richard Schiro	Law Offices of Richard B. Schiro
TAC Member	Bryan Blevins	Provost Umphrey LLC
TAC Member	Russell Budd	Baron & Budd, P.C.
TAC Member	Steven Baron	Silber Pearlman, LLP
Trust Counsel	Jo Hartwick	Stutzman, Bromberg, Esserman & Plifka

Estimated Initial Funding of Trust ($ millions)

	Funding for Claims Paid Through Trust	Funding for Claims Paid Outside Trust
Cash from debtor(s)	6.5	0
Stock from debtors(s)	0.0	0
Insurance settlements	225.8	0
Other assets	0.2	0
Total	232.5	0

J.T. Thorpe Company Successor Trust (continued)

Trust Financial Statement ($)

	Pre-2006	2006	2007	2008
Beginning trust assets	0	154,796,670	162,379,529	186,116,290
Additions				
Cash from debtors	4,223,793	0	0	0
Stock from debtors	0	0	0	0
Insurance settlements	231,437,285	11,318,921	37,825,000	500,000
Investment gains	1,140,718	2,206,490	-371,082	-33,176,612
Investment income	5,429,110	7,475,709	9,815,348	7,311,686
Other additions	0	0	127,375	135,858
Deductions				
Trust expenses	25,473,540	4,364,731	1,320,430	998,337
Claim processing costs	n.a.	n.a.	n.a.	n.a.
Investment fees	n.a.	n.a.	n.a.	n.a.
All other expenses	n.a.	n.a.	n.a.	n.a.
Taxes	113,512	0	-113,512	0
Claim payments	59,648,580	9,053,530	22,452,962	3,862,409
Other deductions	2,198,604	0	0	0
Ending trust assets	154,796,670	162,379,529	186,116,290	156,026,476
Gross claimant compensation as a percentage of deductions				
Lower bound	68.2%	67.5%	94.9%	79.5%
Upper bound	70.7%	67.5%	94.9%	79.5%

Claim Valuation for JT Thorpe claims

Disease level	Scheduled Value	Average Value	Maximum Value
Mesothelioma	100,000	n.appl.	n.appl.
Lung Cancer 1	25,000	n.appl.	n.appl.
Lung Cancer 2	10,000	n.appl.	n.appl.
Other Cancer	10,000	n.appl.	n.appl.
Severe Asbestosis	25,000	n.appl.	n.appl.
Asbestosis / Pleural Disease II	9,000	n.appl.	n.appl.
Asbestosis / Pleural Disease I	4,000	n.appl.	n.appl.

Payment percentage			
Initial payment percentage	18.5%		
Current payment percentage	38.0%		

Claim payment ratio			
Malignancies and severe asbestosis	n.appl.		
Asbestosis and pleural disease	n.appl.		

J.T. Thorpe Company Successor Trust (continued)

Claim Activity

	Pre-2006	2006	2007	2008	Total
Pre-petition pending and post-petition claims					
Claims filed [a]					
Malignant	n.a.	n.a.	0	0	n.a.
Non-malignant	n.a.	n.a.	0	0	n.a.
Not specified	n.a.	n.a.	1,666	1,196	n.a.
All disease types	n.a.	n.a.	1,666	1,196	n.a.
Claims paid					
Malignant	n.a.	n.a.	n.a.	n.a.	n.a.
Non-malignant	n.a.	n.a.	n.a.	n.a.	n.a.
Not specified	105	n.a.	2,541	659	n.a.
All disease types	105	n.a.	2,541	659	n.a.
Claim payments ($)					
Malignant	n.a.	n.a.	n.a.	n.a.	n.a.
Non-malignant	n.a.	n.a.	n.a.	n.a.	n.a.
Not specified	3,683,305	9,053,530	22,452,962 [b]	3,862,409	39,052,206
All disease types	3,683,305	9,053,530	22,452,962 [b]	3,862,409	39,052,206
Average payment per claim ($)					
Malignant	–	–	–	–	–
Non-malignant	–	–	–	–	–
Not specified	35,079	–	1,025 [c]	5,861	n.a.
All disease types	35,079	–	1,025 [c]	5,861	n.a.
Claims settled but not paid pre-petition					
Claims filed [a]					
Malignant	0	0	0	0	0
Non-malignant	0	0	0	0	0
Not specified	0	0	0	0	0
All disease types	0	0	0	0	0
Claims paid					
Malignant	0	0	0	0	0
Non-malignant	0	0	0	0	0
Not specified	366	0	0	0	366
All disease types	366	0	0	0	366
Claim payments ($)					
Malignant	0	0	0	0	0
Non-malignant	0	0	0	0	0
Not specified	55,965,275	0	0	0	55,965,275
All disease types	55,965,275	0	0	0	55,965,275
Average payment per claim ($)					
Malignant	–	–	–	–	–
Non-malignant	–	–	–	–	–
Not specified	152,911	–	–	–	152,911
All disease types	152,911	–	–	–	152,911

[a] Claims filed data incomplete

[b] Includes $13.4 million of payments on past claims to account for changes in the payment percentage

[c] Excludes $13.4 million in payments for past claims

J.T. Thorpe Company Successor Trust (continued)

Claim Approval Criteria for	JT Thorpe claims						
	Meso	LC1	LC2	OC	SA	AP2	AP1
1. Diagnosis requirement (one or more of checked items satisfies requirement)							
a. Physical exam	✔	✔	✔	✔	✔	✔	✔
b. Pathology	✔	✔	✔	✔	✔	✔	✔
c. Medical document review							
2. ILO or x-ray requirement							
a. ILO reading		1/0		1/0	2/1	1/0	1/0
OR b. X-ray, CT scan, or pathology showing one or more of the checked conditions							
(1) Bilateral interstitial fibrosis		✔		✔			✔
(2) Bilateral pleural plaques		✔		✔			✔
(3) Bilateral pleural thickening		✔		✔			✔
(4) Bilateral pleural calcification							
3. Pulmonary function test requirement							
a. TLC < (% of normal)					65	80	
AND FEV1/FVC ratio >							
OR b. DLCO < (% of normal)							
AND FEV1/FVC ratio >							
OR c. FVC < (% of normal)					65	80	
AND FEV1/FVC ratio >					0.65	0.65	
4. Causation statement requirement	No	Yes	Yes	Yes	Yes	Yes	Yes
5. Latency and exposure requirements							
a. Latency	10 yr	10 yr	10 yr	10 yr	10 yr	10 yr	10 yr
b. Company exposure prior to 1983		6 mo	6 mo	6 mo	6 mo	6 mo	6 mo
c. Occupational exposure							
(1) Total		5 yr	5 yr	5 yr	5 yr	5 yr	5 yr
(2) Prior to 1983							

J.T. Thorpe Settlement Trust

J.T. Thorpe Settlement Trust

Bankruptcy Court and Trust Administrative Information

Debtor(s)	J.T. Thorpe, Inc.		
	Thorpe Technologies, Inc.		
	Thorpe Holding Company, Inc.		
Bankruptcy filing date	2/12/02	Confirmation date	1/19/06
Bankruptcy court	Bankr. C.D. Cal.	Bankruptcy judge	Sheri Bluebond
Trust status	Active		
Date trust established	6/29/06		
Classes of claims processed	J.T. Thorpe claims		
Executive Director	Sara Beth Brown		
Claim administrator	Western Asbestos Settlement Trust		
Trust website	jttstrust.com		

Trustees and Advisors

Position	Name	Affiliation
Managing Trustee	Stephen Snyder	Snyder Miller & Orton LLP.
Trustee	John Luikart	Bethany Advisors LLC
Trustee	Sandra Hernandez	The San Francisco Foundation
FCR	Charles Renfrew	Law Offices of Charles B. Renfrew
FCR Counsel	Gary Fergus	Fergus, A Law Office
TAC Member	Alan Brayton	Brayton Purcell, LLP
TAC Member	David Rosen	Rose Klein & Marias LLP
TAC Member	Steven Kazan	Kazan, McClain, Lyons, Greenwood & Harley
TAC Counsel	Michael Ahrens	Sheppard Mullin Richter & Hampton LLP

Estimated Initial Funding of Trust ($ millions)

	Funding for Claims Paid Through Trust	Funding for Claims Paid Outside Trust
Cash from debtor(s)	0.5	0
Stock from debtors(s)	n.a. [a]	0
Insurance settlements	153.4	0
Other assets	0.0	0
Total	153.9	0

[a] The trust received shares of J.T. Thorpe, Inc. and Thorpe Holding Company, Inc., but these shares were closely held and not assigned a value.

J.T. Thorpe Settlement Trust (continued)

Trust Financial Statement ($)

	Pre-2006	2006	2007	2008
Beginning trust assets	0	0	103,073,572	187,206,153
Additions				
Cash from debtors	0	500,000	33,187	0
Stock from debtors	0	0	0	0
Insurance settlements	0	153,370,181	86,000,000	265,499
Investment gains	0	0	1,386,585	-20,457,803
Investment income	0	3,073,174	7,184,846	6,358,087
Other additions	0	0	0	6,100,904
Deductions				
Trust expenses	0	2,108,270	1,110,809	797,836
Claim processing costs	0	123,654	90,242	68,846
Investment fees	0	n.a.	n.a.	n.a.
All other expenses	0	n.a.	n.a.	n.a.
Taxes	0	338,011	2,017,138	0
Claim payments	0	34,937,593	7,344,090	12,355,162
Other deductions	0	16,485,909	0	1,535,248
Ending trust assets	0	103,073,572	187,206,153	164,784,594
Gross claimant compensation as a percentage of deductions				
Lower bound	–	64.9%	70.1%	84.1%
Upper bound	–	95.5%	70.1%	94.6%

Claim Valuation for   J.T. Thorpe claims

Disease level	Base-Case Value [a,b]	Average Value [b]	Maximum Value [b]
Mesothelioma	102,647	150,000	600,000
Lung Cancer	15,278	40,000	160,000
Other Cancer	8,496	25,000	100,000
Grade I Non-Malignancy	6,843	10,000	40,000
Grade II Non-Malignancy	2,374	3,000	12,000

Payment percentage			
Initial payment percentage	50.0%		
Current payment percentage	40.0%		

Claim payment ratio			
Malignancies	90.0%		
Asbestosis and pleural disease	10.0%		

[a] For each claim, base-case values are adjusted using a series of factors that approximate factors which add or substract value to cases in the tort system.

[b] Values have been increased 3.7% above figures shown to account for inflation.

J.T. Thorpe Settlement Trust (continued)

Claim Activity

	Pre-2006	2006	2007	2008	Total
Pre-petition pending and post-petition claims					
Claims filed					
Malignant	0	n.a.	n.a.	n.a.	n.a.
Non-malignant	0	n.a.	n.a.	n.a.	n.a.
Not specified	0	48	1,327	1,725	3,100
All disease types	0	48	1,327	1,725	3,100
Claims paid					
Malignant	0	n.a.	n.a.	n.a.	n.a.
Non-malignant	0	n.a.	n.a.	n.a.	n.a.
Not specified	0	2	98	567	667
All disease types	0	2	98	567	667
Claim payments ($)					
Malignant	0	n.a.	n.a.	n.a.	n.a.
Non-malignant	0	n.a.	n.a.	n.a.	n.a.
Not specified	0	128,437	5,406,731	12,447,911	17,983,079
All disease types	0	128,437	5,406,731	12,447,911	17,983,079
Average payment per claim ($)					
Malignant	–	–	–	–	–
Non-malignant	–	–	–	–	–
Not specified	–	64,219	55,171	21,954	26,961
All disease types	–	64,219	55,171	21,954	26,961
Claims settled but not paid pre-petition					
Claims filed					
Malignant	0	n.a.	n.a.	n.a.	n.a.
Non-malignant	0	n.a.	n.a.	n.a.	n.a.
Not specified	0	1,474	0	0	1,474
All disease types	0	1,474	0	0	1,474
Claims paid					
Malignant	0	n.a.	n.a.	n.a.	n.a.
Non-malignant	0	n.a.	n.a.	n.a.	n.a.
Not specified	0	1,297	120	5	1,422
All disease types	0	1,297	120	5	1,422
Claim payments ($)					
Malignant	0	n.a.	n.a.	n.a.	n.a.
Non-malignant	0	n.a.	n.a.	n.a.	n.a.
Not specified	0	31,294,191	2,280,062	72,403	33,646,656
All disease types	0	31,294,191	2,280,062	72,403	33,646,656
Average payment per claim ($)					
Malignant	–	–	–	–	–
Non-malignant	–	–	–	–	–
Not specified	–	24,128	19,001	14,481	23,662
All disease types	–	24,128	19,001	14,481	23,662

J.T. Thorpe Settlement Trust (continued)

Claim Approval Criteria for	J.T. Thorpe California claims						
	Meso	LC	OC	G1NM-BC [a]	G1NM-E [b]	G1NM-SA [c]	G2NM
1. Diagnosis requirement (one or more of checked items satisfies requirement)							
a. Physical exam	✔	✔	✔	✔	✔	✔	✔
b. Pathology	✔	✔	✔	✔	✔	✔	✔
c. Medical document review							
2. ILO or x-ray requirement							
a. ILO reading		1/0	1/0	1/0	1/1	2/2	1/0
OR b. X-ray, CT scan, or pathology showing one or more of the checked conditions							
(1) Bilateral interstitial fibrosis				✔	✔		✔
(2) Bilateral pleural plaques							
(3) Bilateral pleural thickening							
(4) Bilateral pleural calcification							
3. Pulmonary function test requirement [d]							
a. TLC < (% of normal)				80	70		
AND FEV1/FVC ratio >							
OR b. DLCO < (% of normal)				75	60		
AND FEV1/FVC ratio >				0.65	0.65		
OR c. FVC < (% of normal)				80	60		
AND FEV1/FVC ratio >				0.65	0.65		
4. Causation statement requirement	No	No	No	No	No	No	No
5. Latency and exposure requirements							
a. Latency	10 yr	10 yr	10 yr	10 yr	10 yr	10 yr	10 yr
b. Company exposure prior to 1983	3 mo	1 yr	1 yr	1 yr	1 yr	1 yr	1 yr
c. Occupational exposure							
(1) Total							
(2) Prior to 1983							

[a] Grade I non-malignancy, base case

[b] Grade I non-malignancy, enhanced

[c] Grade I non-malignancy, serious asbestosis

[d] Claimant assumed to be at least 70 years old

Kaiser Aluminum & Chemical Corporation Asbestos Personal Injury Trust

Kaiser Aluminum & Chemical Corporation Asbestos Personal Injury Trust

Bankruptcy Court and Trust Administrative Information

Debtor(s)	Kaiser Aluminum & Chemical Corporation		
Bankruptcy filing date	2/12/02	Confirmation date	5/11/06
Bankruptcy court	Bankr. D. Del.	Bankruptcy judge	Judith Fitzgerald

Trust status	Active
Date trust established	7/6/06
Classes of claims processed	Kaiser claims
Claim administrator	Verus Claims Services
Trust website	www.kaiserasbestostrust.com

Trustees and Advisors

Position	Name	Affiliation
Trustee	Ken Kawaichi	Retired California judge
Trustee	Mark Gleason	Gleason & Associates, P.C.
Trustee	Robert Marcis	unknown
FCR	Martin Murphy	Davis & Young
TAC Member	Matthew Bergman	Bergman Draper & Frockt, PLLC
TAC Member	Alan Brayton	Brayton Purcell
TAC Member	John Cooney	Cooney & Conway
TAC Member	Perry Weitz	Weitz & Luxenburg
TAC Member	Steven Kazan	Kazan, McClain, Lyons, Greenwood & Harley
Trust Counsel	Joseph Frank	Frank/Gecker LLP
FCR Counsel	Sharon Zieg	Young Conaway Stargatt & Taylor LLP

Estimated Initial Funding of Trust ($ millions)

	Funding for Claims Paid Through Trust	Funding for Claims Paid Outside Trust
Cash from debtor(s)	13.0	0
Stock from debtors(s)	48.4	0
Insurance settlements	1,156.7	0
Other assets	0.0	0
Total	1,218.1	0

Kaiser Aluminum & Chemical Corporation Asbestos Personal Injury Trust (continued)

Trust Financial Statement ($)

	Pre-2006	2006	2007	2008
Beginning trust assets	0	0	1,232,139,271	1,196,852,983
Additions				
Cash from debtors	0	311,526,421	78,180,655	119,549,884
Stock from debtors	0	48,375,215	1,276,811	0
Insurance settlements	0	0	0	0
Investment gains	0	14,175,003	1,149,828	-63,872,973
Investment income	0	2,837,487	16,901,762	18,767,794
Other additions [a]	0	858,205,659	-72,000,639	-114,502,061
Deductions				
Trust expenses	0	2,980,514	4,134,780	3,671,040
Claim processing costs	0	290,000	1,054,086	1,087,668
Investment fees	0	0	0	0
All other expenses	0	2,690,514	3,080,694	2,583,372
Taxes	0	0	3,599,636	-3,788,282
Claim payments	0	0	53,060,289	62,880,974
Other deductions	0	0	0	0
Ending trust assets	0	1,232,139,271	1,196,852,983	1,094,031,895
Gross claimant compensation as a percentage of deductions				
Lower bound	–	0.0%	87.3%	94.5%
Upper bound	–	0.0%	87.3%	94.5%

Claim Valuation for Kaiser claims

Disease level	Scheduled Value	Average Value	Maximum Value
Mesothelioma	70,000	104,000	380,000
Lung Cancer 1	27,500	33,000	85,000
Lung Cancer 2	n.appl.	7,000	20,000
Other Cancer	13,800	17,300	40,000
Severe Asbestosis	20,750	22,000	55,000
Asbestosis / Pleural Disease II	4,850	n.appl.	n.appl.
Asbestosis / Pleural Disease I	700	n.appl.	n.appl.
Other Asbestos Disease	200 *	n.appl.	n.appl.

Payment percentage	
Initial payment percentage	39.5%
Current payment percentage	39.5%

Claim payment ratio	
Malignancies and severe asbestosis	70.0%
Asbestosis and pleural disease	30.0%

*Payment percentage does not apply

[a] Reductions in 2007 and 2008 are offset by cash from debtors.

Kaiser Aluminum & Chemical Corporation Asbestos Personal Injury Trust (continued)

Claim Activity

	Pre-2006	2006	2007	2008	Total
Pre-petition pending and post-petition claims					
Claims filed					
Malignant [a]	0	152	18,509	6,082	24,743
Non-malignant	0	286	87,123	26,782	114,191
Not specified	0	2	314	1,031	1,347
All disease types	0	440	105,946	33,895	140,281
Claims paid					
Malignant	0	0	1,779	2,294	4,073
Non-malignant	0	0	14,469	15,558	30,027
Not specified	0	0	0	0	0
All disease types	0	0	16,248	17,852	34,100
Claim payments ($)					
Malignant	0	0	28,958,003	47,193,372	76,151,375
Non-malignant	0	0	14,703,094	14,150,462	28,853,556
Not specified	0	0	0	0	0
All disease types	0	0	43,661,097	61,343,834	105,004,931
Average payment per claim ($)					
Malignant	–	–	16,278	20,573	18,697
Non-malignant	–	–	1,016	910	961
Not specified	–	–	–	–	–
All disease types	–	–	2,687	3,436	3,079
Claims settled but not paid pre-petition					
Claims filed					
Malignant	0	n.a.	n.a.	n.a.	n.a.
Non-malignant	0	n.a.	n.a.	n.a.	n.a.
Not specified	0	11,169	0	0	11,169
All disease types	0	11,169	0	0	11,169
Claims paid					
Malignant	0	n.a.	n.a.	n.a.	n.a.
Non-malignant	0	n.a.	n.a.	n.a.	n.a.
Not specified	0	0	8,944	904	9,848
All disease types	0	0	8,944	904	9,848
Claim payments ($)					
Malignant	0	n.a.	n.a.	n.a.	n.a.
Non-malignant	0	n.a.	n.a.	n.a.	n.a.
Not specified	0	0	9,392,088	1,537,992	10,930,080
All disease types	0	0	9,392,088	1,537,992	10,930,080
Average payment per claim ($)					
Malignant	–	–	–	–	–
Non-malignant	–	–	–	–	–
Not specified	–	–	1,050	1,701	1,110
All disease types	–	–	1,050	1,701	1,110

[a] Malignant claims for this trust include severe asbestosis claims.

Kaiser Aluminum & Chemical Corporation Asbestos Personal Injury Trust (continued)

Claim Approval Criteria for	Kaiser claims							
	Meso	LC1	LC2	OC	SA	AP1	AP2	OAD
1. Diagnosis requirement (one or more of checked items satisfies requirement)								
a. Physical exam	✔	✔	✔	✔	✔	✔	✔	✔
b. Pathology	✔	✔	✔	✔	✔	✔	✔	✔
c. Medical document review								
2. ILO or x-ray requirement								
a. ILO reading		1/0		1/0	2/1	1/0	1/0	1/0
OR b. X-ray, CT scan, or pathology showing one or more of the checked conditions								
(1) Bilateral interstitial fibrosis		✔		✔		✔	✔	✔
(2) Bilateral pleural plaques		✔		✔		✔	✔	✔
(3) Bilateral pleural thickening		✔		✔		✔	✔	✔
(4) Bilateral pleural calcification		✔		✔		✔	✔	✔
3. Pulmonary function test requirement								
a. TLC < (% of normal)					65	80		
AND FEV1/FVC ratio >								
OR b. DLCO < (% of normal)								
AND FEV1/FVC ratio >								
OR c. FVC < (% of normal)					65	80		
AND FEV1/FVC ratio >					0.65	0.65		
4. Causation statement requirement	No	Yes	Yes	Yes	Yes	Yes	No	No
5. Latency and exposure requirements								
a. Latency	10 yr	10 yr	10 yr	10 yr	10 yr	10 yr	10 yr	10 yr
b. Company exposure prior to 1983	1 day	6 mo	1 day	6 mo	6 mo	6 mo	6 mo	1 day
c. Occupational exposure								
(1) Total		5 yr		5 yr	5 yr	5 yr	5 yr	
(2) Prior to 1983	1 day	2 yr	1 day	2 yr	2 yr	2 yr	6 mo	1 day

Manville Personal Injury Settlement Trust

Manville Personal Injury Settlement Trust

Bankruptcy Court and Trust Administrative Information

Debtor(s)	Johns-Manville Corp.		
	Philadelphia Asbestos Corp. (Pacor)		
Bankruptcy filing date	8/1/82	Confirmation date	7/15/87
Bankruptcy court	Bankr. E.D. N.Y.	Bankruptcy judge	Burton Lifland
Trust status	Active		
Date trust established	11/28/88		
Classes of claims processed	Manville claims		
Claim administrator	Claims Resolution Management Corporation		
Trust website	www.mantrust.org		

Trustees and Advisors

Position	Name	Affiliation
Trustee	Robert Falise	Chair, Manville Trust
Trustee	Mark Peterson	Legal Analysis Systems
Trustee	Frank Macchiarola	St. Francis College
Trust Counsel	David Austern	Claims Resolution Management Corporation

Estimated Initial Funding of Trust ($ millions)

	Funding for Claims Paid Through Trust	Funding for Claims Paid Outside Trust
Cash from debtor(s)	n.a.	0
Stock from debtors(s)	n.a.	0
Insurance settlements	n.a.	0
Other assets	n.a.	0
Total	2,500	0

Manville Personal Injury Settlement Trust (continued)

Trust Financial Statement ($)

	Pre-2006	2006	2007	2008
Beginning trust assets	n.a.	1,631,697,081	1,741,502,894	1,778,033,708
Additions				
Cash from debtors	n.a.	0	0	0
Stock from debtors	n.a.	0	0	0
Insurance settlements	n.a.	0	0	0
Investment gains	n.a.	126,514,659	46,485,857	-332,797,421
Investment income	n.a.	47,316,328	53,204,278	44,641,131
Other additions	n.a.	2,422,729	492,300	504,640
Deductions				
Trust expenses	n.a.	5,714,275	5,367,920	5,820,633
Claim processing costs	n.a.	n.a.	n.a.	n.a.
Investment fees	n.a.	n.a.	n.a.	n.a.
All other expenses	n.a.	n.a.	n.a.	n.a.
Taxes	n.a.	7,450,800	9,922,200	9,278,800
Claim payments	3,313,553,508	52,690,236	47,876,548	467,209,590
Other deductions	n.a.	592,592	484,953	3,187,230
Ending trust assets	1,631,697,081	1,741,502,894	1,778,033,708	1,004,885,805

Gross claimant compensation as a percentage of deductions				
Lower bound	–	79.3%	75.2%	96.2%
Upper bound	–	80.2%	76.0%	96.9%

Claim Valuation for   Manville claims

Disease level	Scheduled Value	Average Value	Maximum Value
Mesothelioma	350,000	n.appl.	750,000
Lung Cancer 1	95,000	n.appl.	400,000
Lung Cancer 2	n.appl.	40,000	50,000
Other Cancer	45,000	n.appl.	200,000
Severe Asbestosis	95,000	n.appl.	400,000
Asbestosis / Pleural Disease II	25,000	n.appl.	40,000
Asbestosis / Pleural Disease I	12,000	n.appl.	30,000
Other Asbestos Disease	600 *	n.appl.	600 *

Payment percentage	
Initial payment percentage	100.0%
Current payment percentage	7.5%

Claim payment ratio	
Malignancies and severe asbestosis	n.appl.
Asbestosis and pleural disease	n.appl.

*Payment percentage does not apply

Manville Personal Injury Settlement Trust (continued)

Claim Activity

	Pre-2006	2006	2007	2008	Total
Pre-petition pending and post-petition claims					
Claims filed					
Malignant	n.a.	n.a.	n.a.	n.a.	n.a.
Non-malignant	n.a.	n.a.	n.a.	n.a.	n.a.
Not specified	767,700	10,500	10,097	13,442	801,739
All disease types	767,700	10,500	10,097	13,442	801,739
Claims paid					
Malignant	n.a.	n.a.	n.a.	n.a.	n.a.
Non-malignant	n.a.	n.a.	n.a.	n.a.	n.a.
Not specified	659,982	12,231	10,103	12,415	694,731
All disease types	659,982	12,231	10,103	12,415	694,731
Claim payments ($)					
Malignant	n.a.	n.a.	n.a.	n.a.	n.a.
Non-malignant	n.a.	n.a.	n.a.	n.a.	n.a.
Not specified	3,360,733,676	52,690,236	47,646,174	420,259,796 [a]	3,881,329,882
All disease types	3,360,733,676	52,690,236	47,646,174	420,259,796	3,881,329,882
Average payment per claim ($)					
Malignant	–	–	–	–	–
Non-malignant	–	–	–	–	–
Not specified	5,092 [b]	4,308 [b]	4,716 [b]	6,908 [c]	5,587
All disease types	5,092	4,308	4,716	6,908	5,587
Claims settled but not paid pre-petition					
Claims filed					
Malignant	0	0	0	0	0
Non-malignant	0	0	0	0	0
Not specified	0	0	0	0	0
All disease types	0	0	0	0	0
Claims paid					
Malignant	0	0	0	0	0
Non-malignant	0	0	0	0	0
Not specified	0	0	0	0	0
All disease types	0	0	0	0	0
Claim payments ($)					
Malignant	0	0	0	0	0
Non-malignant	0	0	0	0	0
Not specified	0	0	0	0	0
All disease types	0	0	0	0	0
Average payment per claim ($)					
Malignant	–	–	–	–	–
Non-malignant	–	–	–	–	–
Not specified	–	–	–	–	–
All disease types	–	–	–	–	–

[a] Includes $334.5 million in retroactive payments to approximately 225,000 claimants to account for the increase in payment percentage from 5 percent to 7.5 percent in 2008.

[b] Does not include retroactive payments made in 2008.

[c] Excludes $334.5 million in retroactive payments made in 2008.

Manville Personal Injury Settlement Trust (continued)

Claim Approval Criteria for	Meso	LC1	LC2	OC	SA	AP2	AP1	OAD
1. Diagnosis requirement (one or more of checked items satisfies requirement)								
a. Physical exam	✔	✔	✔	✔	✔	✔	✔	✔
b. Pathology	✔	✔	✔	✔	✔	✔	✔	✔
c. Medical document review								
2. ILO or x-ray requirement								
a. ILO reading		1/0		1/0	2/1	1/0	1/0	1/0
OR b. X-ray, CT scan, or pathology showing one or more of the checked conditions								
(1) Bilateral interstitial fibrosis		✔		✔			✔	✔
(2) Bilateral pleural plaques		✔		✔			✔	✔
(3) Bilateral pleural thickening		✔		✔			✔	✔
(4) Bilateral pleural calcification								
3. Pulmonary function test requirement								
a. TLC < (% of normal)					65	80		
AND FEV1/FVC ratio >								
OR b. DLCO < (% of normal)								
AND FEV1/FVC ratio >					65	80		
OR c. FVC < (% of normal)					65	80		
AND FEV1/FVC ratio >					0.65	0.65		
4. Causation statement requirement	No	Yes	Yes	Yes	Yes	Yes	No	No
5. Latency and exposure requirements								
a. Latency	10 yr	10 yr	10 yr	10 yr	10 yr	10 yr	10 yr	10 yr
b. Company exposure	1 day	6 mo	1 day	6 mo	6 mo	6 mo	6 mo	1 day
c. Occupational exposure								
(1) Total		5 yr		5 yr	5 yr	5 yr	5 yr	
(2) Prior to 1983	1 day	6 mo	1 day	6 mo	6 mo	6 mo	6 mo	1 day

NGC Bodily Injury Trust

NGC Bodily Injury Trust

Bankruptcy Court and Trust Administrative Information

Debtor(s)	National Gypsum		
	Asbestos Claims Management Corp. (ACMC)		
Bankruptcy filing date	10/28/90	Confirmation date	3/9/93
Bankruptcy court	Bankr. N.D. Tex.	Bankruptcy judge	Harlin DeWayne Hale

Trust status	Active
Date trust established	1993
Classes of claims processed	NGC Bodily Injury Trust claims
Executive Director	W.D. Hilton, Jr.
Claim administrator	Trust Services, Inc.
Trust website	www.ngcbitrust.org

Trustees and Advisors

Position	Name	Affiliation
Trustee	Anne Ferazzi	unknown
Trustee	Anne Foreman	Geo Group Inc
Trustee	Walter Taggart	Villanova University School of Law
TAC Member	Robert Steinberg	Rose, Klein & Marias, LLP.
TAC Member	Russell Budd	Baron & Budd, P.C.
TAC Member	Mark Iola	Stanley, Mandel & Iola, LLP
Trust Counsel	Aaron York	Sacks Tierney, P.A.

Estimated Initial Funding of Trust ($ millions)

	Funding for Claims Paid Through Trust	Funding for Claims Paid Outside Trust
Cash from debtor(s)	373.4	0
Stock from debtors(s)	0.0	0
Insurance settlements	63.0	0
Other assets	9.9	0
Total	446.3	0

NGC Bodily Injury Trust (continued)

Trust Financial Statement ($)

	Pre-2006 [a]	2006	2007	2008
Beginning trust assets	0	603,660,490	543,330,853	513,990,993
Additions				
Cash from debtors	486,372,232	0	0	0
Stock from debtors	0	0	0	0
Insurance settlements	66,843,688	6,190,817	1,042,161	26,425
Investment gains	15,541,275	5,674,268	8,035,485	-61,364,284
Investment income	27,576,868	23,495,218	27,121,850	15,317,121
Other additions	36,339,280	0	0	0
Deductions				
Trust expenses	16,490,213	6,448,120	5,966,337	6,570,547
Claim processing costs	n.a.	n.a.	n.a.	n.a.
Investment fees	n.a.	n.a.	n.a.	n.a.
All other expenses	n.a.	n.a.	n.a.	n.a.
Taxes	-1,477,834	3,154,814	5,533,675	-22,612,160
Claim payments	14,000,474	86,087,006	54,039,344	48,775,188
Other deductions	0	0	0	0
Ending trust assets	603,660,490	543,330,853	513,990,993	435,236,680
Gross claimant compensation as a percentage of deductions				
Lower bound	48.3%	90.0%	82.5%	88.1%
Upper bound	48.3%	90.0%	82.5%	88.1%

[a] Data for pre-2006 period incomplete.

Claim Valuation for NGC Bodily Injury Trust claims

Disease level	Scheduled Value	Average Value	Maximum Value
Mesothelioma	22,500	45,000	180,000
Lung Cancer	3,750	7,500	30,000
Other Cancer	1,600	3,200	12,800
Non-Malignant I	1,000	2,000	8,000
Non-Malignant II	500	1,000	4,000
Non-Malignant III	250 *	n.appl.	n.appl.

Payment percentage	
Initial payment percentage	n.a.
Current payment percentage	55.6%

Claim payment ratio	
Malignancies and severe asbestosis	n.appl.
Asbestosis and pleural disease	n.appl.

*Payment percentage does not apply

NGC Bodily Injury Trust (continued)

Claim Activity

	Pre-2006 [a]	2006	2007	2008	Total
Pre-petition pending and post-petition claims					
Claims filed					
Malignant	n.a.	n.a.	n.a.	n.a.	n.a.
Non-malignant	n.a.	n.a.	n.a.	n.a.	n.a.
Not specified	n.a.	n.a.	n.a.	n.a.	n.a.
All disease types	n.a.	n.a.	n.a.	n.a.	n.a.
Claims paid					
Malignant	n.a.	n.a.	n.a.	n.a.	n.a.
Non-malignant	n.a.	n.a.	n.a.	n.a.	n.a.
Not specified	n.a.	n.a.	n.a.	n.a.	n.a.
All disease types	n.a.	n.a.	n.a.	n.a.	n.a.
Claim payments ($)					
Malignant	n.a.	n.a.	n.a.	n.a.	n.a.
Non-malignant	n.a.	n.a.	n.a.	n.a.	n.a.
Not specified	14,000,474	86,087,006	54,039,344	48,775,188	202,902,012
All disease types	14,000,474	86,087,006	54,039,344	48,775,188	202,902,012
Average payment per claim ($)					
Malignant	–	–	–	–	–
Non-malignant	–	–	–	–	–
Not specified	–	–	–	–	–
All disease types	–	–	–	–	–
Claims settled but not paid pre-petition					
Claims filed					
Malignant	0	0	0	0	0
Non-malignant	0	0	0	0	0
Not specified	0	0	0	0	0
All disease types	0	0	0	0	0
Claims paid					
Malignant	0	0	0	0	0
Non-malignant	0	0	0	0	0
Not specified	0	0	0	0	0
All disease types	0	0	0	0	0
Claim payments ($)					
Malignant	0	0	0	0	0
Non-malignant	0	0	0	0	0
Not specified	0	0	0	0	0
All disease types	0	0	0	0	0
Average payment per claim ($)					
Malignant	–	–	–	–	–
Non-malignant	–	–	–	–	–
Not specified	–	–	–	–	–
All disease types	–	–	–	–	–

[a] Data for pre-2006 period incomplete

NGC Bodily Injury Trust (continued)

Claim Approval Criteria for	NGC Bodily Injury Trust claims					
	Meso	LC	OC	NM1A [a]	NM1B [b]	NM1C [c]
1. Diagnosis requirement (one or more of checked items satisfies requirement)						
a. Physical exam	✔	✔	✔	✔	✔	✔
b. Pathology	✔	✔	✔	✔	✔	✔
c. Medical document review						
2. ILO or x-ray requirement						
a. ILO reading		B	1/0	2/1	1/0	B2/C1
OR b. X-ray, CT scan, or pathology showing one or more of the checked conditions						
(1) Bilateral interstitial fibrosis		✔	✔		✔	
(2) Bilateral pleural plaques		✔				
(3) Bilateral pleural thickening		✔	✔			
(4) Bilateral pleural calcification						
3. Pulmonary function test requirement						
a. TLC < (% of normal)				70	80	80
AND FEV1/FVC ratio >						
OR b. DLCO < (% of normal)					76	
AND FEV1/FVC ratio >					0.72	
OR c. FVC < (% of normal)				70	80	80
AND FEV1/FVC ratio >					0.72	0.72
4. Causation statement requirement	No	No	No	No	No	No
5. Latency and exposure requirements						
a. Latency	10 yr	10 yr	10 yr	10 yr	10 yr	10 yr
b. Company exposure	1 day	1 day	1 day	1 day	1 day	1 day
c. Occupational exposure						
(1) Total	10 yr					
(2) Prior to 1983						

[a] Non-Malignant I, Asbestosis I-A

[b] Non-Malignant I, Asbestosis I-B

[c] Non-Malignant I, Diffuse Pleural Thickening I

NGC Bodily Injury Trust (continued)

Claim Approval Criteria for	NGC Bodily Injury Trust claims			
	NM2A [a]	NM2B [b]	NM3A [c]	NM3B [d]
1. Diagnosis requirement (one or more of checked items satisfies requirement)				
a. Physical exam	✔	✔	✔	✔
b. Pathology	✔	✔	✔	✔
c. Medical document review				
2. ILO or x-ray requirement				
a. ILO reading	1/0	B2/C1	1/0	0
OR b. X-ray, CT scan, or pathology showing one or more of the checked conditions				
(1) Bilateral interstitial fibrosis				
(2) Bilateral pleural plaques				✔
(3) Bilateral pleural thickening				✔
(4) Bilateral pleural calcification				
3. Pulmonary function test requirement				
a. TLC < (% of normal)				
AND FEV1/FVC ratio >				
OR b. DLCO < (% of normal)				
AND FEV1/FVC ratio >				
OR c. FVC < (% of normal)				
AND FEV1/FVC ratio >				
4. Causation statement requirement	No	Yes	Yes	Yes
5. Latency and exposure requirements				
a. Latency	10 yr	10 yr	10 yr	10 yr
b. Company exposure	1 day	1 day	1 day	1 day
c. Occupational exposure				
(1) Total				
(2) Prior to 1983				

[a] Non–Malignant II, Asbestosis II

[b] Non–Malignant II, Pleural Thickening II

[c] Non–Malignant III, Fibrosis III

[d] Non–Malignant III, Pleural Changes III

North American Refractories Company Asbestos Personal Injury Settlement Trust

North American Refractories Company Asbestos Personal Injury Settlement Trust

Bankruptcy Court and Trust Administrative Information

Debtor(s)	North American Refractories Corp. (NARCO)		
Bankruptcy filing date	1/4/02	Confirmation date	7/25/08
Bankruptcy court	Bankr. W.D. Pa.	Bankruptcy judge	Judith Fitzgerald
Trust status	Proposed		
Date trust established	–		
Classes of claims processed	North American Refractories Company claims		
Claim administrator	Not yet selected		
Trust website	www.rhireorg.com		

Trustees and Advisors

Position	Name	Affiliation
FCR	Lawrence Fitzpatrick	Asbestos Claims Facility
FCR Counsel	James Patton	Young Conaway Stargatt & Taylor LLP
FCR Counsel	Joel Helmrich	Dinsmore & Shohl LLP
FCR Counsel	Edwin J. Harron	Young Conaway Stargatt & Taylor LLP

Estimated Initial Funding of Trust ($ millions) [a]

	Funding for Claims Paid Through Trust	Funding for Claims Paid Outside Trust
Cash from debtor(s)	6,320.0	1,978.0
Stock from debtors(s)	0.0	0.0
Insurance settlements	0.0	0.0
Other assets	0.0	0.0
Total	6,320.0	1,978.0

[a] Proposed

North American Refractories Company Asbestos Personal Injury Settlement Trust (continued)

Trust Financial Statement ($)

	Pre-2006	2006	2007	2008
Beginning trust assets				
Additions				
Cash from debtors				
Stock from debtors				
Insurance settlements				
Investment gains				
Investment income				
Other additions				
Deductions		TRUST NOT YET OPEN		
Trust expenses				
Claim processing costs				
Investment fees				
All other expenses				
Taxes				
Claim payments				
Other deductions				
Ending trust assets				
Gross claimant compensation as a percentage of deductions				
Lower bound	–	–	–	–
Upper bound	–	–	–	–

Claim Valuation for a	North American Refractories Company claims		
	Scheduled	Average	Maximum
Disease level	Value	Value	Value
Mesothelioma	75,000	200,000	1,000,000
Lung Cancer 1	18,000	50,000	200,000
Lung Cancer 2	n.appl.	15,000	50,000
Other Cancer	9,000	25,000	100,000
Severe Asbestosis	18,000	50,000	100,000
Asbestosis / Pleural Disease II	7,500	n.appl.	n.appl.
Asbestosis / Pleural Disease I	1,200	n.appl.	n.appl.

Payment percentage	
Initial payment percentage	100.0%
Current payment percentage	100.0%

Claim payment ratio	
Malignancies and severe asbestosis	60.0%
Asbestosis and pleural disease	40.0%

[a] Proposed

North American Refractories Company Asbestos Personal Injury Settlement Trust (continued)

Claim Activity

	Pre-2006	2006	2007	2008	Total
Pre-petition pending and post-petition claims					
Claims filed					
Malignant					
Non-malignant					
Not specified					
All disease types					
Claims paid					
Malignant					
Non-malignant					
Not specified					
All disease types					
Claim payments ($)					
Malignant					
Non-malignant					
Not specified					
All disease types					
Average payment per claim ($)					
Malignant					
Non-malignant					
Not specified					
All disease types					
Claims settled but not paid pre-petition					
Claims filed					
Malignant					
Non-malignant					
Not specified					
All disease types					
Claims paid					
Malignant					
Non-malignant					
Not specified					
All disease types					
Claim payments ($)					
Malignant					
Non-malignant					
Not specified					
All disease types					
Average payment per claim ($)					
Malignant					
Non-malignant					
Not specified					
All disease types					

TRUST NOT YET OPEN

North American Refractories Company Asbestos Personal Injury Settlement Trust (continued)

Claim Approval Criteria for	North American Refractories Company claims						
	Meso	LC1	LC2	OC	SA	AP2	AP1
1. Diagnosis requirement (one or more of checked items satisfies requirement)							
a. Physical exam	✔	✔	✔	✔	✔	✔	✔
b. Pathology	✔	✔	✔	✔	✔	✔	✔
c. Medical document review							
2. ILO or x-ray requirement							
a. ILO reading		1/0		1/0	2/1	1/0	1/0
OR b. X-ray, CT scan, or pathology showing one or more of the checked conditions							
(1) Bilateral interstitial fibrosis		✔		✔		✔	✔
(2) Bilateral pleural plaques		✔		✔		✔	✔
(3) Bilateral pleural thickening		✔		✔		✔	✔
(4) Bilateral pleural calcification		✔		✔		✔	✔
3. Pulmonary function test requirement							
a. TLC < (% of normal)					65	80	
AND FEV1/FVC ratio >							
OR b. DLCO < (% of normal)							
AND FEV1/FVC ratio >							
OR c. FVC < (% of normal)					65	80	
AND FEV1/FVC ratio >					0.65	0.65	
4. Causation statement requirement	No	Yes	Yes	Yes	Yes	Yes	No
5. Latency and exposure requirements							
a. Latency	10 yr	10 yr	10 yr	10 yr	10 yr	10 yr	10 yr
b. Company exposure prior to 1983	1 day	1 day	1 day	1 day	1 day	1 day	1 day
c. Occupational exposure							
(1) Total		5 yr		5 yr	5 yr	5 yr	5 yr
(2) Prior to 1983							

Owens Corning Fibreboard Asbestos Personal Injury Trust—Fibreboard Subfund

Owens Corning Fibreboard Asbestos Personal Injury Trust - Fibreboard Subfund

Bankruptcy Court and Trust Administrative Information

Debtor(s)	Fibreboard		
Bankruptcy filing date	10/5/00	Confirmation date	10/31/06
Bankruptcy court	Bankr. D. Del.	Bankruptcy judge	Judith Fitzgerald

Trust status	Active
Date trust established	2006
Classes of claims processed	Fibreboard claims
Claim administrator	Delaware Claims Processing Facility
Trust website	www.ocfbasbestostrust.com

Trustees and Advisors

Position	Name	Affiliation
Managing Trustee	Dean Trafelet	Retired Cook County Circuit Court Judge
Trustee	Harry Huge	Harry Huge Law Firm, LLP
Trustee	LeAnne Jackson	formerly at Baron & Budd, current affilation unknown
FCR	Michael Crames	Peter J. Solomon Company
TAC Member	Armand Volta	Peter G. Angelos
TAC Member	James Ferrano	Kelley & Ferraro, LLC
TAC Member	John Cooney	Cooney & Conway
TAC Member	Joseph Rice	Motley Rice, LLC
TAC Member	Matthew Bergman	Bergman Draper & Frockt, PLLC
TAC Member	Perry Weitz	Weitz & Luxenburg
TAC Member	Russell Budd	Baron & Budd, P.C.
TAC Member	Steven Kazan	Kazan, McClain, Abrams, Fernandez, Lyons, Farrise & Greenwood, P.C.
TAC Member	Theodore Goldberg	Goldberg, Persky & White P.C.
Trust Counsel	Douglas A. Campbell	Campbell & Levine, LLC
Trust Counsel	Philip E. Milch	Campbell & Levine, LLC
Trust Counsel	Marla R. Eskin	Campbell & Levine, LLC
FCR Counsel	Andrew Kress	Kaye Scholer LLP
TAC Counsel	Elihu Inselbuch	Caplin & Drysdale

Estimated Initial Funding of Trust ($ millions)

	Funding for Claims Paid Through Trust	Funding for Claims Paid Outside Trust
Cash from debtor(s)	1,524.9	0
Stock from debtors(s)	0.0	0
Insurance settlements	31.2	0
Other assets	0.0	0
Total	1,556.1	0

Owens Corning Fibreboard Asbestos Personal Injury Trust - Fibreboard Subfund (continued)

Trust Financial Statement ($)

	Pre-2006	2006	2007	2008
Beginning trust assets	0	0	1,418,778,749	1,487,025,977
Additions				
Cash from debtors	0	1,442,100,041	82,813,605	0
Stock from debtors	0	0	0	0
Insurance settlements	0	0	31,152,490	0
Investment gains	0	-48,542,828	25,416,230	-129,844,630
Investment income	0	27,078,245	36,353,043	52,429,085
Other additions	0	0	0	0
Deductions				
Trust expenses	0	1,856,709	9,781,985	14,740,896
Claim processing costs	0	485,451	3,016,356	7,312,285
Investment fees	0	54,774	3,312,185	3,824,624
All other expenses	0	1,316,484	3,453,444	3,603,987
Taxes	0	0	0	0
Claim payments	0	0	97,706,155	262,889,010
Other deductions	0	0	0	0
Ending trust assets	0	1,418,778,749	1,487,025,977	1,131,980,526
Gross claimant compensation as a percentage of deductions				
Lower bound	–	0.0%	90.9%	94.7%
Upper bound	–	0.0%	90.9%	94.7%

Claim Valuation for Fibreboard claims

Disease level	Scheduled Value	Average Value	Maximum Value
Mesothelioma	135,000	180,000	450,000
Lung Cancer I	27,000	35,000	90,000
Lung Cancer II	n.appl.	12,000	30,000
Other Cancer	12,000	15,000	36,000
Severe Asbestosis	29,000	30,000	90,000
Asbestosis / Plueral Disease II	11,500	12,000	21,000
Asbestosis / Plueral Disease I	4,500	5,400	12,000
Other Asbestos Disease	240 *	n.appl.	n.appl.

Payment percentage

Initial payment percentage	25.0%
Current payment percentage	11.0%

Claim payment ratio

Malignancies and severe asbestosis	65.0%
Asbestosis and pleural disease	35.0%

*Payment percentage does not apply

Owens Corning Fibreboard Asbestos Personal Injury Trust - Fibreboard Subfund (continued)

Claim Activity

	Pre-2006	2006	2007	2008	Total
Pre-petition pending and post-petition claims					
Claims filed					
Malignant	0	0	n.a.	n.a.	n.a.
Non-malignant	0	0	n.a.	n.a.	n.a.
Not specified	0	0	116,725	102,471	219,196
All disease types	0	0	116,725	102,471	219,196
Claims paid					
Malignant	0	0	82	6,164	6,246
Non-malignant	0	0	854	45,564	46,418
Not specified	0	0	0	1,000	1,000
All disease types	0	0	936	52,728	53,664
Claim payments ($)					
Malignant	0	0	825,000	140,538,000	141,363,000
Non-malignant	0	0	1,375,000	93,692,000	95,067,000
Not specified	0	0	0	0	0
All disease types	0	0	2,200,000	234,230,000	236,430,000
Average payment per claim ($)					
Malignant	–	–	10,061	22,800	22,633
Non-malignant	–	–	1,610	2,056	2,048
Not specified	–	–	–	0	0
All disease types	–	–	2,350	4,442	4,406
Claims settled but not paid pre-petition					
Claims filed [a]					
Malignant	0	0	n.a.	n.a.	n.a.
Non-malignant	0	0	n.a.	n.a.	n.a.
Not specified	0	0	31,249	0	31,249
All disease types	0	0	31,249	0	31,249
Claims paid					
Malignant	0	0	2,631	783	3,414
Non-malignant	0	0	28,401	7,316	35,717
Not specified	0	0	0	0	0
All disease types	0	0	31,032	8,099	39,131
Claim payments ($)					
Malignant	0	0	57,000,000	15,035,000	72,035,000
Non-malignant	0	0	38,000,000	15,035,000	53,035,000
Not specified	0	0	0	0	0
All disease types	0	0	95,000,000	30,070,000	125,070,000
Average payment per claim ($)					
Malignant	–	–	21,665	19,202	21,100
Non-malignant	–	–	1,338	2,055	1,485
Not specified	–	–	–	–	–
All disease types	–	–	3,061	3,713	3,196

[a] Claims filed data incomplete

Owens Corning Fibreboard Asbestos Personal Injury Trust - Fibreboard Subfund (continued)

Claim Approval Criteria for	Fibreboard claims							
	Meso	LC1	LC2	OC	SA	AP2	AP1	OAD
1. Diagnosis requirement (one or more of checked items satisfies requirement)								
a. Physical exam	✔	✔	✔	✔	✔	✔	✔	✔
b. Pathology	✔	✔	✔	✔	✔	✔	✔	✔
c. Medical document review								
2. ILO or x-ray requirement								
a. ILO reading		1/0		1/0	2/1	1/0	1/0	1/0
OR b. X-ray, CT scan, or pathology showing one or more of the checked conditions								
(1) Bilateral interstitial fibrosis		✔		✔		✔	✔	✔
(2) Bilateral pleural plaques		✔		✔		✔	✔	✔
(3) Bilateral pleural thickening		✔		✔		✔	✔	✔
(4) Bilateral pleural calcification		✔		✔		✔	✔	✔
3. Pulmonary function test requirement								
a. TLC < (% of normal)					65	80		
AND FEV1/FVC ratio >								
OR b. DLCO < (% of normal)								
AND FEV1/FVC ratio >								
OR c. FVC < (% of normal)					65	80		
AND FEV1/FVC ratio >					0.65	0.65		
4. Causation statement requirement	No	Yes	Yes	Yes	Yes	Yes	Yes	No
5. Latency and exposure requirements								
a. Latency	10 yr	10 yr	10 yr	10 yr	10 yr	10 yr	10 yr	10 yr
b. Company exposure prior to 1983	1 day	6 mo	1 day	6 mo	6 mo	6 mo	6 mo	1 day
c. Occupational exposure								
(1) Total		5 yr		5 yr	5 yr	5 yr	5 yr	
(2) Prior to 1983	1 day	2 yr	1 day	2 yr	2 yr	2 yr	6 mo	1 day

Owens Corning Fibreboard Asbestos Personal Injury Trust—Owens Corning Subfund

Owens Corning Fibreboard Asbestos Personal Injury Trust - Owens Corning Subfund

Bankruptcy Court and Trust Administrative Information

Debtor(s)	Owens Corning Corp.		
Bankruptcy filing date	10/5/00	Confirmation date	10/31/06
Bankruptcy court	Bankr. D. Del.	Bankruptcy judge	Judith Fitzgerald

Trust status	Active
Date trust established	2006
Classes of claims processed	Owens Corning claims
Claim administrator	Delaware Claims Processing Facility
Trust website	www.ocfbasbestostrust.com

Trustees and Advisors

Position	Name	Affiliation
Managing Trustee	Dean Trafelet	Retired Cook County Circuit Court Judge
Trustee	Harry Huge	Harry Huge Law Firm, LLP
Trustee	LeAnne Jackson	formerly at Baron & Budd, current affilation unknown
FCR	Michael Crames	Peter J. Solomon Company
TAC Member	Armand Volta	Peter G. Angelos
TAC Member	James Ferrano	Kelley & Ferraro, LLC
TAC Member	John Cooney	Cooney & Conway
TAC Member	Joseph Rice	Motley Rice, LLC
TAC Member	Matthew Bergman	Bergman Draper & Frockt, PLLC
TAC Member	Perry Weitz	Weitz & Luxenburg
TAC Member	Russell Budd	Baron & Budd, P.C.
TAC Member	Steven Kazan	Kazan, McClain, Abrams, Fernandez, Lyons, Farrise & Greenwood, P.C.
TAC Member	Theodore Goldberg	Goldberg, Persky & White P.C.
Trust Counsel	Douglas A. Campbell	Campbell & Levine, LLC
Trust Counsel	Philip E. Milch	Campbell & Levine, LLC
Trust Counsel	Marla R. Eskin	Campbell & Levine, LLC
FCR Counsel	Andrew Kress	Kaye Scholer LLP
TAC Counsel	Elihu Inselbuch	Caplin & Drysdale

Estimated Initial Funding of Trust ($ millions)

	Funding for Claims Paid Through Trust	Funding for Claims Paid Outside Trust
Cash from debtor(s)	2,603.0	0
Stock from debtors(s)	820.3	0
Insurance settlements	0.0	0
Other assets	0.0	0
Total	3,423.3	0

Owens Corning Fibreboard Asbestos Personal Injury Trust - Owens Corning Subfund (continued)

Trust Financial Statement ($)

	Pre-2006	2006	2007	2008
Beginning trust assets	0	0	1,280,852,658	2,989,424,297
Additions				
Cash from debtors	0	1,276,131,074	1,326,822,945	0
Stock from debtors	0	0	820,338,000	0
Insurance settlements	0	0	11,440,000	19,360,000
Investment gains	0	-4,393,544	-242,269,263	-300,569,226
Investment income	0	10,884,120	96,081,075	80,987,703
Other additions	0	0	0	0
Deductions				
Trust expenses	0	1,768,992	10,644,145	15,376,692
Claim processing costs	0	485,449	3,016,357	7,390,898
Investment fees	0	51,269	3,734,263	4,111,490
All other expenses	0	1,232,274	3,893,525	3,874,304
Taxes	0	0	0	0
Claim payments	0	0	293,196,973	802,505,337
Other deductions	0	0	0	0
Ending trust assets	0	1,280,852,658	2,989,424,297	1,971,320,745
Gross claimant compensation as a percentage of deductions				
Lower bound	–	0.0%	96.5%	98.1%
Upper bound	–	0.0%	96.5%	98.1%

Claim Valuation for — Owens Corning claims

Disease level	Scheduled Value	Average Value	Maximum Value
Mesothelioma	215,000	270,000	650,000
Lung Cancer 1	40,000	50,000	150,000
Lung Cancer 2	n.appl.	20,000	50,000
Other Cancer	22,000	25,000	60,000
Severe Asbestosis	42,000	50,000	150,000
Asbestosis / Pleural Disease II	19,000	20,000	35,000
Asbestosis / Pleural Disease I	8,000	9,000	20,000
Other Asbestos Disease	400 *	n.appl.	n.appl.

Payment percentage

Initial payment percentage	40.0%
Current payment percentage	10.0%

Claim payment ratio

Malignancies and severe asbestosis	65.0%
Asbestosis and pleural disease	35.0%

*Payment percentage does not apply

Owens Corning Fibreboard Asbestos Personal Injury Trust - Owens Corning Subfund (continued)

Claim Activity

	Pre-2006	2006	2007	2008	Total
Pre-petition pending and post-petition claims					
Claims filed					
Malignant	0	0	n.a.	n.a.	n.a.
Non-malignant	0	0	n.a.	n.a.	n.a.
Not specified	0	0	141,056	107,101	248,157
All disease types	0	0	141,056	107,101	248,157
Claims paid					
Malignant	0	0	131	7,633	7,764
Non-malignant	0	0	1,451	61,946	63,397
Not specified	0	0	0	0	0
All disease types	0	0	1,582	69,579	71,161
Claim payments ($)					
Malignant	0	0	4,667,000	373,400,000	378,067,000
Non-malignant	0	0	9,333,000	373,400,000	382,733,000
Not specified	0	0	0	0	0
All disease types	0	0	14,000,000	746,800,000	760,800,000
Average payment per claim ($)					
Malignant	–	–	35,626	48,919	48,695
Non-malignant	–	–	6,432	6,028	6,037
Not specified	–	–	–	–	–
All disease types	–	–	8,850	10,733	10,691
Claims settled but not paid pre-petition					
Claims filed [a]					
Malignant	0	0	n.a.	n.a.	n.a.
Non-malignant	0	0	n.a.	n.a.	n.a.
Not specified	0	0	36,970	0	36,970
All disease types	0	0	36,970	0	36,970
Claims paid					
Malignant	0	0	3,794	839	4,633
Non-malignant	0	0	32,987	7,701	40,688
Not specified	0	0	0	0	0
All disease types	0	0	36,781	8,540	45,321
Claim payments ($)					
Malignant	0	0	166,800,000	23,267,143	190,067,143
Non-malignant	0	0	111,200,000	31,022,857	142,222,857
Not specified	0	0	0	0	0
All disease types	0	0	278,000,000	54,290,000	332,290,000
Average payment per claim ($)					
Malignant	–	–	43,964	27,732	41,025
Non-malignant	–	–	3,371	4,028	3,495
Not specified	–	–	–	–	–
All disease types	–	–	7,558	6,357	7,332

[a] Claims filed data are incomplete

Owens Corning Fibreboard Asbestos Personal Injury Trust - Owens Corning Subfund (continued)

Claim Approval Criteria for	Owens Corning claims							
	Meso	LC1	LC2	OC	SA	AP2	AP1	OAD
1. Diagnosis requirement (one or more of checked items satisfies requirement)								
a. Physical exam	✔	✔	✔	✔	✔	✔	✔	✔
b. Pathology	✔	✔	✔	✔	✔	✔	✔	✔
c. Medical document review								
2. ILO or x-ray requirement								
a. ILO reading		1/0		1/0	2/1	1/0	1/0	1/0
OR b. X-ray, CT scan, or pathology showing one or more of the checked conditions								
(1) Bilateral interstitial fibrosis		✔		✔		✔	✔	✔
(2) Bilateral pleural plaques		✔		✔		✔	✔	✔
(3) Bilateral pleural thickening		✔		✔		✔	✔	✔
(4) Bilateral pleural calcification		✔		✔		✔	✔	✔
3. Pulmonary function test requirement								
a. TLC < (% of normal)					65	80		
AND FEV1/FVC ratio >								
OR b. DLCO < (% of normal)								
AND FEV1/FVC ratio >								
OR c. FVC < (% of normal)					65	80		
AND FEV1/FVC ratio >					0.65	0.65		
4. Causation statement requirement	No	Yes	Yes	Yes	Yes	Yes	Yes	No
5. Latency and exposure requirements								
a. Latency	10 yr	10 yr	10 yr	10 yr	10 yr	10 yr	10 yr	10 yr
b. Company exposure prior to 1983	1 day	6 mo	1 day	6 mo	6 mo	6 mo	6 mo	1 day
c. Occupational exposure								
(1) Total		5 yr		5 yr	5 yr	5 yr	5 yr	
(2) Prior to 1983	1 day	2 yr	1 day	2 yr	2 yr	2 yr	6 mo	1 day

Pittsburgh Corning Corporation Asbestos PI Trust

Pittsburgh Corning Corporation Asbestos PI Trust

Bankruptcy Court and Trust Administrative Information

Debtor(s)	Pittsburgh Corning		
Bankruptcy filing date	4/16/00	Confirmation date	Not confirmed
Bankruptcy court	Bankr. W.D. Pa	Bankruptcy judge	Judith Fitzgerald
Trust status	Proposed		
Date trust established	–		
Classes of claims processed	Pittsburgh Corning claims		
Claim administrator	Not selected		
Trust website	None		

Trustees and Advisors

Position	Name	Affiliation
FCR	Lawrence Fitzpatrick	Asbestos Claims Facility
FCR Counsel	James Patton	Young Conaway Stargatt & Taylor LLP
FCR Counsel	Joel Helmrich	Dinsmore & Shohl LLP

Estimated Initial Funding of Trust ($ millions) [a]

	Funding for Claims Paid Through Trust	Funding for Claims Paid Outside Trust
Cash from debtor(s)	1,174.9	0
Stock from debtors(s)	311.7	0
Insurance settlements	1,892.7	0
Other assets	28.2	0
Total	3,407.4	0

[a] Proposed

Pittsburgh Corning Corporation Asbestos PI Trust (continued)

Trust Financial Statement ($)

	Pre-2006	2006	2007	2008
Beginning trust assets				
Additions				
Cash from debtors				
Stock from debtors				
Insurance settlements				
Investment gains				
Investment income				
Other additions				
Deductions		TRUST NOT YET OPEN		
Trust expenses				
Claim processing costs				
Investment fees				
All other expenses				
Taxes				
Claim payments				
Other deductions				
Ending trust assets				
Gross claimant compensation as a percentage of deductions				
Lower bound	–	–	–	–
Upper bound	–	–	–	–

Claim Valuation for [a] — **Pittsburgh Corning claims**

Disease level	Scheduled Value	Average Value	Maximum Value
Mesothelioma	175,000	200,000	500,000
Lung Cancer 1	47,500	50,000	100,000
Lung Cancer 2	n.appl.	20,000	50,000
Other Cancer	27,500	30,000	100,000
Severe Asbestosis	47,500	50,000	100,000
Asbestosis / Pleural Disease II	11,750	12,500	22,500
Asbestosis / Pleural Disease I	5,500	6,000	10,000
Other Asbestos Disease	400 *	n.appl.	n.appl.

Payment percentage	
Initial payment percentage	37.0%
Current payment percentage	37.0%

Claim payment ratio	
Malignancies and severe asbestosis	60.0%
Asbestosis and pleural disease	40.0%

*Payment percentage does not apply
[a] Proposed

Pittsburgh Corning Corporation Asbestos PI Trust (continued)

Claim Activity					
	Pre-2006	2006	2007	2008	Total
Pre-petition pending and post-petition claims					
Claims filed					
Malignant					
Non-malignant					
Not specified					
All disease types					
Claims paid					
Malignant					
Non-malignant					
Not specified					
All disease types					
Claim payments ($)					
Malignant					
Non-malignant					
Not specified					
All disease types					
Average payment per claim ($)					
Malignant					
Non-malignant					
Not specified					
All disease types					
			TRUST NOT YET OPEN		
Claims settled but not paid pre-petition					
Claims filed					
Malignant					
Non-malignant					
Not specified					
All disease types					
Claims paid					
Malignant					
Non-malignant					
Not specified					
All disease types					
Claim payments ($)					
Malignant					
Non-malignant					
Not specified					
All disease types					
Average payment per claim ($)					
Malignant					
Non-malignant					
Not specified					
All disease types					

Pittsburgh Corning Corporation Asbestos PI Trust (continued)

Claim Approval Criteria for [a]	Pittsburgh Corning claims							
	Meso	LC1	LC2	OC	SA	AP2	AP1	OAD
1. Diagnosis requirement (one or more of checked items satisfies requirement)								
a. Physical exam	✔	✔	✔	✔	✔	✔	✔	✔
b. Pathology	✔	✔	✔	✔	✔	✔	✔	✔
c. Medical document review								
2. ILO or x-ray requirement								
a. ILO reading		1/0		1/0	2/1	1/0	1/0	1/0
OR b. X-ray, CT scan, or pathology showing one or more of the checked conditions								
(1) Bilateral interstitial fibrosis		✔		✔		✔	✔	✔
(2) Bilateral pleural plaques		✔		✔		✔	✔	✔
(3) Bilateral pleural thickening		✔		✔		✔	✔	✔
(4) Bilateral pleural calcification		✔		✔		✔	✔	✔
3. Pulmonary function test requirement								
a. TLC < (% of normal)					65	80		
AND FEV1/FVC ratio >								
OR b. DLCO < (% of normal)								
AND FEV1/FVC ratio >								
OR c. FVC < (% of normal)					65	80		
AND FEV1/FVC ratio >					0.65	0.65		
4. Causation statement requirement	No	Yes	Yes	Yes	Yes	Yes	No	No
5. Latency and exposure requirements								
a. Latency	10 yr	10 yr	10 yr	10 yr	10 yr	10 yr	10 yr	10 yr
b. Company exposure prior to 1093	1 day	6 mo	1 day	6 mo	6 mo	6 mo	6 mo	1 day
c. Occupational exposure								
(1) Total		5 yr		5 yr	5 yr	5 yr	5 yr	
(2) Prior to 1983	1 day	2 yr	1 day	2 yr	2 yr	2 yr	6 mo	1 day

[a] Proposed

Plibrico 524(g) Trust

Plibrico 524(g) Trust

Bankruptcy Court and Trust Administrative Information

Debtor(s)	Plibrico Co.		
	Plibrico Sales & Services, Inc.		
Bankruptcy filing date	3/13/02	Confirmation date	1/30/06
Bankruptcy court	Bankr. N.D. Ill.	Bankruptcy judge	John Squires
Trust status	Active		
Date trust established	3/8/06		
Classes of claims processed	Plibrico claims		
Claim administrator	Verus Claims Services		
Trust website	www.verusllc.com/plibrico/plibrico.htm		

Trustees and Advisors

Position	Name	Affiliation
Trustee	Alfred Wolin	Saiber LLC
FCR	Dean Trafelet	Retired Cook County Circuit Court Judge
TAC Member	John Cooney	Cooney & Conway
TAC Member	Steven Baron	Silber Pearlman, LLP
TAC Member	Steven Kazan	Kazan, McClain, Abrams, Fernandez, Lyons, Farrise & Greenwood, P.C.
TAC Member	Thomas Wilson	Kelley & Ferraro, LLC
TAC Member	James Bedortha	Goldberg, Persky & White, P.C.
Trust Counsel	Kevin Irwin	Keating Muething & Klekamp PLL

Estimated Initial Funding of Trust ($ millions)

	Funding for Claims Paid Through Trust	Funding for Claims Paid Outside Trust
Cash from debtor(s)	0.0	0
Stock from debtors(s)	0.0	0
Insurance settlements	205.6	0
Other assets	0.0	0
Total	205.6	0

Plibrico 524(g) Trust (continued)

Trust Financial Statement ($)

	Pre-2006	2006	2007	2008
Beginning trust assets	0	0	54,709,664	197,885,441
Additions				
Cash from debtors	0	0	0	0
Stock from debtors	0	0	0	0
Insurance settlements	0	58,850,000	146,700,000	208,724
Investment gains	0	-3,700	1,769,894	-18,544,572
Investment income	0	837,653	5,308,135	9,743,304
Other additions	0	133,428	136,571	-287,215
Deductions				
Trust expenses	0	5,858,940	1,734,091	1,141,412
Claim processing costs	0	134,171	281,871	529,088
Investment fees	0	56,548	210,686	287,215
All other expenses	0	5,668,221	1,241,534	325,109
Taxes	0	0	0	0
Claim payments	0	0	9,004,733	59,954,748
Other deductions	0	81,665	0	0
Ending trust assets	0	53,876,776	197,885,440	127,909,522
Gross claimant compensation as a percentage of deductions				
Lower bound	–	0.0%	83.9%	98.1%
Upper bound	–	1.4%	83.9%	98.1%

Claim Valuation for Plibrico claims

Disease level	Scheduled Value	Average Value	Maximum Value
Mesothelioma	350,000	425,000	750,000
Lung Cancer 1	120,000	135,000	200,000
Lung Cancer 2	n.appl.	45,000	135,000
Other Cancer	65,000	70,000	100,000
Severe Asbestosis	120,000	135,000	200,000
Asbestosis / Pleural Disease II	15,000	n.appl.	15,000
Asbestosis / Pleural Disease I	1,500	n.appl.	1,500

Payment percentage	
Initial payment percentage	1.1%
Current payment percentage	8.5%

Claim payment ratio	
Malignancies and severe asbestosis	65.0%
Asbestosis and pleural disease	35.0%

Plibrico 524(g) Trust (continued)

Claim Activity					
	Pre-2006	2006	2007	2008	Total
Pre-petition pending and post-petition claims					
Claims filed					
Malignant	0	0	5,674	7,789	13,463
Non-malignant	0	0	18,454	20,136	38,590
Not specified	0	0	193	1,053	1,246
All disease types	0	0	24,321	28,978	53,299
Claims paid					
Malignant	0	0	311	1,585	1,896
Non-malignant	0	0	1,488	9,813	11,301
Not specified	0	0	0	0	0
All disease types	0	0	1,799	11,398	13,197
Claim payments ($)					
Malignant	0	0	6,100,328	38,187,033	44,287,361
Non-malignant	0	0	959,820	4,679,887	5,639,707
Not specified	0	0	0	0	0
All disease types	0	0	7,060,148	42,866,920	49,927,068
Average payment per claim ($)					
Malignant	–	–	19,615	24,093	23,358
Non-malignant	–	–	645	477	499
Not specified	–	–	–	–	–
All disease types	–	–	3,924	3,761	3,783
Claims settled but not paid pre-petition					
Claims filed					
Malignant	0	0	0	0	0
Non-malignant	0	0	0	0	0
Not specified	0	0	0	0	0
All disease types	0	0	0	0	0
Claims paid					
Malignant	0	0	0	0	0
Non-malignant	0	0	0	0	0
Not specified	0	0	0	0	0
All disease types	0	0	0	0	0
Claim payments ($)					
Malignant	0	0	0	0	0
Non-malignant	0	0	0	0	0
Not specified	0	0	0	0	0
All disease types	0	0	0	0	0
Average payment per claim ($)					
Malignant	–	–	–	–	–
Non-malignant	–	–	–	–	–
Not specified	–	–	–	–	–
All disease types	–	–	–	–	–

Plibrico 524(g) Trust (continued)

Claim Activity by Disease Level

	2006	2007	2008	Total
Pre-petition pending and post-petition claims				
Claims paid				
Mesothelioma	0	151	757	908
Lung cancer 1	0	128	557	685
Lung cancer 2	0	0	52	52
Other cancer	0	32	219	251
Severe asbestosis	0	13	21	34
Asbestosis/pleural disease I	0	557	2,791	3,348
Asbestosis/pleural disease II	0	918	7,001	7,919
Unknown	0	0	0	0
Claims payments ($)				
Mesothelioma	0	4,617,928	30,735,904	35,353,832
Lung cancer 1	0	1,305,600	5,983,579	7,289,179
Lung cancer 2	0	0	220,176	220,176
Other cancer	0	176,800	1,247,374	1,424,174
Severe asbestosis	0	132,600	228,734	361,334
Asbestosis/pleural disease I	0	710,175	3,558,525	4,268,700
Asbestosis/pleural disease II	0	117,045	892,628	1,009,673
Unknown	0	0	0	0
Average payment per claim ($)				
Mesothelioma	–	30,582	40,602	38,936
Lung cancer 1	–	10,200	10,743	10,641
Lung cancer 2	–	–	4,234	4,234
Other cancer	–	5,525	5,696	5,674
Severe asbestosis	–	10,200	10,892	10,627
Asbestosis/pleural disease I	–	1,275	1,275	1,275
Asbestosis/pleural disease II	–	128	128	128
Unknown	–	–	–	–

Plibrico 524(g) Trust (continued)

Claim Approval Criteria for	Plibrico claims						
	Meso	_LC1_	_LC2_	_OC_	_SA_	_AP2_	_AP1_
1. Diagnosis requirement (one or more of checked items satisfies requirement)							
a. Physical exam	✔	✔	✔	✔	✔	✔	✔
b. Pathology	✔	✔	✔	✔	✔	✔	✔
c. Medical document review							
2. ILO or x-ray requirement							
a. ILO reading		1/0		1/0	2/1	1/0	1/0
OR b. X-ray, CT scan, or pathology showing one or more of the checked conditions							
(1) Bilateral interstitial fibrosis		✔		✔			✔
(2) Bilateral pleural plaques		✔		✔			✔
(3) Bilateral pleural thickening		✔		✔			✔
(4) Bilateral pleural calcification		✔		✔			✔
3. Pulmonary function test requirement							
a. TLC < (% of normal)					65	80	
AND FEV1/FVC ratio >							
OR b. DLCO < (% of normal)							
AND FEV1/FVC ratio >							
OR c. FVC < (% of normal)					65	80	
AND FEV1/FVC ratio >					0.65	0.65	
4. Causation statement requirement	No	Yes	Yes	Yes	Yes	Yes	No
5. Latency and exposure requirements							
a. Latency	10 yr	10 yr	10 yr	10 yr	10 yr	10 yr	10 yr
b. Company exposure prior to 1983	1 day	6 mo	1 day	6 mo	6 mo	6 mo	1 day
c. Occupational exposure							
(1) Total		5 yr		5 yr	5 yr	5 yr	5 yr
(2) Prior to 1983	1 day	6 mo	1 day	6 mo	6 mo	6 mo	1 day

Swan Asbestos and Silica Settlement Trust

Swan Asbestos and Silica Settlement Trust

Bankruptcy Court and Trust Administrative Information

Debtor(s)	Swan Transportation Co.		
Bankruptcy filing date	12/20/01	Confirmation date	7/21/03
Bankruptcy court	Bankr. D. Del.	Bankruptcy judge	Judith Fitzgerald

Trust status	Active
Date trust established	2003
Classes of claims processed	Swan Asbestos claims
Claim administrator	Trust Services, Inc.
Trust website	Unknown

Trustees and Advisors

Position	Name	Affiliation
FCR Counsel	Richard B. Schiro	Unknown
TAC Member	Russell Budd	Baron & Budd, P.C.
TAC Member	Jimmy Negem	Negem Bickham & Worthinton
TAC Member	Shelton Smith	Shelton Smith & Associates
Trust Counsel	Sander Esserman	Stutzman, Bromberg, Esserman & Plifka
Trust Counsel	Rachel Mersky	Monzack Mersky McLaughlin and Browder, P.A.

Estimated Initial Funding of Trust ($ millions)

	Funding for Claims Paid Through Trust	Funding for Claims Paid Outside Trust
Cash from debtor(s)	1.6	0
Stock from debtors(s)	0.0	0
Insurance settlements	118.3	0
Other assets	0.0	0
Total	119.9	0

Swan Asbestos and Silica Settlement Trust (continued)

Trust Financial Statement ($)

	Pre-2006	2006	2007	2008
Beginning trust assets	0	22,088,782	25,952,921	26,058,082
Additions				
Cash from debtors	1,655,408	0	0	0
Stock from debtors	0	0	0	0
Insurance settlements	120,041,750	5,464,357	0	0
Investment gains	0	0	0	0
Investment income	583,767	986,084	1,188,818	423,337
Other additions	0	0	0	0
Deductions				
Trust expenses	3,034,838	543,702	845,257	893,091
Claim processing costs	n.a.	n.a.	n.a.	n.a.
Investment fees	n.a.	n.a.	n.a.	n.a.
All other expenses	n.a.	n.a.	n.a.	n.a.
Taxes	0	0	0	0
Claim payments [a]	97,157,305	2,042,600	238,400	1,998,360
Other deductions	0	0	0	0
Ending trust assets	22,088,782	25,952,921	26,058,082	23,589,968
Gross claimant compensation as a percentage of deductions				
Lower bound	97.0%	79.0%	22.0%	69.1%
Upper bound	97.0%	79.0%	22.0%	69.1%

[a] Includes some payments for silica claims. Payments for silica claims are likely a small percentage of the total.

Claim Valuation for Swan Asbestos claims

Disease level	Scheduled Value	Average Value	Maximum Value
Mesothelioma	1,200,000	n.appl.	n.appl.
Lung Cancer	600,000	n.appl.	n.appl.
Other Cancer	400,000	n.appl.	n.appl.
Severe Asbestosis	600,000	n.appl.	n.appl.
Asbestosis / Pleural Disease	200,000	n.appl.	n.appl.
Payment percentage			
Initial payment percentage	n.a.		
Current payment percentage	20.0%		
Claim payment ratio			
Malignancies and severe asbestosis	n.appl.		
Asbestosis and pleural disease	n.appl.		

Swan Asbestos and Silica Settlement Trust (continued)

Claim Activity

	Pre-2006	2006	2007	2008	Total
Pre-petition pending and post-petition claims					
Claims filed					
Malignant	n.a.	n.a.	n.a.	n.a.	n.a.
Non-malignant	n.a.	n.a.	n.a.	n.a.	n.a.
Not specified	n.a.	n.a.	n.a.	n.a.	n.a.
Non-asbestos	n.a.	n.a.	n.a.	n.a.	n.a.
All disease types	n.a.	n.a.	n.a.	n.a.	n.a.
Claims paid					
Malignant	65	15	4	9	93
Non-malignant	2,266	459	7	8	2,740
Not specified	0	0	0	0	0
Non-asbestos	1,038	292	1	7	1,338
All disease types	3,369	766	12	24	4,171
Claim payments ($)					
Malignant	n.a.	n.a.	n.a.	n.a.	n.a.
Non-malignant	n.a.	n.a.	n.a.	n.a.	n.a.
Not specified	97,157,305	2,042,600	238,400	1,998,360	101,436,665
Non-asbestos	n.a.	n.a.	n.a.	n.a.	n.a.
All disease types	97,157,305	2,042,600	238,400	1,998,360	101,436,665
Average payment per claim ($)					
Malignant	–	–	–	–	–
Non-malignant	–	–	–	–	–
Not specified	–	–	–	–	–
Non-asbestos	–	–	–	–	–
All disease types	28,839	2,667	19,867	83,265	24,320
Claims settled but not paid pre-petition					
Claims filed					
Malignant	0	0	0	0	0
Non-malignant	0	0	0	0	0
Not specified	0	0	0	0	0
Non-asbestos	0	0	0	0	0
All disease types	0	0	0	0	0
Claims paid					
Malignant	0	0	0	0	0
Non-malignant	0	0	0	0	0
Not specified	0	0	0	0	0
Non-asbestos	0	0	0	0	0
All disease types	0	0	0	0	0
Claim payments ($)					
Malignant	0	0	0	0	0
Non-malignant	0	0	0	0	0
Not specified	0	0	0	0	0
Non-asbestos	0	0	0	0	0
All disease types	0	0	0	0	0
Average payment per claim ($)					
Malignant	–	–	–	–	–
Non-malignant	–	–	–	–	–
Not specified	–	–	–	–	–
Non-asbestos					
All disease types	–	–	–	–	–

Swan Asbestos and Silica Settlement Trust (continued)

Claim Activity by Disease Level

	2006	2007	2008	Total
Pre-petition pending and post-petition claims				
Claims paid				
Mesothelioma	2	0	3	5
Lung cancer	11	3	6	20
Other cancer	2	1	0	3
Severe asbestosis	159	2	3	164
Asbestosis/pleural disease	264	4	4	272
Asbestosis/pleural disease 2	36	1	1	38
Unknown	0	0	0	0
Claims payments ($)				
Mesothelioma	n.a.	n.a.	n.a.	n.a.
Lung cancer	n.a.	n.a.	n.a.	n.a.
Other cancer	n.a.	n.a.	n.a.	n.a.
Severe asbestosis	n.a.	n.a.	n.a.	n.a.
Asbestosis/pleural disease	n.a.	n.a.	n.a.	n.a.
Asbestosis/pleural disease 2	n.a.	n.a.	n.a.	n.a.
Unknown	2,042,600	238,400	1,998,360	4,279,360
Average payment per claim ($)				
Mesothelioma	–	–	–	–
Lung cancer	–	–	–	–
Other cancer	–	–	–	–
Severe asbestosis	–	–	–	–
Asbestosis/pleural disease	–	–	–	–
Asbestosis/pleural disease 2	–	–	–	–
Unknown	–	–	–	–

Swan Asbestos and Silica Settlement Trust (continued)

Claim Approval Criteria for	Swan asbestos claims				
	Meso	LC	OC	SA	APD
1. Diagnosis requirement (one or more of checked items satisfies requirement)					
a. Physical exam	✔	✔	✔	✔	✔
b. Pathology	✔	✔	✔	✔	✔
c. Medical document review					
2. ILO or x-ray requirement					
a. ILO reading				1/0	1/0
OR b. X-ray, CT scan, or pathology showing one or more of the checked conditions					
(1) Bilateral interstitial fibrosis					
(2) Bilateral pleural plaques					
(3) Bilateral pleural thickening					
(4) Bilateral pleural calcification					
3. Pulmonary function test requirement					
a. TLC < (% of normal)					
AND FEV1/FVC ratio >					
OR b. DLCO < (% of normal)					
AND FEV1/FVC ratio >					
OR c. FVC < (% of normal)				59	
AND FEV1/FVC ratio >					
4. Causation statement requirement	Yes	Yes	Yes	No	No
5. Latency and exposure requirements					
a. Latency	10 yr	10 yr	10 yr	10 yr	10 yr
b. Company exposure prior to 1983	1 day	1 day	1 day	1 day	1 day
c. Occupational exposure					
(1) Total					
(2) Prior to 1983					

T. H. Agriculture & Nutrition, LLC Asbestos Personal Injury Trust

T. H. Agriculture & Nutrition, LLC Asbestos Personal Injury Trust

Bankruptcy Court and Trust Administrative Information

Debtor(s)	T. H. Agriculture & Nutrition, LLC (THAN)		
Bankruptcy filing date	11/24/08	Confirmation date	10/26/09
Bankruptcy court	Bankr. S.D. N.Y.	Bankruptcy judge	Robert Gerber

Trust status	Active
Date trust established	2009
Classes of claims processed	THAN claims
Claim administrator	Not selected
Trust website	None

Trustees and Advisors

Position	Name	Affiliation
Trustee	Alfred Wolin	Retired U.S. District Court Judge
Trustee	Charles A. Koppelman	Unknown
Trustee	David F. Levi	Retired U.S. District Court Judge
FCR	Samuel Issacharoff	NYU Law
TAC Member	Alan Brayton	Brayton Purcell
TAC Member	John Cooney	Cooney & Conway
TAC Member	Peter Kraus	Waters & Kraus, LLP
TAC Member	Steven Kazan	Kazan, McClain, Abrams, Fernandez, Lyons, Farrise & Greenwood, P.C.
TAC Member	Matthew Bergman	Bergman Draper & Frockt, PLLC
Trust Counsel	Steven Felsenthal	Stutzman, Bromberg, Esserman & Plifka

Estimated Initial Funding of Trust ($ millions)

	Funding for Claims Paid Through Trust	Funding for Claims Paid Outside Trust
Cash from debtor(s)	901.0	0
Stock from debtors(s)	0.0	0
Insurance settlements	0.0	0
Other assets	0.0	0
Total	901.0	0

T. H. Agriculture & Nutrition, LLC Asbestos Personal Injury Trust (continued)

Trust Financial Statement ($)

	Pre-2006	2006	2007	2008
Beginning trust assets				
Additions				
Cash from debtors				
Stock from debtors				
Insurance settlements				
Investment gains				
Investment income				
Other additions				
Deductions		TRUST NOT ESTABLISHED UNTIL 2009		
Trust expenses				
Claim processing costs				
Investment fees				
All other expenses				
Taxes				
Claim payments				
Other deductions				
Ending trust assets				
Gross claimant compensation as a percentage of deductions				
Lower bound	-	-	-	-
Upper bound	-	-	-	-

Claim Valuation for THAN claims

Disease level	Scheduled Value	Average Value	Maximum Value
Mesothelioma	150,000	238,000	900,000
Lung Cancer 1	65,000	89,900	250,000
Lung Cancer 2	n.appl.	20,000	75,000
Other Cancer	30,000	50,000	70,000
Severe Asbestosis	60,000	67,600	250,000
Asbestosis / Pleural Disease II	8,000	8,600	15,000
Asbestosis / Pleural Disease I	3,800	4,200	8,000
Other Asbestos Disease	500 *	n.appl.	n.appl.

Payment percentage	
Initial payment percentage	100.0%
Current payment percentage	100.0%

Claim payment ratio	
Malignancies and severe asbestosis	80.0%
Asbestosis and pleural disease	20.0%

*Payment percentage does not apply

T. H. Agriculture & Nutrition, LLC Asbestos Personal Injury Trust (continued)

Claim Activity

	Pre-2006	2006	2007	2008	Total
Pre-petition pending and post-petition claims					
Claims filed					
Malignant					
Non-malignant					
Not specified					
All disease types					
Claims paid					
Malignant					
Non-malignant					
Not specified					
All disease types					
Claim payments ($)					
Malignant					
Non-malignant					
Not specified					
All disease types					
Average payment per claim ($)					
Malignant					
Non-malignant					
Not specified					
All disease types					
		TRUST NOT ESTABLISHED UNTIL 2009			
Claims settled but not paid pre-petition					
Claims filed					
Malignant					
Non-malignant					
Not specified					
All disease types					
Claims paid					
Malignant					
Non-malignant					
Not specified					
All disease types					
Claim payments ($)					
Malignant					
Non-malignant					
Not specified					
All disease types					
Average payment per claim ($)					
Malignant					
Non-malignant					
Not specified					
All disease types					

T. H. Agriculture & Nutrition, LLC Asbestos Personal Injury Trust (continued)

Claim Approval Criteria for	THAN claims							
	Meso	LC1	LC2	OC	SA	AP2	AP1	OAD
1. Diagnosis requirement (one or more of checked items satisfies requirement)								
a. Physical exam	✔	✔	✔	✔	✔	✔	✔	✔
b. Pathology	✔	✔	✔	✔	✔	✔	✔	✔
c. Medical document review								
2. ILO or x-ray requirement								
a. ILO reading		1/0		1/0	2/1	1/0	1/0	1/0
OR b. X-ray, CT scan, or pathology showing one or more of the checked conditions								
(1) Bilateral interstitial fibrosis		✔		✔		✔	✔	✔
(2) Bilateral pleural plaques		✔		✔		✔	✔	✔
(3) Bilateral pleural thickening		✔		✔		✔	✔	✔
(4) Bilateral pleural calcification		✔		✔		✔	✔	✔
3. Pulmonary function test requirement								
a. TLC < (% of normal)					65	80		
AND FEV1/FVC ratio >								
OR b. DLCO < (% of normal)								
AND FEV1/FVC ratio >								
OR c. FVC < (% of normal)					65	80		
AND FEV1/FVC ratio >					0.65	0.65		
4. Causation statement requirement	No	Yes	Yes	Yes	Yes	Yes	No	No
5. Latency and exposure requirements								
a. Latency	10 yr	10 yr	10 yr	10 yr	10 yr	10 yr	10 yr	10 yr
b. Company exposure prior to 1987	1 day	6 mo	1 day	6 mo	6 mo	6 mo	6 mo	1 day
c. Occupational exposure								
(1) Total		5 yr		5 yr	5 yr	5 yr	5 yr	
(2) Prior to 1983								

United States Gypsum Asbestos Personal Injury Settlement Trust

United States Gypsum Asbestos Personal Injury Settlement Trust

Bankruptcy Court and Trust Administrative Information

Debtor(s)	USG Corp.		
Bankruptcy filing date	6/25/01	Confirmation date	6/15/06
Bankruptcy court	Bankr. D. Del.	Bankruptcy judge	Judith Fitzgerald
Trust status	Active		
Date trust established	6/20/06		
Classes of claims processed	United States Gypsum claims		
Claim administrator	Delaware Claims Processing Facility		
Trust website	www.usgasbestostrust.com		

Trustees and Advisors

Position	Name	Affiliation
Managing Trustee	Philip Pahigian	Retired from Wilentz, Goldman & Spitzer
Trustee	Charles Koppelman	Martha Stewart Living Omnimedia
Trustee	Lewis Sifford	Anderson & Co., P.C.
FCR	Dean Trafelet	Retired Cook County Circuit Court Judge
TAC Member	John Cooney	Cooney & Conway
TAC Member	Perry Weitz	Weitz & Luxenburg
TAC Member	Russell Budd	Baron & Budd, P.C.
TAC Member	Steven Kazan	Kazan, McClain, Abrams, Fernandez, Lyons, Farrise & Greenwood, P.C.
TAC Member	Theodore Goldberg	Goldberg, Persky & White, P.C.
Trust Counsel	Douglas Campbell	Campbell & Levine, LLC
Trust Counsel	Marla Eskin	Campbell & Levine, LLC
Trust Counsel	Philip Milch	Campbell & Levine, LLC
TAC Counsel	Elihu Inselbuch	Caplin & Drysdale
FCR Counsel	Andrew Kress	Kaye Scholer LLP

Estimated Initial Funding of Trust ($ millions)

	Funding for Claims Paid Through Trust	Funding for Claims Paid Outside Trust
Cash from debtor(s)	3,950.0	0
Stock from debtors(s)	0.0	0
Insurance settlements	4.2	0
Other assets	2.5	0
Total	3,956.7	0

United States Gypsum Asbestos Personal Injury Settlement Trust (continued)

Trust Financial Statement ($)

	Pre-2006	2006	2007	2008
Beginning trust assets	0	0	3,975,184,899	4,089,038,836
Additions				
Cash from debtors	0	3,952,500,000	0	0
Stock from debtors	0	0	0	0
Insurance settlements	0	4,223,000	0	0
Investment gains	0	13,148	30,518,702	-246,886,861
Investment income	0	21,536,208	157,817,936	123,548,594
Other additions	0	0	0	0
Deductions				
Trust expenses	0	2,857,457	10,758,701	16,678,382
Claim processing costs	0	585,500	3,797,746	6,268,215
Investment fees	0	0	2,844,085	5,903,739
All other expenses	0	2,271,957	4,116,870	4,506,428
Taxes	0	230,000	17,768,905	24,359
Claim payments	0	0	45,955,095	566,176,688
Other deductions	0	0	0	0
Ending trust assets	0	3,975,184,899	4,089,038,836	3,382,821,140
Gross claimant compensation as a percentage of deductions				
Lower bound	–	0.0%	61.7%	97.1%
Upper bound	–	0.0%	61.7%	97.1%

Claim Valuation for United States Gypsum and A.P. Green claims

Disease level	Scheduled Value	Average Value	Maximum Value
Mesothelioma	155,000	225,000	450,000
Lung Cancer 1	45,000	55,000	100,000
Lung Cancer 2	n.appl.	15,000	35,000
Other Cancer	15,000	18,000	35,000
Severe Asbestosis	30,000	35,000	50,000
Asbestosis / Pleural Disease II	8,300	n.appl.	n.appl.
Asbestosis / Pleural Disease I	2,625	n.appl.	n.appl.
Other Asbestos Disease	400 *	n.appl.	n.appl.

Payment percentage	
Initial payment percentage	45.0%
Current payment percentage	45.0%

Claim payment ratio	
Malignancies and severe asbestosis	85.0%
Asbestosis and pleural disease	15.0%

*Payment percentage does not apply

United States Gypsum Asbestos Personal Injury Settlement Trust (continued)

Claim Activity

	Pre-2006	2006	2007	2008	Total
Pre-petition pending and post-petition claims					
Claims filed					
Malignant	0	0	n.a.	n.a.	n.a.
Non-malignant	0	0	n.a.	n.a.	n.a.
Not specified	0	0	123,783	90,756	214,539
All disease types	0	0	123,783	90,756	214,539
Claims paid					
Malignant	0	0	504	7,146	7,650
Non-malignant	0	0	4,777	42,659	47,436
Not specified	0	0	0	0	0
All disease types	0	0	5,281	49,805	55,086
Claim payments ($)					
Malignant	0	0	23,333,000	450,368,000	473,701,000
Non-malignant	0	0	11,667,000	112,592,000	124,259,000
Not specified	0	0	0	0	0
All disease types	0	0	35,000,000	562,960,000	597,960,000
Average payment per claim ($)					
Malignant	–	–	46,296	63,024	61,922
Non-malignant	–	–	2,442	2,639	2,620
Not specified	–	–	–	–	–
All disease types	–	–	6,628	11,303	10,855
Claims settled but not paid pre-petition					
Claims filed					
Malignant	0	2,686	n.a.	0	2,686
Non-malignant	0	11,287	n.a.	0	11,287
Not specified	0	0	413	0	413
All disease types	0	13,973	413	0	14,386
Claims paid					
Malignant	0	0	69	73	142
Non-malignant	0	0	354	1,656	2,010
Not specified	0	0	0	0	0
All disease types	0	0	423	1,729	2,152
Claim payments ($)					
Malignant	0	0	6,400,000	1,730,000	8,130,000
Non-malignant	0	0	1,600,000	1,730,000	3,330,000
Not specified	0	0	0	0	0
All disease types	0	0	8,000,000	3,460,000	11,460,000
Average payment per claim ($)					
Malignant	–	–	92,754	23,699	57,254
Non-malignant	–	–	4,520	1,045	1,657
Not specified	–	–	–	–	–
All disease types	–	–	18,913	2,001	5,325

United States Gypsum Asbestos Personal Injury Settlement Trust (continued)

Claim Approval Criteria for	United States Gypsum and A.P. Green claims							
	Meso	LC1	LC2	OC	SA	AP2	AP1	OAD
1. Diagnosis requirement (one or more of checked items satisfies requirement)								
a. Physical exam	✔	✔	✔	✔	✔	✔	✔	✔
b. Pathology	✔	✔	✔	✔	✔	✔	✔	✔
c. Medical document review								
2. ILO or x-ray requirement								
a. ILO reading		1/0		1/0	2/1	1/0	1/0	1/0
OR b. X-ray, CT scan, or pathology showing one or more of the checked conditions								
(1) Bilateral interstitial fibrosis		✔		✔		✔	✔	✔
(2) Bilateral pleural plaques		✔		✔		✔	✔	✔
(3) Bilateral pleural thickening		✔		✔		✔	✔	✔
(4) Bilateral pleural calcification		✔		✔		✔	✔	✔
3. Pulmonary function test requirement								
a. TLC < (% of normal)					65	80		
AND FEV1/FVC ratio >								
OR b. DLCO < (% of normal)								
AND FEV1/FVC ratio >								
OR c. FVC < (% of normal)					65	80		
AND FEV1/FVC ratio >					0.65	0.65		
4. Causation statement requirement	No	Yes	Yes	Yes	Yes	Yes	No	No
5. Latency and exposure requirements								
a. Latency	10 yr	10 yr	10 yr	10 yr	10 yr	10 yr	10 yr	10 yr
b. Company exposure prior to 1983 [a]	1 day	6 mo	1 day	6 mo	6 mo	6 mo	6 mo	1 day
c. Occupational exposure								
(1) Total		5 yr		5 yr	5 yr	5 yr	5 yr	
(2) Prior to 1983	1 day	2 yr	1 day	2 yr	2 yr	2 yr	6 mo	1 day

[a] Exposure must be prior to January 2, 1968 for A.P. Green claims

UNR Asbestos-Disease Claims Trust

UNR Asbestos-Disease Claims Trust

Bankruptcy Court and Trust Administrative Information

Debtor(s)   UNR Industries
                                  Unarco

Bankruptcy filing date   7/29/82   Confirmation date   6/2/89
Bankruptcy court   Bankr. N.D. Ill.   Bankruptcy judge   Eugene Wedoff

Trust status   Active
Date trust established   2/25/90
Classes of claims processed UNR (UNARCO) claims
Executive director   David E. Maxam
Claim administrator   Claims Processing Facility
Trust website   www.cpf-inc.com

Trustees and Advisors

Position	Name	Affiliation
Managing Trustee	Michael Levine	NYU Law School
Trustee	Alison Overseth	Franklin and Eleanor Roosevelt Institute, PASE
TAC Member	Gene Locks	Locks Law Firm
TAC Member	Robert Steinberg	Rose, Klein & Marias, LLP.
TAC Member	Stanley Levy	Levy Phillips & Konigsberg
Trust Counsel	Kevin E. Irwin	Keating Muething & Klekamp PLL

Estimated Initial Funding of Trust ($ millions)

	Funding for Claims Paid Through Trust	Funding for Claims Paid Outside Trust
Cash from debtor(s)		
Stock from debtors(s)		
Insurance settlements	DATA NOT AVAILABLE	
Other assets		
Total		

UNR Asbestos-Disease Claims Trust (continued)

Trust Financial Statement ($)

	Pre-2006	2006	2007	2008
Beginning trust assets	0	17,929,262	17,129,535	16,941,510
Additions				
Cash from debtors	0	0	0	0
Stock from debtors	130,626,075	0	0	0
Insurance settlements	0	0	0	0
Investment gains	-104,783,270	14,298	60,296	-25,580
Investment income	328,086,253	816,250	703,543	645,061
Other additions	3,161,795	144,230	85,580	84,400
Deductions				
Trust expenses	45,533,140	742,081	495,215	440,774
Claim processing costs	n.a.	212,150	96,000	96,000
Investment fees	n.a.	36,341	11,459	20,320
All other expenses	n.a.	493,590	387,756	324,454
Taxes	33,090,050	0	0	0
Claim payments	259,184,954	1,032,424	542,229	665,497
Other deductions	1,354,077	0	0	0
Ending trust assets	17,929,262	17,129,535	16,941,510	16,539,120

Gross claimant compensation as a percentage of deductions				
Lower bound	76.4%	58.2%	52.3%	60.2%
Upper bound	76.8%	58.2%	52.3%	60.2%

Claim Valuation for — UNR (UNARCO) claims

Disease level	Scheduled Value	Average Value	Maximum Value
Mesothelioma	n.a.	n.a.	n.a.
Lung cancer 1	n.a.	n.a.	n.a.
Lung cancer 2	n.a.	n.a.	n.a.
Other cancer	n.a.	n.a.	n.a.
Severe asbestosis	n.a.	n.a.	n.a.
Asbestosis/pleural disease	n.a.	n.a.	n.a.
Asbestosis/pleural disease	n.a.	n.a.	n.a.
Other asbestos disease	n.a.	n.a.	n.a.

Payment percentage	
Initial payment percentage	17.2%
Current payment percentage	1.1%

Claim payment ratio	
Malignancies and severe asbestosis	n.appl.
Asbestosis and pleural disease	n.appl.

UNR Asbestos-Disease Claims Trust (continued)

Claim Activity

	Pre-2006	2006	2007	2008	Total
Pre-petition pending and post-petition claims					
Claims filed [a]					
Malignant	n.a.	n.a.	n.a.	n.a.	n.a.
Non-malignant	n.a.	n.a.	n.a.	n.a.	n.a.
Not specified	437,622	n.a.	n.a.	n.a.	n.a.
All disease types	437,622	n.a.	n.a.	n.a.	n.a.
Claims paid					
Malignant	n.a.	n.a.	n.a.	n.a.	n.a.
Non-malignant	n.a.	n.a.	n.a.	n.a.	n.a.
Not specified	303,756	1,194	768	755	306,473
All disease types	303,756	1,194	768	755	306,473
Claim payments ($)					
Malignant	n.a.	n.a.	n.a.	n.a.	n.a.
Non-malignant	n.a.	n.a.	n.a.	n.a.	n.a.
Not specified	259,184,954	1,097,612	547,972	634,345	261,464,883
All disease types	259,184,954	1,097,612	547,972	634,345	261,464,883
Average payment per claim ($)					
Malignant	–	–	–	–	–
Non-malignant	–	–	–	–	–
Not specified	853	919	714	840	853
All disease types	853	919	714	840	853
Claims settled but not paid pre-petition					
Claims filed					
Malignant	0	0	0	0	0
Non-malignant	0	0	0	0	0
Not specified	0	0	0	0	0
All disease types	0	0	0	0	0
Claims paid					
Malignant	0	0	0	0	0
Non-malignant	0	0	0	0	0
Not specified	0	0	0	0	0
All disease types	0	0	0	0	0
Claim payments ($)					
Malignant	0	0	0	0	0
Non-malignant	0	0	0	0	0
Not specified	0	0	0	0	0
All disease types	0	0	0	0	0
Average payment per claim ($)					
Malignant	–	–	–	–	–
Non-malignant	–	–	–	–	–
Not specified	–	–	–	–	–
All disease types	–	–	–	–	–

[a] Claims filed data are incomplete.

UNR Asbestos-Disease Claims Trust (continued)

Claim Approval Criteria for   UNR and UNARCO claims

"In order to qualify for the exercise of this opinion [applies both to the expedited cash option and to the indvidualized resolution option], the claimant must make a conclusive demonstration of exposure to a UNR asbestos-containing product and submit a medical report from a qualified physician containing a diagnosis of an asbestos-related disease or injury and outlining the condition, symptoms, work history and/or exposure of the injured person." (Excerpted from UNR Claims Resolution Procedures)

Western Asbestos Settlement Trust

Western Asbestos Settlement Trust

Bankruptcy Court and Trust Administrative Information

Debtor(s)	Western Asbestos Company		
	Western MacArthur Co.		
	MacArthur Co.		
Bankruptcy filing date	11/22/02	Confirmation date	1/27/04
Bankruptcy court	Bankr. N.D. Cal.	Bankruptcy judge	Leslie Tchaikovsky
Trust status	Active		
Date trust established	4/22/04		
Classes of claims processed	Mac Arthur Co. - Minnesota claims		
	Mac Arthur Co. - North Dakota claims		
	Western MacArthur-Western Asbestos - California		
Executive director	Sara Beth Brown		
Claim administrator	Western Asbestos Settlement Trust		
Trust website	www.wastrust.com		

Trustees and Advisors

Position	Name	Affiliation
Managing Trustee	Stephen Snyder	Snyder Miller & Orton LLP.
Trustee	John Luikart	Bethany Advisors LLC
Trustee	Sandra Hernandez	The San Francisco Foundation
FCR	Charles Renfrew	Law Offices of Charles B. Renfrew
TAC Member	Alan Brayton	Brayton Purcell, LLP
TAC Member	David McClain	Kazan, McClain, Lyons, Greenwood & Harley
TAC Member	Michael Sieben	Sieben Polk, P.A.
TAC Member	Jack Clapper	Clapper, Patti, Schweizer & Mason
TAC Member	Jerry Paul	Paul & Hartley LLP
Trust Counsel	Janet Chubb	Jones Vargas
TAC Counsel	Michael Ahrens	Sheppard Mullin Richter & Hampton LLP
FCR Counsel	Gary Fergus	Fergus, A Law Office

Estimated Initial Funding of Trust ($ millions)

	Funding for Claims Paid Through Trust	Funding for Claims Paid Outside Trust
Cash from debtor(s)	0.5	0
Stock from debtors(s)	0.0	0
Insurance settlements	2,000.4	0
Other assets	0.0	0
Total	2,000.9	0

Western Asbestos Settlement Trust (continued)

Trust Financial Statement ($)				
	Pre-2006	2006	2007	2008
Beginning trust assets	0	161,412,077	1,150,877,094	980,270,462
Additions				
Cash from debtors	500,000	0	4,041	0
Stock from debtors	0	0	0	0
Insurance settlements	2,000,368,050	0	0	0
Investment gains	-3,812,864	29,559,324	15,738,730	-117,791,033
Investment income	47,033,607	42,558,920	40,644,401	32,826,096
Other additions	7,388,357	199,248	1,685,050	38,279,408
Deductions				
Trust expenses	18,484,448	1,663,514	2,655,094	6,454,391
Claim processing costs	1,393,091	378,868	444,848	486,512
Investment fees	n.a.	n.a.	n.a.	n.a.
All other expenses	n.a.	n.a.	n.a.	n.a.
Taxes	2,545,469	17,879,129	11,468,672	0
Claim payments	768,456,867	62,127,398	213,697,340	47,635,162
Other deductions	100,578,292	1,182,434	857,748	235,448
Ending trust assets	1,161,412,074	1,150,877,094	980,270,462	879,259,932
Gross claimant compensation as a percentage of deductions				
Lower bound	86.3%	75.0%	93.4%	87.7%
Upper bound	97.6%	76.4%	93.8%	88.1%

Western Asbestos Settlement Trust (continued)

Claim Valuation for	Mac Arthur Co. - Minnesota claims		
	Base-Case	Average	Maximum
Disease level	Value a,b	Value b	Value b
Mesothelioma	148,678	316,250	1,265,000
Lung Cancer	41,211	137,050	548,200
Other Cancer	21,222	73,800	295,200
Grade I Non-Malignancy	30,868	57,200	228,800
Grade II Non-Malignancy	21,875	30,150	120,600
Payment percentage			
Initial payment percentage	31.5%		
Current payment percentage	44.0%		
Claim payment ratio			
Malignancies	71.5%		
Asbestosis and pleural disease	28.5%		

Claim Valuation for	Mac Arthur Co. - North Dakota claims		
	Base-Case	Average	Maximum
Disease level	Value a,b	Value b	Value b
Mesothelioma	58,544	117,087	468,348
Lung Cancer	13,569	44,777	179,108
Other Cancer	4,894	16,884	67,536
Grade I Non-Malignancy	9,764	16,500	66,000
Grade II Non-Malignancy	8,219	12,000	48,000
Payment percentage			
Initial payment percentage	31.5%		
Current payment percentage	44.0%		
Claim payment ratio			
Malignancies	71.5%		
Asbestosis and pleural disease	28.5%		

Claim Valuation for	Western MacArthur-Western Asbestos - California		
	Base-Case	Average	Maximum
Disease level	Value a,b	Value b	Value b
Mesothelioma	276,479	524,025	2,096,100
Lung Cancer	62,046	199,195	796,780
Other Cancer	22,298	75,000	300,000
Grade I Non-Malignancy	32,131	51,557	206,228
Grade II Non-Malignancy	18,574	21,816	87,264
Payment percentage			
Initial payment percentage	31.5%		
Current payment percentage	44.0%		
Claim payment ratio			
Malignancies	84.0%		
Asbestosis and pleural disease	16.0%		

[a] For each claim, base-case values are adjusted using a series of factors that approximate factors which add or substract value to cases in the tort system.

[b] Trust has increased values 10.1% above figures shown to account for inflation.

Western Asbestos Settlement Trust (continued)

Claim Activity	Pre-2006	2006	2007	2008	Total
Pre-petition pending and post-petition claims					
Claims filed					
Malignant	n.a.	n.a.	n.a.	n.a.	n.a.
Non-malignant	n.a.	n.a.	n.a.	n.a.	n.a.
Not specified	3,179	1,626	937	864	6,606
All disease types	3,179	1,626	937	864	6,606
Claims paid					
Malignant	n.a.	n.a.	n.a.	n.a.	n.a.
Non-malignant	n.a.	n.a.	n.a.	n.a.	n.a.
Not specified	1,180	1,408	917	897	4,402
All disease types	1,180	1,408	917	897	4,402
Claim payments ($)					
Malignant	n.a.	n.a.	n.a.	n.a.	n.a.
Non-malignant	n.a.	n.a.	n.a.	n.a.	n.a.
Not specified	122,161,180	52,332,752	53,926,911	45,311,265	273,732,108
All disease types	122,161,180	52,332,752	53,926,911	45,311,265	273,732,108
Average payment per claim ($)					
Malignant	–	–	–	–	–
Non-malignant	–	–	–	–	–
Not specified	103,526	37,168	58,808	50,514	62,184
All disease types	103,526	37,168	58,808	50,514	62,184
Claims settled but not paid pre-petition					
Claims filed					
Malignant	n.a.	n.a.	n.a.	n.a.	n.a.
Non-malignant	n.a.	n.a.	n.a.	n.a.	n.a.
Not specified	5,448	0	0	0	5,448
All disease types	5,448	0	0	0	5,448
Claims paid					
Malignant	n.a.	n.a.	n.a.	n.a.	n.a.
Non-malignant	n.a.	n.a.	n.a.	n.a.	n.a.
Not specified	5,417	0	2	1	5,420
All disease types	5,417	0	2	1	5,420
Claim payments ($)					
Malignant	n.a.	n.a.	n.a.	n.a.	n.a.
Non-malignant	n.a.	n.a.	n.a.	n.a.	n.a.
Not specified	646,714,878	72,135,428 [a]	159,729,591 [a]	21,105	878,601,002
All disease types	646,714,878	72,135,428	159,729,591	21,105	878,601,002
Average payment per claim ($)					
Malignant	–	–	–	–	–
Non-malignant	–	–	–	–	–
Not specified	119,386	–	–	21,105	162,104
All disease types	119,386	–	–	21,105	162,104

[a] Includes additonal payments on previously paid claims.

Western Asbestos Settlement Trust (continued)

Claim Approval Criteria for	Mac Arthur Co. - All claims						
	Meso	LC	OC	G1NM-BC [a]	G1NM-E [b]	G1NM-SA [c]	G2NM
1. Diagnosis requirement (one or more of checked items satisfies requirement)							
a. Physical exam	✔	✔	✔	✔	✔	✔	✔
b. Pathology	✔	✔	✔	✔	✔	✔	✔
c. Medical document review							
2. ILO or x-ray requirement							
a. ILO reading		1/0	1/0	1/0	1/1	2/2	1/0
OR b. X-ray, CT scan, or pathology showing one or more of the checked conditions							
(1) Bilateral interstitial fibrosis				✔	✔		✔
(2) Bilateral pleural plaques							
(3) Bilateral pleural thickening							
(4) Bilateral pleural calcification							
3. Pulmonary function test requirement [d]							
a. TLC < (% of normal)				80	70		
AND FEV1/FVC ratio >							
OR b. DLCO < (% of normal)				75	60		
AND FEV1/FVC ratio >				0.65	0.65		
OR c. FVC < (% of normal)				80	60		
AND FEV1/FVC ratio >				0.65	0.65		
4. Causation statement requirement	No	No	No	No	No	No	No
5. Latency and exposure requirements							
a. Latency	10 yr	10 yr	10 yr	10 yr	10 yr	10 yr	10 yr
b. Company exposure prior to 1983	3 mo	1 yr	1 yr	1 yr	1 yr	1 yr	1 yr
c. Occupational exposure							
(1) Total							
(2) Prior to 1983							

[a] Grade I non-malignancy, base case
[b] Grade I non-malignancy, enhanced
[c] Grade I non-malignancy, serious asbestosis
[d] Claimant assumed to be at least 70 years old

W.R. Grace & Co. Asbestos Personal Injury Settlement Trust

W.R. Grace & Co. Asbestos Personal Injury Settlement Trust

Bankruptcy Court and Trust Administrative Information

Debtor(s)	W.R. Grace		
Bankruptcy filing date	4/1/01	Confirmation date	Not confirmed
Bankruptcy court	Bankr. D. Del.	Bankruptcy judge	Judith Fitzgerald
Trust status	Proposed		
Date trust established	Trust not established		
Classes of claims processed	W.R. Grace claims		
Claim administrator	Not selected		
Trust website	None		

Trustees and Advisors

Position	Name	Affiliation
FCR	David Austern	Claims Resolution Management Corporation
FCR Counsel	John Phillips	Phillips Parker Orberson & Moore PLC
FCR Counsel	Roger Frankel	Orrick, Herrington & Sutcliffe LLP
FCR Counsel	Debra Felder	Orrick, Herrington & Sutcliffe LLP
FCR Counsel	Richard Wyron	Orrick, Herrington & Sutcliffe LLP

Estimated Initial Funding of Trust ($ millions)

	Funding for Claims Paid Through Trust	Funding for Claims Paid Outside Trust
Cash from debtor(s)	2,315.5	0
Stock from debtors(s)	662.8	0
Insurance settlements	0.0	0
Other assets	0.0	0
Total	2,978.3	0

W.R. Grace & Co. Asbestos Personal Injury Settlement Trust (continued)

Trust Financial Statement ($)

	Pre-2006	2006	2007	2008
Beginning trust assets				
Additions				
Cash from debtors				
Stock from debtors				
Insurance settlements				
Investment gains				
Investment income				
Other additions				
Deductions		TRUST NOT YET ESTABLISHED		
Trust expenses				
Claim processing costs				
Investment fees				
All other expenses				
Taxes				
Claim payments				
Other deductions				
Ending trust assets				
Gross claimant compensation as a percentage of deductions				
Lower bound	–	–	–	–
Upper bound	–	–	–	–

Claim Valuation for [a]

W.R. Grace claims

Disease level	Scheduled Value	Average Value	Maximum Value
Mesothelioma	180,000	225,000	450,000
Lung Cancer 1	42,000	45,000	95,000
Lung Cancer 2	n.appl.	14,000	33,000
Other Cancer	20,000	20,500	35,000
Severe Asbestosis	50,000	62,240	100,000
Asbestosis / Pleural Disease II	7,500	8,500	15,000
Asbestosis / Pleural Disease I	2,500	3,000	5,000
Other Asbestos Disease	300 *	n.appl.	n.appl.

Payment percentage	
Initial payment percentage	30.0%
Current payment percentage	30.0%

Claim payment ratio	
Malignancies and severe asbestosis	88.0%
Asbestosis and pleural disease	12.0%

*Payment percentage does not apply

[a] Proposed

W.R. Grace & Co. Asbestos Personal Injury Settlement Trust (continued)

Claim Activity	Pre-2006	2006	2007	2008	Total
Pre-petition pending and post-petition claims					
Claims filed					
Malignant					
Non-malignant					
Not specified					
All disease types					
Claims paid					
Malignant					
Non-malignant					
Not specified					
All disease types					
Claim payments ($)					
Malignant					
Non-malignant					
Not specified					
All disease types					
Average payment per claim ($)					
Malignant					
Non-malignant					
Not specified					
All disease types					
		TRUST NOT YET ESTABLISHED			
Claims settled but not paid pre-petition					
Claims filed					
Malignant					
Non-malignant					
Not specified					
All disease types					
Claims paid					
Malignant					
Non-malignant					
Not specified					
All disease types					
Claim payments ($)					
Malignant					
Non-malignant					
Not specified					
All disease types					
Average payment per claim ($)					
Malignant					
Non-malignant					
Not specified					
All disease types					

W.R. Grace & Co. Asbestos Personal Injury Settlement Trust (continued)

Claim Approval Criteria for [a]	W.R. Grace claims							
	Meso	LC1	LC2	OC	SA	AP2	AP1	OAD
1. Diagnosis requirement (one or more of checked items satisfies requirement)								
a. Physical exam	✔	✔	✔	✔	✔	✔	✔	✔
b. Pathology	✔	✔	✔	✔	✔	✔	✔	✔
c. Medical document review								
2. ILO or x-ray requirement								
a. ILO reading		1/0		1/0	2/1	1/0	1/0	1/0
OR b. X-ray, CT scan, or pathology showing one or more of the checked conditions								
(1) Bilateral interstitial fibrosis		✔		✔	✔	✔	✔	✔
(2) Bilateral pleural plaques		✔		✔	✔	✔	✔	✔
(3) Bilateral pleural thickening		✔		✔	✔	✔	✔	✔
(4) Bilateral pleural calcification		✔		✔	✔	✔	✔	✔
3. Pulmonary function test requirement								
a. TLC < (% of normal)					65	80		
AND FEV1/FVC ratio >								
OR b. DLCO < (% of normal)								
AND FEV1/FVC ratio >								
OR c. FVC < (% of normal)					65	80		
AND FEV1/FVC ratio >					0.65	0.65		
4. Causation statement requirement	No	Yes	Yes	Yes	Yes	Yes	No	No
5. Latency and exposure requirements								
a. Latency	10 yr	10 yr	10 yr	10 yr	10 yr	10 yr	10 yr	10 yr
b. Company exposure prior to 1983	1 day	6 mo	1 day	6 mo	6 mo	6 mo	6 mo	1 day
c. Occupational exposure								
(1) Total		5 yr		5 yr	5 yr	5 yr	5 yr	
(2) Prior to 1983	1 day	2 yr	1 day	2 yr	2 yr	2 yr	6 mo	1 day

[a] Proposed

References

Allen, Lucy P., and Mary Elizabeth Stern, *Snapshot of Recent Trends in Asbestos Litigation*, NERA Economic Consulting, June 16, 2009.

Amchem Prods. v. Windsor, Supreme Court of the United States, 521 U.S. 591, 117 S. Ct. 2231, June 25, 1997.

American Academy of Actuaries, Mass Torts Subcommittee, *Overview of Asbestos Claims Issues and Trends*, Washington, D.C., August 2007. As of July 2, 2010:
http://www.actuary.org/pdf/casualty/asbestos_aug07.pdf

Armstrong World Industries, *Amended and Restated Armstrong World Industries, Inc. Asbestos Personal Injury Settlement Trust Distribution Procedures*, 2008.

Babcock and Wilcox Company, *Asbestos Personal Injury Settlement Trust: Instructions for Filing a Claim—Updated 8/5/2009*, August 5, 2009. As of July 2, 2010:
http://www.bwasbestostrust.com/files/BWClaimantInstructionLetterFinal8_4_09a.pdf

Barliant, Ronald, Dimitri G. Karcazes, and Anne M. Sherry, "From Free-Fall to Free-for-All: The Rise of Pre-Packaged Asbestos Bankruptcies," *American Bankruptcy Institute Law Review*, Vol. 12, No. 2, Winter 2004, pp. 441–471.

Bates, Charles E., and Charles Mullin, "Having Your Tort and Eating It Too?" *Mealey's Litigation Report: Asbestos*, Vol. 6, No. 4, November 2006.

Bates, Charles E., Charles H. Mullin, and A. Rachel Marquardt, "The Naming Game," *Mealey's Litigation Report*, Vol. 24, No. 15, 2009, pp. 1–7.

Bates, Charles E., Charles H. Mullin, and Marc C. Scarcella, "The Claiming Game," *Mealey's Litigation Report*, Vol. 25, No. 1, February 2010, pp. 1–8.

Behrens, Mark A., "What's New in Asbestos Litigation?" *Review of Litigation*, Vol. 28, No. 3, Spring 2009, pp. 500–557.

Borel v. Fibreboard Paper Products Corp., U.S. Court of Appeals for the Fifth Circuit, 493 F.2d 1076, September 10, 1973.

Borg-Warner Corp. v. Flores, Supreme Court of Texas, 232 S.W.3d 765, argued September 29, 2006, opinion delivered June 8, 2007, released for publication October 12, 2007; rehearing denied by *Borg-Warner Corp. v. Flores*, 2007 Tex. LEXIS 930, Tex., October 12, 2007.

Brown, S. Todd, "Section 524(g) Without Compromise: Voting Rights and the Asbestos Bankruptcy Paradox," *Columbia Business Law Review*, Vol. 2008, No. 3, 2008, pp. 841–933.

Carroll, Stephen J., Lloyd Dixon, James M. Anderson, Thor Hogan, and Elizabeth M. Sloss, *The Abuse of Medical Diagnostic Practices in Mass Litigation: The Case of Silica*, Santa Monica, Calif.: RAND Corporation, TR-774-ICJ, 2009. As of July 3, 2010:
http://www.rand.org/pubs/technical_reports/TR774/

Carroll, Stephen J., Deborah R. Hensler, Jennifer Gross, Elizabeth M. Sloss, Matthias Schonlau, Allan Abrahamse, and J. Scott Ashwood, *Asbestos Litigation*, Santa Monica, Calif.: RAND Corporation, MG-162-ICJ, 2005. As of March 23, 2010:
http://www.rand.org/pubs/monographs/MG162/

C. E. Thurston and Sons, *Asbestos Trust Agreement*, undated. As of July 3, 2010:
http://www.claimsres.com/CET%20docs/Trust%20Agreement%20-%20Executed.pdf

Crowell and Moring, "Chart 1: Company Name and Year of Bankruptcy Filing (Chronologically)," revised June 5, 2010. As of March 24, 2010:
http://www.crowell.com/pdf/AsbestosChart1.pdf

Effross, Walter A., "The Bankruptcy Reform Act of 1994: Something for Everyone," *American Bankruptcy Institute Journal*, Vol. 13, No. 10, December 1994.

Ehrenfeld, Joshua A., "Quieting the Rebellion: Eliminating Payment of Prepetition Debts Prior to Chapter 11 Reorganizations," *University of Chicago Law Review*, Vol. 70, No. 2, Spring 2003, pp. 621–638.

Esserman, Sander L., and David J. Parsons, "The Case for Broad Access to 11 U.S.C. Section 524(g) in Light of the Third Circuit's Ongoing Business Requirement Dicta in Combustion Engineering," *New York University Annual Survey of American Law*, Vol. 62, No. 2, 2006, pp. 187–222.

Falise, Robert A., chair and managing trustee, Manville Personal Injury Settlement Trust, letter to Hon. Jack B. Weinstein, senior judge, U.S. District Court, Eastern District of New York, and Hon. Burton R. Lifland, U.S. Bankruptcy Court, Southern District of New York, October 30, 2009. As of July 3, 2010:
http://www.mantrust.org/FTP/thirdQ09.pdf

Green, Eric D., Lawrence Fitzpatrick, James L. Patton Jr., Edwin J. Harron, and Travis N. Turner, "Prepackaged Asbestos Bankruptcies: Down but Not Out," *New York University Annual Survey of American Law*, Vol. 63, No. 4, 2007–2008, pp. 727–772.

H. K. Porter Company, *Asbestos Trust Agreement*, c. 1998. As of March 23, 2010:
http://www.hkporterasbestostrust.org/Resources.htm

Hensler, Deborah R., William L. F. Felstiner, Molly Selvin, and Patricia A. Ebener, *Asbestos in the Courts: The Challenge of Mass Toxic Torts*, Santa Monica, Calif.: RAND Corporation, R-3324-ICJ, 1985. As of July 8, 2010:
http://www.rand.org/pubs/reports/R3324/

In re Combustion Eng'g., Inc., U.S. Court of Appeals for the Third Circuit, 391 F.3d 190, argued June 3, 2004, filed December 2, 2004, as amended February 23, 2005.

In re Fuller-Austin Insulation, U.S. District Court for the District of Delaware, 1998 U.S. Dist. LEXIS 18340, decided November 10, 1998, findings of fact/conclusions of law at In re Fuller-Austin Insulation Co., 1998 U.S. Dist. LEXIS 23567, D. Del., November 13, 1998.

In re Johns-Manville Corp., U.S. Bankruptcy Court for the Southern District of New York, 68 B.R. 618, decided December 18, 1986, amended December 19, 1986, amended December 23, 1986; affirmed by *In re Johns-Manville Corp.*, 78 B.R. 407, Southern District of New York, 1987; affirmed sub nomine by *Kane v. Johns-Manville Corp.*, 843 F.2d 636, Second Circuit of New York, 1988.

In re Joint E. & S. Dist. Asbestos Litig., U.S. District Court for the Eastern District of New York, U.S. District Court for the Southern District of New York, U.S. Bankruptcy Court for the Southern District of New York, 129 B.R. 710, filed June 27, 1991, as amended August 5, 1991.

In re Joint E. & S. Dists. Asbestos Litig. v. Falise, U.S. District Court for the Eastern District of New York and Southern District of New York, 878 F. Supp. 473, decided January 19, 1995, filed January 18, 1995, entered January 19, 1995; affirmed in part, vacated in part, and remanded by *In re Joint E. & S. Dist. Asbestos Litig.*, 78 F.3d 764, 2d Cir. N.Y., 1996; affirmed without opinion by *Findley v. Falise (In re Joint E. & S. Dist. Asbestos Litig.)*, 100 F.3d 944, 2d Cir. N.Y., 1996; affirmed without opinion by *Findley v. Falise (In re Joint E. & S. Dist. Asbestos Litig.)*, 100 F.3d 945, 2d Cir. N.Y., 1996.

Inselbuch, Elihu, "Some Key Issues in Asbestos Bankruptcies," *South Texas Law Review*, Vol. 44, No. 4, Fall 2003, pp. 1037–1044.

Issacharoff, Samuel, "'Shocked': Mass Torts and Aggregate Asbestos Litigation After Amchem and Ortiz," *Texas Law Review*, Vol. 80, No. 7, June 2002, pp. 1925–1942.

J. T. Thorpe Settlement Trust, *Fourth Amendment to and Complete Restatement of J. T. Thorpe Settlement Trust Agreement*, April 21, 2010. As of July 8, 2010:
http://jttstrust.com/pdf/Fourth%20Amendment%20to%20and%20Complete%20Restatement%20of%20 J.T.%20Thorpe%20Settlement%20Trust%20Agreement,%20April%2021,%202010.pdf

Kaiser Aluminum and Chemical Corporation, *Third Amended Asbestos Trust Distribution Procedures*, November 20, 2007. As of July 3, 2010:
http://www.kaiserasbestostrust.com/Files/ Third%20Amended%20Trust%20Distribution%20Procedures%2000013238.pdf

Mabey, Ralph R., and Peter A. Zisser, "Improving Treatment of Future Claims: The Unfinished Business Left by the Manville Amendments," *American Bankruptcy Law Journal*, Vol. 69, No. 4, Fall 1995, pp. 487–514.

Macchiarola, Frank J., "The Manville Personal Injury Settlement Trust: Lessons for the Future," *Cardozo Law Review*, Vol. 17, No. 3, January 1996, pp. 583–628.

Manville Personal Injury Settlement Trust, "History," c. 1996. As of March 23, 2010:
http://mantrust.org/history.htm

———, claim history provided to the authors by Claims Resolution Management Corporation, August 2007.

McGovern, Francis E., "The Tragedy of the Asbestos Commons," *Virginia Law Review*, Vol. 88, No. 8, December 2002, pp. 1721–1756.

———, "The Evolution of Asbestos Bankruptcy Trust Distribution Plans," *New York University Annual Survey of American Law*, Vol. 62, No 2, 2006, pp. 163–186.

NGC Bodily Injury Trust, *Seventh Amended Claims Resolution Procedures*, December 12, 2002. As of July 3, 2010:
http://www.ngcbitrust.org/DownloadableForms/CRP.pdf

Ortiz v. Fibreboard Corp., Supreme Court of the United States, 527 U.S. 815, 119 S. Ct. 2295, June 23, 1999.

Parloff, Roger, "Welcome to the New Asbestos Scandal," *Fortune*, September 6, 2004, p. 186. As of July 3, 2010:
http://money.cnn.com/magazines/fortune/fortune_archive/2004/09/06/380311/index.htm

Peterson, Mark A., "Giving Away Money: Comparative Comments on Claims Resolution Facilities," *Law and Contemporary Problems*, Vol. 3, No. 4, Autumn 1990, pp. 113–136.

Plevin, Mark D., Leslie A. Davis, and Noah S. Bloomberg, "Where Are They Now, Part Five: An Update on Developments in Asbestos-Related Bankruptcy Cases," *Mealey's Asbestos Bankruptcy Report*, Vol. 8, No. 8, March 2009, pp. 1–35. As of July 3, 2010:
http://www.crowell.com/documents/Where-Are-They-Now-Part-5_Asbestos-Related-Bankruptcy.pdf

Plevin, Mark D., Robert T. Ebert, and Leslie A. Epley, "Pre-Packed Asbestos Bankruptcies: A Flawed Solution," *South Texas Law Review*, Vol. 44, No. 4, Fall 2003, pp. 883–924.

Plevin, Mark D., Leslie A. Epley, and Clifton S. Elgarten, "The Future Claims Representative in Prepackaged Asbestos Bankruptcies: Conflicts of Interest, Strange Alliances, and Unfamiliar Duties for Burdened Bankruptcy Courts," *New York University Annual Survey of American Law*, Vol. 62, No. 2, 2006, pp. 271–328.

Plevin, Mark D., and Paul W. Kalish, "Where Are They Now? A History of the Companies That Have Sought Bankruptcy Protection Due to Asbestos Claims," *Mealey's Asbestos Bankruptcy Report*, Vol. 1, No. 1, August 2001, pp. 1–9. As of July 3, 2010:
http://www.crowell.com/documents/DOCASSOCFKTYPE_ARTICLES_424.pdf

Plevin, Mark D., Paul W. Kalish, and Kelly R. Cusick, "Where Are They Now, Part Four: A Continuing History of the Companies That Have Sought Bankruptcy Protection Due to Asbestos Claims," *Mealey's Asbestos Bankruptcy Report*, Vol. 6, No. 7, February 2007, pp. 1–41. As of July 3, 2010:
http://www.crowell.com/documents/DOCASSOCFKTYPE_ARTICLES_592.pdf

Plevin, Mark D., Paul W. Kalish, and Leslie A. Epley, "Where Are They Now? Part Two: A Continuing History of the Companies That Have Sought Bankruptcy Protection Due to Asbestos Claims," *Mealey's Asbestos Bankruptcy Report*, Vol. 17, No. 20, November 15, 2002. As of July 3, 2010:
http://www.crowell.com/documents/DOCASSOCFKTYPE_ARTICLES_422.pdf

————, "Where Are They Now, Part Three: A Continuing History of the Companies That Have Sought Bankruptcy Protection Due to Asbestos Claims," *Mealey's Asbestos Bankruptcy Report*, Vol. 5, No. 4, November 2005, pp. 1–35. As of July 3, 2010:
http://www.crowell.com/documents/DOCASSOCFKTYPE_ARTICLES_419.pdf

Public Law 103-394, Bankruptcy Reform Act of 1994, October 22, 1994. As of July 4, 2010:
http://frwebgate.access.gpo.gov/cgi-bin/getdoc.cgi?dbname=103_cong_bills&docid=f:h5116enr.txt.pdf

Shelley, William P., Jacob C. Cohn, and Joseph A. Arnold, "The Need for Transparency Between the Tort System and Section 524(g) Asbestos Trusts," *Norton Journal of Bankruptcy Law and Practice*, Vol. 17, No. 2, 2008, pp. 257–295. As of July 3, 2010:
http://www.cozen.com/admin/files/publications/JBLP_v17n2_ShelleyCohnArnold_sent%20040208.pdf

Silverstein, Joshua M., "Overlooking Tort Claimants' Best Interests: Non-Debtor Releases in Asbestos Bankruptcies," *University of Missouri, Kansas City, Law Review*, Vol. 78, No. 1, Fall 2009, pp. 1–100.

Snyder, Todd R., and Deanne C. Siemer, "Reply to Barliant: Asbestos Pre-Packaged Bankruptcies: Apply the Brakes Carefully and Retain Flexibility for Debtors," *American Bankruptcy Institute Law Review*, Vol. 13, No. 2, Winter 2005, pp. 801–808.

Stengel, James L., "The Asbestos End-Game," *New York University Annual Survey of American Law*, Vol. 62, No. 2, 2006, pp. 223–270.

Taylor, Mark D., "How Congress Can Solve the 'Great Asbestos Bankruptcy Heist,'" *Mealey's Asbestos Bankruptcy Report*, Vol. 4, No. 9, April 2005, pp. 1–5. As of July 3, 2010:
http://www.arentfox.com/pdf_notReady/asbestos_bankruptcy_report.pdf

Tomplait v. Combustion Eng'g, Inc., No. C.A. 5402, Eastern District of Tex., 1967.

UNR Asbestos-Disease Claims Trust, "2008 Annual Report," c. 2009. On file with the authors.

U.S. Code, Title 11, Bankruptcy; Chapter 7, Liquidation.

————, Title 11, Bankruptcy.

————, Title 11, Bankruptcy; Chapter 11, Reorganization.

————, Title 11, Bankruptcy; Chapter 5, Creditors, the Debtor, and the Estate; Subchapter II, Debtors Duties and Benefits; Section 524, Effect of Discharge.

U.S. House of Representatives, Asbestos Health Hazards Compensation Act, H.R. 8689, introduced August 2, 1977.

————, report 103-835, H.R. 5116, October 4, 1994.